MIDDLE CLASS: AN INTELLECTUAL HISTORY THROUGH SOCIAL SCIENCES

Studies in Critical Social Sciences Book Series

Haymarket Books is proud to be working with Brill Academic Publishers (www.brill.nl) to republish the *Studies in Critical Social Sciences* book series in paperback editions. This peer-reviewed book series offers insights into our current reality by exploring the content and consequences of power relationships under capitalism, and by considering the spaces of opposition and resistance to these changes that have been defining our new age. Our full catalog of *SCSS* volumes can be viewed at https://www.haymarketbooks .org/series_collections/4-studies-in-critical-social-sciences.

MIDDLE CLASS: AN INTELLECTUAL HISTORY THROUGH SOCIAL SCIENCES

An American Fetish from Its Origins to Globalization

MATTEO BATTISTINI

Haymarket Books
Chicago, IL

First published in 2022 by Brill Academic Publishers, The Netherlands
© 2022 Koninklijke Brill NV, Leiden, The Netherlands

Published in paperback in 2023 by
Haymarket Books
P.O. Box 180165
Chicago, IL 60618
773-583-7884
www.haymarketbooks.org

ISBN: 979-8-88890-007-9

Distributed to the trade in the US through Consortium Book Sales and
Distribution (www.cbsd.com) and internationally through Ingram Publisher
Services International (www.ingramcontent.com).

This book was published with the generous support of Lannan Foundation,
Wallace Action Fund, and the Marguerite Casey Foundation.

Special discounts are available for bulk purchases by organizations and
institutions. Please call 773-583-7884 or email info@haymarketbooks.org for more
information.

Cover design by Jamie Kerry and Ragina Johnson.

Printed in the United States.

Library of Congress Cataloging-in-Publication data is available.

We don't need your magazines
We don't need your fashion show
We don't need your TV
We don't wanna know

We don't need we get our fill
It's esoteric overkill
It's a shiny new aesthetic
Get us out of vogue

Middle Class, *Out of Vogue*, 1978

• •
•

Contents

Preface

Over the last decade, publications, but also scientific studies and research, have obsessively announced the decline of the American middle class, its disappearance, or its end. This is not a new debate. Similar pronouncements marked the public and political debate in the 1930s, on the occasion of the first major crisis of capitalism on a world scale, and then again in the 1980s when the topics were the economic changes following the period of stagnation and inflation linked to the oil crises as well as President Ronald Reagan's neoliberal and anti-union policies. The same was true again in the nineties, when the 'new economy', supported by the Democratic administration of Bill Clinton, produced increasing results in terms of productivity and profit. Unlike those historical moments, today the question is faced in light of a field of tension opened by globalisation which has exploded due to the 2008 financial and economic collapse. Income inequality, polarisation of the labour market, and a change in the role of the state are transnational processes which are related to one other and invoked in order to explain the crisis of the American middle class.

Today it is a well-established fact that 80% of homeowners have access to less than half of national annual income, while the richest 1% have more than doubled their share since the 1980s. Impoverished at home, the American middle class is not even the richest in the world, especially when one considers the ascent of a middle class in China, Asia, and Latin America. In this way, if globalisation was greeted with optimism in the 1990s due to the potential for growth and prosperity that seemed to come with it, in the new millennium it represents a darkened horizon. The space for criticism that the no-global movement had opened during the beginning of the century was closed by the neoconservatism of President George W. Bush, and today globalisation appears to be a nightmare in the imagination of the new alternative right which led to the election of Donald Trump. Today, political and technocratic elites, both Republicans and Democrats, are accused of being globalists, and globalisation is presented as a plot against America and its middle class.

The nightmare of globalisation also emerges in the transnational process of the polarisation of the labour market. Since the 1980s, there has been a change in the employment structure of the United States, which has occurred according to a centrifugal dynamic that has accelerated over the last decade. The number of creative, highly professional, and highly paid jobs for full-time scientists, engineers, and managers have increased. The number of those working part-time, hired with specific tasks as well as routine de-skilled tasks, has also

X   PREFACE

grown. On the other hand, the skilled and semi-skilled occupations of the last century (middle-level managers, administrators, professionals, office clerks, and skilled workers) are decreasing and have been drastically downsized by the entrepreneurial strategies implemented to offset the social and labour mobilisation of the 1960s and 1970s. These strategies include the introduction of technological innovations (automation and digitalisation), domestic and international outsourcing in search of a poor and non-unionised workforce, and the devaluation of labour in terms of wages, tasks, and prestige through the use of migrant labour.

President Barack Obama's middle-class economics have also been ineffective, since the economic recovery, which also characterised his second term, did not reverse this trend. The decrease in unemployment did not coincide with the return of a significant number of middle-skill jobs. In considerable numbers, new generations especially are finding increasingly low-skill, low-wage jobs such as services and personal care, which, since they are mainly provided by migrants, minorities, and women, heighten the sense of impoverishment of the male breadwinner of white America. The difficulties encountered by the first African American president in keeping a nation divided along lines of class, race and sex unified thus coincided with the sublimation of the nightmare of globalisation into the reactionary dream of 'America First'. This dream envisions America's future as a return to the mythical nation of the origins (with its racial and sexual connotations), one that is closed within the internal and external boundaries identified by white America. The white backlash against minorities and migrants finds in the word *jobs* – a plural term without the polemical tone that had characterised the meaning labour in the twentieth century – its reason for governing.

To explain the decline of the middle class, liberal commentators and scholars finally call into question the transnational process of changing the role of the state with the abandonment of the redistributive character of taxation, the reduction in the policies of social security, and the change in the objectives of assistance. Even though in the thirty years following the Great Depression of the 1930s – both in the European language of social rights and in the American language of entitlement – an expansive vision of the public guarantee of benefits had become established, today the residual supply of assistance is aimed at the mere reproduction of the working poor. To use the words of President Clinton, the 'end of welfare as we have known it' was followed by 'welfare to work', namely assistance programs which forced people to accept any job (even if it was precarious and poor) in order to continue receiving benefits. These programs guide people onto the labour market in an inferior position that favours the compression of the average wage.

There is a widespread belief in public opinion that these transnational processes have caused the 'crisis of the American century', the collapse of the trust that Americans have historically placed in the possibility of being part of the middle class from the 1940s, when the magazine *Fortune*, the voice of Americanism inside and outside the United States, regularly published polls showing that approximately 80% of respondents indicated that they belonged to the middle class. The new alternative right, from a racist perspective, has grasped that labour has returned to the fore as a dividing line of the nation. After a decade of recession and weak economic recovery, although about half of Americans still define themselves as middle class, opinion research shows how the percentage of those who consider themselves lower class is growing. But what remains unchanged and undisputed is what Paul Krugman has referred to as the 'fetishization of the middle class'. With this phrase, he defined the historical claim that even today, despite the enormous inequalities and poverty that mark their society, Americans advance to be members of this class, aspiring not only to the wealth that had characterised the middle class of the past century, but also to the sharing and realisation of the ideal of a nation that, precisely because of its middle class, considered itself and still wants to consider itself exceptional. So why do Americans historically recognise themselves as a middle class? This is the basic question that drives the history of the fetish presented in this book.

Differently than Europe, in the United States the association of the two expressions – economic crisis and middle class – defines a decisive character that qualifies the public and political debate. The reason for this is essentially historical. Since the second half of the 1930s, the US social sciences have publicly affirmed a specific and shared political concept of the middle class that has not fully taken hold in Europe. Although influenced by the English, German, and French social sciences, they distanced themselves from the European scientific literature which had linked the end of the liberal order and the Nazi orientation of the middle classes to the crisis of capitalism that occurred between the two world wars. Above all, they denied the Marxist interpretation at its roots, which had identified in the middle class an intermediate (and therefore passive) subject with respect to the possibility of overturning the power relationships that capital projected on society. In other words, for the US social sciences the middle class was not – as Marx called it – an 'incarnate contradiction' destined to be overcome with the advent of communism.

The triumphant middle class of the American century was not defined by the criterion of work. That is, it was not exclusively a class of employees. Instead, it constituted a broad formation, composed of multiple social groups, not only the entrepreneurial and professional petite bourgeoisie, but also white-collar workers who fell into the lower bracket of office work and those who carried out manual work. The specialised and unionised workers who, thanks to their skills and their high salaries, crossed the line between blue collar and white collar to share an adequate level of income, education and consumption, a common lifestyle, and, above all, an 'original' adherence to the American liberal tradition. Unlike its European history, the middle class of the United States did not identify a specific economic and social formation. Instead, it represented a cultural and political identity that established a code of behaviour organised around the value set of white and Protestant America: individualism and work ethic, equality of opportunity and personal responsibility, and competition for success and social mobility. This was the middle class of the golden age of capitalism that characterised the American nation, its exceptionalism, and its international projection. Therefore, it was a generally universal subject, one considered as capable of overcoming the differences of class, race, and sex, thereby denying the possibility of conflict, and ensuring an order based on consent.

This book thus reconstructs the history of the American middle class from its European origins to globalisation, not exclusively in terms of an economic or social history, nor only as a cultural or political history, but as an intellectual history that emerges in the social sciences of the American century. It identifies this intellectual history in their empirical research and theoretical reflections, in their public and political activism, in their institutional commitment in federal agencies, in private foundations, in civic and economic associations, from the progressivism of the early twentieth century to the social contract of the New Deal, from the liberalism of the second postwar period to the neoconservatism and neoliberalism of the seventies and eighties, up to the globalisation of the nineties. This intellectual history gives back the social history of a political concept that assumes a specific scientific content by which it acquires an ideological centrality that has no equal in European history. The US social sciences have freed the middle class from its historical relationship with work in an attempt to emancipate it from the field of tension into which it was continually dragged by class conflict. Their political objective was to erase the polemical meaning it assumed in the behaviour of specific social groups of workers and employees. They did not intend simply to neutralise the conflict, but also to lead it back to a social and institutional solution that would overturn the unacceptable image of opposing forces of labour and capital into a consensual order wherein capitalism and democracy would coexist forever without tension.

In this sense, the middle class actually takes on the appearance of a fetish: a symbolic object of mediation in which Americans recognise themselves regardless of the manual or intellectual work they do. The fetishism of the middle class ideally rewards the condition of subordination and deprivation that impacts American labour during capitalism's moments of crisis, namely in the transitional phases of its becoming global. The history of the fetish – which historiography has not grasped because it has assumed the concept of social sciences without discussing it – does not only allow us to understand why middle class constitutes the essential master key by which Americans try to unravel the tangled skein of the contemporary global crisis. It also provides the key to accessing the secret laboratory of the legitimation of capitalism in which the social sciences have developed the historical project (both scientific and political) of constructing the middle class. Within this scientific laboratory, the American middle class appears turned upside down with respect to its fetish. It is not the subject of timeless power that is the protagonist of national history, but rather the historical figure of the crises of American capitalism.

After retracing the European origins of the concept, taking on the social sciences as a privileged field of investigation, middle class is outlined in the progressive era up to the first postwar period when, in the context of international mercantile competition and growing economic interdependence, the formation of large industry coincided with the decline of the proprietary and professional old middle class and the rise of a new middle class of intellectual work. Then, I examine the middle class in the 1930s and 1940s, when facing the first major global crisis of capitalism, the New Deal responded to the processes of proletarianisation and the self-activity of the working class with policies which, being aimed at the social and institutional integration of skilled and semi-skilled workers and the white-collar work of professionals and salaried employees, found fulfilment in the large middle class after World War II. After this, I turn to the sixties and seventies, when the political response of business to the worker and social mobilisation reaffirmed the dominance of capital over society by launching transnational dynamics, which in the eighties and nineties heralded the contemporary decline of the middle class. The history of the fetish is, therefore, the history of the crises – and the transformations – of the middle class that accompanied globalisation as a historical process which in the last quarter of the twentieth century deprived American capitalism of its own historical source of legitimation.

The historically provisional result of this research shows that, although it still constitutes an obvious reference to US political culture today, the middle class is now an 'illusory' subject which, precisely because it is full of history, is expropriated of the future. It is an out-of-vogue symbol, unable to determine a shared and recognisable, orderly, and ordering mode of social behaviour.

Acknowledgments

This book is the result of many years of research marked by accelerations, slow-downs, suspensions, and recoveries. Many colleagues and friends have helped me. In recent years, I have had the opportunity to make several study trips to the United States to consult bibliographic sources and archival materials held at Yale University, Columbia University and New York University. I would like to thank Mario Del Pero, Eric Foner, Daniel J. Walkowitz and all the library staff of the universities that hosted me, especially Michael Koncewicz and the staff of the Tamiment Library & Robert F. Wagner Labor Archives.

In its various stages, the research has been presented and discussed at conferences and seminars. I am pleased to recall the conferences of the Italian Association for North American Studies (www.aisna.net) and the initiatives of the Interuniversity Center for Euro-American History and Politics (www .cispea.it). In these and other occasions I had the opportunity to consult with Lorenzo Costaguta, Daniele Fiorentino, Jonathan Levy, Marco Mariano, Daniel T. Rodgers, Federico Romero, Angela Santese, Bruno Settis, Marco Sioli, Arnaldo Testi, Elisabetta Vezzosi. Special thanks are addressed to those who discussed the research project and the structure of the book, who read all or part of the manuscript: Fulvio Cammarano, Bruno Cartosio, Monica Cioli, Ferdinando Fasce, Ferruccio Gambino, Mario Piccinini, Pierangelo Schiera, Maurizio Vaudagna. I hope that the result will live up to their advice and criticism. Eleonora Cappuccilli, Michele Cento, Luca Cobbe, Isabella Consolati, Roberta Ferrari, Carolina Marelli, Maurizio Ricciardi and Paola Rudan have not only helped to clarify this work in detail. They are more than just an area of discussion. Raffaella Baritono and Tiziano Bonazzi have continuously fed my commitment to research. With them I share not only an interest in the United States and its social sciences. I would also like to thank David R. Roediger and Graham Cassano for having appreciated my research and strongly supported the idea of publishing it in English. Finally, I want to thank Dave Mesing for his invaluable and tireless help in revising the English.

CHAPTER 1

The Middle Class between History and Social Sciences

In the history of the United States, references to the middle class are much less frequent than contemporary public debates and the historiography of the last century might suggest. Although used generically to reference an intermediate, industrious, and wealthy class in the latter half of the nineteenth century – one which had taken shape with the economic and social relations based on the market and introduced by the first industrial revolution – the term officially entered the US lexicon late with respect to European history. As proof of its lacking importance, the first dictionaries did not include an entry for middle class, but rather 'middle rank' or 'middling sort', entries which repeated the English meaning of those who were 'equally distant from the extremes' (Webster 1828: 126), i.e., the aristocracy and the labouring masses. This was true for Noah Webster's *American Dictionary of the English Language* (first edition 1828), which served as a point of reference for most of the nineteenth century, as well as for the 1859 editions of John Russell Bartlett's *Dictionary of Americanisms* (Russell Bartlett 1848: 270). Even when it was present in dictionaries and encyclopaedias during the late nineteenth century, its meaning did not have any particular US sense, but on the contrary denied that a similar European class distinction was present in the United States. *The Century Dictionary and Cyclopedia*, which was published by Yale University in twelve volumes between 1889 and 1911, still described a 'class of people which is socially and conventionally intermediate between the aristocratic class, or nobility, and the laboring class'. However, it was used in order to identify the set ('well born' or 'wealthy people') of landowners, merchants, professionals, and enterprising or well-off men who, while in continental Europe were included in the term bourgeoisie (thus expressing a strong hierarchical meaning), in the United States seemed to include everyone with the exception of the idle rich and the lazy and dissolute poor. The entry ended, in fact, by stating that 'in the United States no class-distinction of this nature exists' (Whitney and Smith 1901: 3755).[1]

---

1   Cf. Blumin 1985.

Only in the early 1930s does the *Encyclopaedia of the Social Sciences* present an entry for middle class for the first time, explaining the origins and transformations of the American middle class by way of comparing it to European history. Published between 1930 and 1935 under the direction of the economist Edwin Seligman as well as Alvin Johnson – editor of the progressive magazine *The New Republic* and director of the New School for Social Research in New York City – the work was the initiative of several large foundations and major academic associations in the field of the social sciences. The most authoritative US and European scholars were involved in an enterprise that testified to the affirmation of the social sciences in universities, and their increasing multidisciplinary and international inclination. Scientific reflection on the middle class was thus initiated and developed within transnational academic networks that developed above all after World War I. It happened within an intellectual and political horizon that broadened from the specific US field of vision in order to focus on, comprehend, and draw comparisons with the European experiences.[2]

The entry for 'middle class' in the encyclopaedia edited by the German scholar Alfred Meusel clarified the meaning of the concept in light of European historical developments, making particular reference to English literature from which the definition of 'lower middle class' was derived, as well as to German sociology which had introduced the concept of the new middle class, the *Neuer Mittelstand*. The historical account of the American middle class was thus reconstructed by distinguishing between 'old middle class' and 'new middle class'. The first term included the nineteenth-century figures linked to the free professions, and to small agricultural, commercial, artisanal, and manufacturing businesses. These figures were economically independent thanks to the ownership of property and control of their own work. On these bases they distinguished themselves from the labouring class by supporting the processes of industrialisation and democratisation in a way that was not completely unlike what happened in English and French history, albeit still distinct from these. The second signalled instead the presence of a set of workers ('salaried employee') which emerged in the United States as in Europe – in particular, in Great Britain and Germany – between the late nineteenth and early twentieth centuries following the second industrial revolution and the affirmation of large industry ('big business', 'trust', and 'corporation') which delegated decision-making, control, and bureaucratic functions to hired fiduciary assistants. In this sense, the new administrative profile that the progressivist era

---

2 Gemelli 1994.

American state took on by overcoming the laissez-faire policies of the earlier liberal epoch was also important.[3]

The new middle class was therefore made up mostly of 'white-collar' employees who, despite being dependent on the sale of their own labour-power, distinguished themselves from wage earners because they carried out non-manual labour ('brain work' or 'intellectual work') thanks to their training in secondary and vocational schools and universities. White-collar workers were engaged in the leadership ('manager' and 'superintendent') of branches and departments of large companies, in professional and technical services to businesses, especially as clerks, accountants, and office workers at the lower levels of public and private bureaucracies ('lower middle class'). Independence therefore did not pass through the ownership of property and autonomy of work, but rather through adequate levels of income and training which guaranteed a 'standard of living' distinct from that of the working class (Meusel 1933: 407–415). This was, in short, the new physiognomy of the middle class that would also be described in the 1944 *Dictionary of Sociology* and again in the 1959 *Dictionary of Social Sciences* (Pratt Fairchild 1944; Zadrozny 1959).

What was anticipated with respect to a scientific debate, which we will see to be much broader and more articulated, attempts to preliminarily trace the outlines of the American middle class in order to immediately draw attention to the role social sciences had in its definition. The nineteenth-century dictionaries had limited themselves to presenting a term of English vocabulary, denying, or reducing its meaning for US political culture because it alluded to specifically European class distinctions. The encyclopaedia instead pointed out that in order to understand the consequences of the second industrial revolution it was necessary to analyse the transformations large industry was causing in the middle class. Still more importantly, it showed how its formation should be considered within the framework outlined by the historical processes that traversed and joined the two sides of the Atlantic.

It is possible to speak of the Atlantic world first of all because, starting from the end of the nineteenth century, Europe and the United States were marked by a rapid convergence of economic development. Excluding the differences resulting from the different experiences following the epoch of democratic revolutions, two phenomena made the progressive connection of Euro-American states and societies possible. First, recognisable economic processes were emerging on both sides of the ocean. In the constant rush to increase profit margins compressed by competition and the crash of prices in

---

3 Skowroneck 1982.

the final quarter of the nineteenth century, economic forces were aggressive in crossing national borders. The movement of capital by means of increasing industrial and financial investments abroad, the spread of the factory system and production techniques and organisation of work ('scientific management', Taylorism and Fordism), the expansion of trade routes and information networks following the technological development of transportation (rail, naval, and airplane) and communication (telephone and telegraph) sectors, the tendency towards the economic concentration and the affirmation of the figure of the manager, the expansion of corporate bureaucracies and the development of the tertiary sector of private and public services, the birth of large-scale distribution and increase in consumer goods beyond subsistence needs – all of this was transforming and placing national states and their societies into an interdependent world distinguished by expansionist foreign policies and a greater economic competition which saw Germany and the United States grow more quickly than Great Britain and France.[4]

Second, in addition to causing changes in the economic geography of the Atlantic world, these transformations radically changed its social and political architecture. The formation of vast zones of mineral extraction and industrial production, migration towards industrialised societies, the birth of workers' settlements in cities, and the construction of suburban neighbourhoods as residential areas for the new middle class – all of this defined an unprecedented social edifice that was constantly shaken by conflict. Europe and the United States were traversed by a continuous industrial warfare which showed how poverty and strikes were constitutive elements of the new market relations, factory discipline, the organisation of work, and the stratification of societies. In light of the explosion of the social question, different national experiences were also marked by similar analogous tendencies. The end of the liberal era was characterised by policies which were still experimental and uncertain and which, albeit in different ways and at different times, intervened onto the market with regulatory, organisational, and distributive instruments aimed at mediating social conflict. The representation of interests and the integration of interest groups within the decision-making process, the legal and political recognition of unions, the development of reform programs, assistance, and social security all went in this direction. In this sense, a new and old world no longer seemed to exist: the transnational development of economic forces, both contradictory and conflictual, made clear the existence of a new Atlantic world, integrated according to unprecedented social and political coordinates,

---

4   On the category of interdependence, see Ninkovich 2009.

different from those that had characterised its modern formation between the seventeenth and eighteenth centuries.[5]

The economic and political convergences emerged from – and fueled – an ideological and scientific confrontation common to both sides of the ocean. Throughout the nineteenth century, democratisation, with the introduction of electoral systems based on a broad right to vote or universal male suffrage, had opened the doors of politics to the masses. What was witnessed was not only the rise of socialist and communist movements and parties with outcomes that differed from country to country, but also the overcoming of classical liberalism. Although they did not share the same name ('progressive', 'new liberal', 'réformateur social', 'solidariste', 'Sozialliberalen'), intellectuals and politicians who developed and promoted the new economic and social legislation policies expressed a new liberal vocation. This assumed the social question as central in order to integrate it into a coherent and functional horizon for the development of the national and international market, with the objective of avoiding the radicalisation – in a conservative or radical sense – of the political and social field. In this way the economic doctrine of the 'invisible hand' (Manchester School) was called into question, rethinking the role of the state as well as the very political anthropology at the basis of liberalism. It was recognised that the economic transformations placed the individual within complex and bureaucratised entities, where individual freedom could be thought and exercised only in light of increasing mutual dependence. The individual was no longer considered an independent atom, but rather as an expression of an interrelated set of social relations. The possessive and utilitarian individualism of the nineteenth century was therefore reformulated in the direction of a new social ethic which intended to affirm the role of collectivity and the participation of the community.[6]

The social sciences contributed to these institutional and ideological tendencies. Their affirmation as academic disciplines (economics, sociology, anthropology, history, and political science) in European and US universities started training and research networks that fueled the transnational circulation of new methodologies, empirical knowledge, and theories. In this way there emerged specific scientific convergences that transcended the various national cultures. A priori and deductive principles were rejected in favour of an analytic approach that intended to historicise economic and social processes,

---

5 Cf. Rodgers 2000; Battistini 2012.
6 The reference is to 'centrist liberalism' as a political discourse capable of moderating the ideological forces of conservatism and radicalism: Wallerstein 2011 (cf. Kloppenberg 1986; Kelley 1969; Leonhard 2007).

identify causes and consequences of conflicts, and propose adequate solutions because they were supported by findings considered objective and rational. This implied that scientific research did not place the individual itself in the foreground, but rather individuals for how they acted in society, in social groups and classes, and in the political elites. Furthermore, this new attention on collective entities led to portraying society as an articulate, organised, and artificial system, which took shape from the relations between its parts and which could therefore be dissected, controlled, and modeled in order to restore harmony and consensus. Finally, such an assessment made it possible to theorise a determinate capacity for political planning. From the end of the nineteenth century, in Europe (especially Germany) as in the United States, the social sciences took on a specific function of government to the extent that they contributed to the elaboration of public policies, claiming impartiality and the objectivity of the scientific method with respect to a decision-making process marked by the clash between political parties and between classes. The growing direct involvement of social scientists in public administrations showed that the new liberalism took on the guise of a genuine social science. In other words, it defined a political project that had the objective of shaping society on the basis of the results of scientific research.[7]

The new Atlantic world emerged from this complex set of economic processes, social changes, and institutional and ideological tendencies. Above all, the transnational circulation of political knowledge produced by the social sciences made possible a common, or at least commensurable, understanding of the different national histories. As the *Encyclopaedia of the Social Sciences* showed, while acting to control tensions within national states by legitimising and directing government interventions and relations between groups and classes, the social sciences formulated and discussed an unprecedented social and political vocabulary that traversed national borders. Among its terms, as we will see in this first chapter, was that of the middle class. While during the nineteenth century the middle classes were defined in light of national processes of industrialisation and democratisation, from the end of the century the crises that accompanied the second industrial revolution imposed a transnational comparison. Scholars and intellectuals began a reflection on the formation and transformation of the middle class that did not take place exclusively in single nations, nor even only in Europe or the United States, but rather in the Atlantic world that held the two sides of the ocean together. For this reason, it is not a matter of presenting a comparative social history of the middle

---

7   Bonazzi 1982; Schiera 1987; Baritono 1993.

classes, but rather of tracing the historical and conceptual features transversal to different societies, in order to emphasise not only the common dynamics involved in the formation of the American middle class, but also the specificity that marked its rise. Before proceeding to the United States, it is therefore appropriate to reconstruct the histories of the European middle classes.[8]

1   The (Lower) English Middle Class

Early modern England has been considered the birth nation of the middle class. This is the not case because it was the only European society to have an important presence of merchants, artisans, and manufacturers, but rather because these figures were attributed with a noteworthy role in national history. The middle class explained the early entry of the English nation into economic and political modernity to the extent that it had fueled the industrial revolution and supported the political reforms which, from the Glorious Revolution, made it possible to embark upon a path of democratisation that avoided ruptures and upheavals of the constitutional framework (unlike what happened in France). The middle class was mentioned in this sense in the *History of England* by both Thomas B. Macaulay (1848–1855) and George M. Trevelyan (1926), texts which established the liberal canon of the 'whig interpretation of history'. Even at the end of the previous century, 'the making of the English middle class' defined the theme of historical reconstructions which counterbalanced research on the formation of the English working class.[9]

'Middle class' appeared in the English dictionary in the entry for class as a term introduced in order to understand the economic transformations and social changes which marked the end of the eighteenth and early nineteenth century. Before the industrial revolution there was talk of 'sort', 'rank', or 'order' for defining different degrees of respectability and deference within a rigid hierarchical scale that ranged from the nobility to the plebs. From the end of the eighteenth century, the concept of class began to be used to explain an unprecedented historical character of society: since progress depended on the relation between classes, middle class indicated the genesis of an industrious and opulent class of merchants, artisans, manufacturers, and capitalists who broke the traditional links of feudal subordination in favour of new hierarchies determined by the market rather than titles and privilege (Wade 1842). Thus,

---

8   Cf. Grew 1980; Beck 2010; Ross 1997: XIII–XXII; De Grazia 2005: 75–129.
9   Cf. Earle 1989; Briggs 1959; Perkin 1969. See also Cannadine 1998; Gunn 2012: 58–74.

during the French Revolution, while the Tory exponents continued to speak of ranks and orders in defense of monarchical and aristocratic institutions, the reference to the middle class was used with different political meanings by those who intended to make a constitutional change in a democratic sense as well as by those who instead, faced with the Jacobin threat from across the Channel, promoted a limited and moderate reform within the constitutional horizon outlined in 1688.[10]

The reformist perspective prevailed during the nineteenth century also thanks to the affirmation of economic and political liberalism (the Manchester School and utilitarianism), particularly through two of the most influential intellectuals of the era: Richard Cobden and James Mill. While the economic doctrine of 'free trade' and the invisible hand of the market had found confirmation in the rise of the middle class, economic and moral individualism, the theory of representative government, and the appeal to public opinion provided the Whig exponents with a political discourse that consolidated the faith of the middle class in the old English constitution, in this way making possible a reform policy which avoided the insurrectionary tendencies evoked in the words of radicals and Chartists associated with workers' mobilisations. In light of the emerging class conflict, middle class thus assumed a full political significance that held together different groups: manufacturers in the north, merchants and financiers in large urban centres (especially London), professionals linked to university instruction, government, and local institutions. The middle class embodied the national wealth produced by the industrial revolution in a way that was coherent and functional to the vision of society considered unique in Europe because it was distinguished by an unparalleled social mobility. In this sense, even the term 'gentleman' (Marshall 1873) did not identify only the noble landowner, but increasingly anyone who occupied an eminent social position for his entrepreneurial or professional activity. Above all, the public reference to the middle class served to give political voice to a subject on whom the conquest of free trade and suffrage was dependent. While the 1832 Reform Bill excluded the working class from the vote by announcing the possibility of a government of the middle class, the revoking of the Corn Laws (1846–1849) realised the economic interests of manufacturing groups. Following this, the 1867 conservative Reform Act further expanded the vote on the basis of proprietary criterion of 'household', and the successive liberal governments of William Gladstone approved measures which positively responded to consumers and producers against landlord rent. As Walter

---

10   Cf. Seed 1992: 114–135; Wallech 1986: 409–431; Briggs 1967: 43–73; Kramnick 1990.

Bagehot wrote in *The English Constitution* (1867): 'The middle classes are today the despotic power of England'.[11]

For much of the century, economic development and democratisation therefore confirmed the belief that the Victorian era coincided with the triumph of a middle class depicted as the subject of civilisation and the political bulwark against the privileges of the aristocracy as well as the radical tendencies of class conflict and the revolutionary excesses on the other side of the Channel. In this sense, James Mill wrote that the middle class constituted 'the wisest and most virtuous part of the community' that 'will guide the poorer classes' (Mill 1978: 93–94). Since the middle class demanded the broadening of suffrage and free trade while invoking the support of the working class, the reforms institutionalised the entrepreneurial and professional ideal within the constitutional framework. On the one hand, it was maintained that the process of democratisation did not question the property accumulated because labour and capital did not constitute two opposing interests but were instead mutually dependent. On the other hand, Parliament and the courts legislated and administered civil law by producing juridical distinctions which reflected the moral character of the 'gentleman' and formalised the social inferiority of a working class deemed irresponsible and incapable of independence. The 'English middle class' defined the fulcrum of national political culture, the gravitational centre of the nation which coagulated the economic and intellectual forces in the direction of civilisation, progress, and prosperity.[12]

Despite finding precise echoes in the public debate and literature of this period, this historiographical narrative has simplified the social and political architecture of the English nineteenth century. This is so not only because it has weakened the workers' political voice which emerged after 1832 through Chartism, but also because it has smoothed over hierarchies within the middle class by not considering that the financial and mercantile wealth concentrated in London was considerably greater than the wealth accumulated in manufacturing areas of the north. On the institutional level, moreover, the organisation of interests in Victorian politics was more complex and transversal to parties, both conservative and liberal, while the electoral choices did not only have an economic motive, being influenced by different religious affiliations (Anglican and dissident). In light of this, it is possible to overturn the interpretive key which, through the Whig canon of liberal historiography, has associated the middle class with the affirmation of industrial capital, the triumph of economic

---

11   Cf. Perkin 1969: 309–312, 365–380; Adelman 1984: 11–40, 90–115; Hobsbawn 1989: 100–106.
12   Cf. Johnson 1993: 147–169; Adelman 1984: 30–40; Perkin 1969: 365–380.

and political liberalism, and democratisation. Instead of representing the middle class as subject of civilisation, it is possible to consider how the political and economic reforms constituted the crucial factor which allowed for the shaping of an otherwise differentiated and divided middle class along lines determined by the market. The construction of the middle class in national history was the necessary apparatus for the governing of society. In order to understand its historical and conceptual formation, it is therefore important to show how this construction broke out towards the end of the century.[13]

Starting from the final quarter of the nineteenth century, various processes related to the second industrial revolution radically changed the social and political framework. Large industrialists and financiers acquired an economic supremacy which resulted in the rise of a new political elite that integrated landed aristocracy and monetary wealth.[14] It was not as much a matter of the assimilation of bourgeois figures into the aristocracy thanks to the acquisition of the noble title (a phenomenon already present in the first half of the century), but rather the complete affirmation of the monetary criterion to establish hierarchies which were different than the past because they were no longer based on the possession of land from birth. This elite – defined as 'upper class' or negatively as 'plutocracy' – was the expression of processes of economic concentration that had profound consequences on the composition and representation of the middle class. The spread of professions and the rise of salaried managers and administrators particularly in large-scale companies, the increase in office jobs in the industrial and financial sector, as well as the increase in sales employees with the emergence of large-scale distribution, the expansion of the administrative functions of the state, and the increase in public services following the social legislation of the early twentieth century – all of this upset the nineteenth-century physiognomy of the middle class. It was decreasingly composed of merchants, manufacturers, and capitalists, and increasingly of public and private employees ('clerk', 'black-coated worker', 'white collar') who were mostly concentrated in London, Edinburg, Nottingham, Birmingham, Liverpool, Manchester, and Bristol.[15]

These figures embodied what was defined as the lower middle class, a middle class identifiable not according to proprietary, entrepreneurial, and

---

13   Gunn 2004: 29–47; Gunn and Bell 2002; Wahrman 1995. Cf. Stedman Jones 1982: 3–58. By
      the same author see also Stedman Jones 1983.
14   Feuchtwanger 1985: 84–146.
15   From 1891 to 1911, employee figures (both private and public) increased from about 144,000
      to 918,000 unites. Between 1912 and 1954, the figure climbed to 2.4 million (cf. McKibbin
      1998; Crossick 1977).

professional criteria, but rather in relation to other groups in society. While occupying a marginal position with respect to the new economic and political elite, its members distinguished themselves from workers by claiming a superior social position due to the skilled training they received, the non-manual labour ('brain work') based on technical and professional skills, the major level of consumption, and the different lifestyle that characterised suburban residential areas. In 1896, Charles Booth – philanthropist and sociologist, the cousin of Beatrice Potter Webb, author of pioneering studies on poverty and an advocate of social reform – wrote in this sense that the 'undifferentiated labour-power' spoken of by Karl Marx did not exist and could least of all be found among the employees (Booth 1896). Only a little while later, however, it was realised that these lower middle-class figures were suffering from the increasing accumulation of wealth. Above all in moments of economic crisis and inflation, which followed one another between the turn of the century and the interwar period, their career ambitions were frustrated by changes in the labour market and the structure of businesses. If greater access to training fuelled these ambitions, the processes of economic concentration and the hierarchies of private and public bureaucracies limited opportunities for social advancement: non-manual labour became less skilled, more routinised and impersonal.[16]

In light of these economic and social transformations, the English middle class was involved in a cultural and political tension. On the one hand it continued to be defined in opposition to the working class, while on the other it could no longer be identified with the figure of the owner-entrepreneur who had characterised its nineteenth century triumph. While the Victorian view assumed that the middle class was mostly composed of the 'business man', the decline of the entrepreneurial ideal after the second industrial revolution made clear the presence of a middle class that was until then overlooked ('forgotten middle class'): a class composed not only of members of professions whose numbers had grown considerably since the second half of the century (doctors, engineers, architects, teachers, journalists), but above all the new employee figures who could claim training and skills. In this sense, despite never having formed a single and homogenous subject, if not for the greater public visibility of proprietary and entrepreneurial figures who had supported the affirmation of economic and political liberalism, there was talk of the middle class in the plural ('middle classes'). Further, the adjective 'lower' disproved

---

16   Cf. Lockwood 1958: 18; Hobsbawn 1989: 108–118.

the representation of the middle class as the central subject of national history, indicating rather the failure of Victorian aspirations (Masterman 1909: 68–69).[17]

This clearly emerges from the work of Charles Masterman, a journalist and political liberal who in 1909 no longer described the middle class as the economic and social motor of the English nation, nor even as the political bulwark against the growing class conflict. He did not celebrate its triumph, but rather publicly denounced its economic weakness and political inconsistency in relation to the opposing forces of labour and capital. Without the 'channels of communication' through which capitalists and workers exercised power in society, it remained silent or unheard. While the working class was unionised and politically organised, the middle class was not feared because even though it was large, it 'lacked organization, strength, and ideas'. Its values of security and respectability were entirely vulnerable. Even the historical reconstructions that still described it as the 'representation of civilisation' ended with a 'sense of desolation', registering its social fragmentation and the impossibility of defining it according to a common political orientation (Masterman 1909: 68–70, 76, 84–85). While conservatives became the party of land and capital, integrating most of the industrial and financial figures previously linked to the Liberal Party, the presence of a lower middle class influenced the rethinking of classical liberalism and favoured the rise of an independent Labourist force.[18]

At the turn of the century, in the radical press and in various reforming intellectual milieus (such as Toynbee Hall and the Rainbow Circle), and among critics of William Gladstone's liberal leadership, a public debate began which renewed liberalism by introducing elements of theoretical and political novelty in light of the social question. The 'new liberalism' went beyond utilitarianism by integrating the ethics of individual responsibility and private interest into a new vision of community, social cooperation, and the public good. It abandoned the dogma of free trade by shifting attention away from production, naturally regulated by the invisible hand of the market, and to distribution and consumption, which made government intervention possible. The partial loss of faith in civilisation understood as progress and autonomous improvement of society was compensated for by claiming social reform through a broad conception of the functions of the state. In the intentions of economists and sociologists such as John Hobson and John Hobhouse who rejected the evolutionism of Herbert Spencer and radical journalists such as John Hammond (editor of *The Speaker* from 1899–1906) and Henry Massingham (editor of *The*

---

17   Cfr. Perkin 1969: 379–380, 448–450; McLeod 1977: 58–62; Gunn 1988: 17–43. See also Perkin 1989; Malatesta 2011.

18   Guazzaloca 2004: 46–65, 234–256.

Nation from 1907–1923), these new theories served to take distance from conservativism as well as socialism by indicating the new political goal of liberalism in 'pragmatic collectivism'. While nineteenth-century liberalism ('old
liberalism') had originated and at the same time fuelled the battle of the entrepreneurial middle class in order to free the government from noble control,
the 'new liberalism' was the expression of a new professional middle class that
claimed the application of the scientific method and empirical knowledge in
order to intervene in favour of the working masses.[19]

On this intellectual basis, in the decade before World War I, the new leadership of the Liberal Party constructed around Herbert Henry Asquith and David
Lloyd George elaborated social legislation (social security, insurance systems,
and forms of welfare) which, although financed by introducing the principle
of direct and progressive taxation that mainly affected large landowners and
industrialists, produced tensions and divisions among the middle classes.
While the conservative press denounced the 'looting of the middle class', the
liberal debate expressed concerns about the tendency of conservativism to
become the electoral choice for broad intermediate sections of the population.
Those who remained tied to classic liberalism warned the party leadership
that it could not govern without the support of the middle classes. Even those
who promoted the transition to the new liberalism began to fear that the party
was considered a class party, a 'party of the non-proprietary class'. They viewed
a possible compromise with the nascent Labour Party with suspicion because
it was believed that the expansion of suffrage to the working masses should
not involve Parliament in the task of establishing the wage level or working
day by law. What liberalism could do for the working class was to develop public education and implement distributive policies which ensured equity and
opportunities for social advancement. Without undermining the traditional
liberal value of individualism, it was a matter of achieving 'a higher standard
of living for the whole people, largely by the regulative and persuasive action
of the state', in order to forge a 'middle class as large as possible by recruiting
the best of the sad and suffering section beneath it'. The attempt was to make
the lower middle class the backbone of reform or to elaborate a 'middle-class
liberalism' which would convince employee figures to support social legislation (Haldane 1888).[20]

---

19   Adelman 1984: 120–145. Cf. Freeden 1978; Collini 1979.
20   By the same author, see also Haldane 1905. Articles published by Hobson and Masterman
      between 1906 and 1908 in the *Tribune, Nation,* and *Speaker* also go in this direction (cf.
      Freeden 1979: 151–158; Lewis and Maude 1953: 42–50; Adelman 1984: 140–143). On social
      legislation at the beginning of the century, see Feuchtwanger 1985: 335–384.

The translation of new liberalism into public policies did not produce the expected results, however. Except for a short period, the new liberal leadership was unable to consolidate a broad consensus among the various intermediate figures of the population: entrepreneurs, professionals, and employees. At the beginning of the 1920s, the accomplished affirmation of the Labour Party was the clear sign that, despite its rethinking in a social key, liberalism had not been able to understand and politically interpret the economic transformations which had invested and upset the middle class. While pointing out the difficulty in univocally defining the middle class, several publications reproduced the entrepreneurial image of the Victorian era. Others failed to go beyond denouncing the conditions of poverty, cultural frustration, and political impotence which above all marked the inferior figures of the 'white collar' and 'clerk' (Gretton 1919).

After World War I, Masterman described a picture of suburban areas that was even worse than the one presented at the turn of the century. The interwar period emerged as the culmination of the 'slow disintegration and decay of this whole standard of civilisation of Middle Class England'. Inflation and unemployment transferred wealth from debtors to creditors, the decline in income widened the gap between lower rank employees and those who occupied the highest level of public and private bureaucracies (officials, administrators, and managers), a 'new poverty' finally marked a conspicuous decrease in consumption which previously had ensured a higher social position than the working class. Not by chance, it was only in these years that research on middle class consumption and habits began for the first time. Journalists and scholars who referred to the liberal camp thus provided valuable empirical knowledge but were unable to forge a shared political discourse that would allow the middle classes to influence public opinion and the government. On the contrary, they noted that the new liberalism had not taken root in suburban areas, where irritation about social legislation and the related taxation had shifted the vote towards conservatives. While the traditional values of individualism remained intact, reproducing the 'absurd and irrational belief' of the possible alliance between the middle class and the industrial and financial upper class, the middle class was portrayed as being forced 'between two burdens': the proletariat and the capitalist. This image effectively represented not only the 'strange death' of liberalism and the electoral marginality of the Liberal Party which had been ousted by the affirmation of the Labour Party, but also the defeat of a political culture that had legitimised democratisation not as a political outcome of the class conflict, but rather as the natural product of the spread of liberal individualism among the 'aristocracies of labor'

(Masterman 1922: 57–59, 66, 70–81; Masterman 1909: 68–71; 80–81; 84–85; Caradog Jones 1928).[21]

In this sense, significant contributions to the social and political understanding of the lower middle class also came from the socialist and labour forces. In the first decade of the twentieth century, in a series of articles on *Socialism and the Middle Classes* published in *Fortnightly Review*, Bernard Shaw and H.G. Wells rejected the accusation that socialism constituted a 'plan of expropriation' by appealing to the 'more educated middle classes'. In their view, the second industrial revolution had undermined the sense of individual responsibility and individual security. For this reason, the 'middle-class families' who had 'fallen into deprivation' should abandon the individualism of the market in order to make 'common cause' with the working class (Wells 1906). These and other arguments were developed within the Fabian Society, thanks above all to the contributions of its founding leaders Sidney and Beatrice Webb (Shaw 1894; *Fabian Tract 69*, 1896; *Fabian Tract 146*, 1909; Webb 1917).[22] With respect to European socialist experiences, which were also facing the question of the formation of a new middle class, the specificity of their political reflection was to raise the flag of socialism among the new salaried figures which defined the 'intellectual' or 'professional' proletariat. The new professionals – particularly the state civil servant and the technical and administrative frameworks of large companies – indicated a possible alternative to the economic system based on profit. Even when they supported trade union organisations, the Webbs' socialism thus did not rest on the working class, but on the contrary intended to overcome the social conflict by identifying in intellectual labour ('brain work') and the cooperative ethics of the new professions the forces to scientifically organise an administrative management of the economy through the state. In this sense, not unlike the new liberalism, Fabianism was an expression of the reaction of the new middle classes to the end of the Victorian era.[23]

Even as they drew closer to the Labour Party, the Webbs continued to look towards the middle class. In 1920, Sidney Webb distinguished between two middle classes: one which recognised itself in the liberal government of Lloyd George (1916–1922) and one that would govern in the near future. The former was composed of the manufacturing, merchant, and agrarian 'business man' who had accumulated immense wealth during the global conflict thanks to

---

21   On the 'death' of political liberalism in relation to the middle class, see Lewis and Maude 1953: 53. On the political crisis at the turn of the century and the defeat of liberal cultural politics, see Cammarano 2003.
22   Cf. Lewis and Maude 1953: 49; Ferrari 2017.
23   Hobsbawm 1964: 255–271.

the war economy organised around price control and the rationalisation of investments. Opposed to this 'predatory plutocracy', the latter middle class contributed much of the national wealth through the work of managers, designers, superintendents and foremen, sales and other clerks, teachers and professionals, and officials and employees in public administration. This 'large army of the salariat' – with a sober character, moderate income, and an aptitude for saving, cultural aspirations, and a commitment to education – lacked a common public voice that challenged the 'political deference' towards businessmen. The problem of organisation had to be resolved by looking at the forms of worker association: if until the beginning of the century the middle classes were divided between conservative and liberal camps, from the 1920s on it seemed possible to involve in the Labour project (presented in the 1918 pamphlet *Labour and the New Social Order*) at least the employee figures who were experimenting with new forms of union action. As the membership of professional teachers' associations in the Trades Union Congress demonstrated, according to Webb, there was no other way to organise the middle class other than to integrate the 'workers by brain' into the Labour Party (Webb 1920: 13–14).

The history of the middle class, however, took a different direction. The low participation of white-collar employees in the 1926 general strike and the organisation of thousands of volunteers in order to ensure essential services were clear proof of this. In spite of the intellectual and political effort of the socialist and labour forces, the middle classes entrusted a large part of their vote to conservativism, especially in the second half of the 1920s when wages and consumption began to rise again. Only at the beginning of the following decade, after the economic crisis, did communist-oriented intellectuals and scholars initiate a new political reflection on the 'destiny of the middle classes', publishing economic and sociological analyses that argued for their complete proletarianisation and encouraged their unionisation and political identification with the working class.[24]

In conclusion, from the final quarter of the nineteenth century up to the period between the two wars, the English public and political debate overturned the nineteenth-century narrative of the formation of the middle class: 'the making of the English middle class' appeared as an 'un-making', or as an inverse process of social and political decline that prevented the centrality that classic liberalism had attributed to the middle class from updating in the

---

[24]   See Hobsawm 1989: 122–123, and Samuel 1983. Examples of studies on the English middle class with a communist orientation include Klingender 1935 and Brown 1936. On the electoral orientation of the English middle class, see Bonham 1954 and Kocka 1980: 267–275.

new century. From the confrontation within the liberal, socialist, and labour camp, the image that emerged was plural, economically insecure, socially disarticulated, and culturally and politically disoriented in the face of the opposing forces of labour and capital. If during the nineteenth century the reference to the middle class had served to forge and support a shared liberal political project contrary to both aristocratic privilege and worker protagonism, when the growing weight of class conflict undermined liberal political hegemony, the middle class showed divisions and tensions that the new liberalism could not recompose and overcome. There was no lack of associations such as the Middle Class Defense Organization (1906) and the Middle Classes Union (1919), as well as the National Citizen Union from 1921, which acted autonomously from liberals, conservatives, and labour. Their impact was negligible, however. Composed above all of residual entrepreneurial figures, since they did not involve the new lower middle classes, these associations were unable to reconstruct the nineteenth-century public opinion that John Stuart Mill had intended to coincide with the middle class on a new basis (Mill 1859). To paraphrase Bagehot, the middle class no longer constituted the despotic power of the English nation.[25]

There are a number of reasons that explain a similar social and political decline: the economic transformations that pushed towards a polarisation of wealth, the affirmation of an aggressive syndicalism that also mobilised less skilled manual labour, and the rise of an independent labour political force. Still more important is that these reasons find confirmation in the failure to elaborate a specific reflection on the middle class, capable not only of describing and denouncing its precarious economic conditions, but also defining a shared political vocabulary that would allow it to communicate with and unify the different social and cultural aspirations of its members. At least until the interwar period, both liberalism and labourism failed on this terrain or were marked only by partial successes. In this sense, the weak academic development of the social sciences was decisive. This is not the place to examine the historiographical debate on the absence of English sociology, a debate which has often underestimated the works of scholars such as Spencer, Stuart Mill, and Hobhouse. However, it is useful to highlight the contribution that scientific associations, such as the National Association of Social Science, made in renewing liberal discourse in the direction of social reform. Not unlike the German and US scientific experiences of the period (particularly, as we will see, the Verein für Socialpolitik and the American Social Science Association),

---

25   Cf. Habermas 1991 and McKibbin 1998.

these associations formed a kind of public forum of the educated middle classes, giving voice to their knowledge and skills, and their aspiration to govern society. In this way they forged a strong unity between science, politics, and reform that shaped the liberal and labour need to establish an 'alliance' between 'brains' and 'numbers'. Unlike what happened on the European continent, however, sociological analyses and empirical research aimed specifically at the study of the middle class were not initiated across the Channel. Those linked to the liberal political field were concentrated on the working class, while the London School of Economics, founded by the Webbs in 1895, favoured above all the development of economic and administrative disciplines. Since it was limited to the political polemic, the reference to the middle class thus lacked an adequate scientific depth which would make it authoritative, and therefore capable of defining a cornerstone of political culture and public opinion. Consequently, in the first half of the twentieth century, the middle class become an equivocal and indefinite signifier. Only in the aftermath of World War II would it assume a new centrality in the English vocabulary through the scientific and popular audience works that borrowed its meaning from the US social sciences.[26]

2 Bourgeoisie and *Classe Moyenne*

We see in the examination of nineteenth-century dictionaries and encyclopaedias that the term bourgeoisie was not part of the US vocabulary. There was also no significant reference within English history. Rather, 'higher class' or 'upper class' was spoken in order to indicate a process of integration between 'gentry' and 'common' which, moving from the bottom towards the top, prevented the consolidation of an impermeable class: in this way the bourgeois nature of English society was rejected. The continental history of the middle class emerged instead in a complex relation with the bourgeoisie that matured particularly in France and Germany in the period between the age of revolutions and the end of the liberal age.[27]

In France, reference to the middle class was present starting from the revolutionary events of the late eighteenth century. Taken from French translation of Aristotle's *Politics*, which had identified in the middle class the sure foundation for avoiding the degenerative cycle of forms of government by

26   Goldman 1986; Goldman 1987; Goldman 2004. Cf. Cole 1955; Stearns 1979; Crossick 1977; Mayer 1975.
27   Hobsbawm 1989: 124–125; Kocka 1995; Romanelli 1989.

ensuring duration and balance to the constitution, *classe mytoyenne* – soon replaced with *classe moyenne* – was used in the political debate on the electoral census by moderate members of the National Assembly gathered around Antoine Barnave. During the drafting of the Thermidorian Constitution (1795), the Aristotelian argument also served to ward off the fear of the Terror, supporting the expansion of suffrage according to a certain census in order to guarantee in this way the supremacy of a class that – it was argued – loved order and harboured an aversion to constant revolutions. The concept therefore immediately appeared with a strong political meaning, in continuity with the expression *tiers état*, as this was formulated by Emmanuel Sieyès on the eve of the revolution. In this sense, in his historical writings, Augustine Thierry broadened the reference to the bourgeois as an inhabitant of the city in order to involve the indistinct people, from the countryside to the cities, in the battle against noble privilege. In the *Histoire de la civilization en France*, published close to the July Monarchy, François Guizot wrote that the Third Estate was so extensive that it absorbed all other classes, determining the direction and character of French civilisation. A few years later, in a speech delivered before the Legislative Assembly, Guizot attributed the same historical function to the *classe moyenne*: a proprietary and independent class whose members were not forced into manual labour, nor dependent on wages and thus could devote their own time for public affairs (Thierry 1827, particularly *Letter XV*; Guizot 1829–1832).[28]

In the period between the parliamentary monarchy and the Second Republic there thus emerged a political notion of the middle class which – with a meaning coextensive to that of the bourgeoisie – identified and united all the forces opposed to the nobility, while avoiding the result of the government of the nation ending up in popular and workers' hands. It was instead a different situation at the beginning of the Third Republic, when *classe moyenne* carried an ambiguous meaning. On the one hand, it was used as a synonym for bourgeoisie by those who rejected universal suffrage because it would have undermined the possibility of restoring the constitutional balance after the Second Empire of Napoleon III and the experience of the Paris Commune (1871). On the other, it was used in the political debate with the aim of identifying a broader social subject that, by involving artisanal figures, would claim and legitimise the conquest of representative democracy against the census regime. This was the meaning of the 'national recovery' of the Republic in the short government of Léon Gambetta following the

---

28   Cf. Sick 1993: 14–16.

1881 elections. Beyond the polemic between democratic and non-democratic republicans, in the final quarter of the century *classe moyenne* maintained the shared meaning of the historical motor of French civilisation. Not unlike the English events, the social and political affirmation of the bourgeoisie coincided with the elaboration of a national history that had the middle class at its centre: since it held together different figures who shared a common progressive vision of the nation, speaking of the *classe moyenne* purged the political debate of the polemical character that the concept of the bourgeoisie had assumed in socialist and communist literature. As could be read in an article entitled 'Middle-Class Life in France' published in *The North American Review*, that did not mean that the bourgeoisie no longer existed. The bourgeois still identified those who were linked to their profession, trade, savings, and the accumulation of wealth. And yet, referring to the bourgeoisie no longer made any sense: 'now that everybody may become a gentleman, as the English say, we have no more nobles, no more bourgeoisie, nor any more Third Estate' (Lola de San Carlos 1893: 478).

Even in this case, however, it is a matter of historical representation strongly vitiated by political events. *Classe moyenne* did not so much identify a social group but was rather a political notion that performed a precise function of the legitimation of a liberal order that continually derailed from the progressive vision of national history that intellectuals, historians, and politicians had traced starting from the July Monarchy. Not by chance, the reference to the middle class was imposed in the public and political debate especially in moments of constitutional transition: in order to celebrate the success of the parliamentary monarchy against the restoration of absolutism, the affirmation of the Second Republic after the workers' uprisings in June 1848, and the institution of the Third Republic after the Second Empire and the experience of the Commune. With this meaning, still in the second half of the twentieth century, the rise of the *classe moyenne* was at the centre of historiographical reconstructions which have traced the progressive formation of French democracy, from the revolutionary period until the second postwar period. Against the interpretations that have emphasised most of all the nineteenth-century permanence of the landed aristocracies, the role of the state functionaries, and the mercantile and industrial weakness in comparison to the English economy, these reconstructions have associated industrialists, landowners, professionals, administers, and state officials with the *classe moyenne*: even if in the short term these intermediate figures were divided by conflicting interests and diverging political positions, in the long term they would still have the merit of keeping society open and mobile against the reactionary closure of the constitutional system, of promoting policies on a rational rather than traditional basis, and of fuelling the economic and social development of the nation.[29]

These historiographical reconstructions have therefore reproduced the narrative of the first half of the nineteenth century according to which the middle class acted in a univocal and linear way in the civilisation of the French nation. In this sense, they have not considered the 'other history' of the *classe moyenne* presented in the pages of the *18th Brumaire of Luigi Bonaparte* (1852), where Marx emphasises how the French middle class has abdicated its 'political emancipation', entrusting the 'executive power' in the hands of Napoleon III in order to guarantee a 'bourgeois order' otherwise threatened by workers' forces: 'industry and commerce, hence the business affairs of the middle class, are to prosper in hothouse fashion under the strong government' (Marx 1979: 194–195). Only in this way, during the Second Empire, did Paris become the *ville lumière* with its large department stores and the national economy opened to the second industrial revolution. While for Thierry and Guizot bourgeoisie and *classe moyenne* converged at the centre of a national history represented as continuous and progressive, for Marx the experience of the Commune showed how the middle class had given up its own capacity for political initiative. In his view, *classe moyenne* did not mark the civilisation of the nation and the democratisation of the republic, but rather the political death of the bourgeoisie, the fulfilment of its historical mission (Marx 1986: 480–485).

Beyond the historical and historiographical comparison, all of this highlights the growing discontinuity of meaning between the terms bourgeoisie and *classe moyenne*, above all from the end of the century. On the one hand, the negative image of the new *féodalité financière* and the explosion of the social question made clear the profound cultural and political disorietation of the bourgeoisie, or its inability to understand how its liberal vision of society and the state was no longer adequate to the changes imposed by the second industrialisation. On the other hand, the same economic and political transformations affected the composition of a middle class made up of less and less of property owning and independent figures – '*isolés*', according to the first official classification of the census in the late the nineteenth century – and increasingly of state officials of different levels, professionals, and simple employees of departments in large industries and distribution (*cadres* and *employée*), whose main characteristic was to depend on the market in a way not different

---

29   O'Noyle 1966; Pilbeam 1990. Cf. Thomson 1952; Palmer 1959; Pinkey 1964; Cobban 1967.

from the waged workers (*salarié*).[30] If for most of the nineteenth century *classe moyenne* had intended to incorporate the entire bourgeoisie, representing in this way the liberal ideal of the rational and progressive conquest of civil and political freedom, at the end of the century it became increasingly difficult to consider capitalists, entrepreneurs, and managers of large businesses as part of the middle class. Above all, while the bourgeoisie no longer constituted the cornerstone of the political legitimacy of a liberal order in the process of transformation, the reference to the middle class escaped a coherent and shared definition that allowed the representing of a subject capable of interpreting and governing social changes: the growing tension between bourgeoisie and middle class reflected the end of the liberal era.

Faced with this situation – this is what distinguishes the history of the French middle class from the English middle class – the social sciences attributed a specific scientific meaning to the concept *classe moyenne*. Influenced by the scholar and reformer Pierre-Guillaume-Frédéric Le Play (1806–1882) and his social Catholicism, French and Belgian scholars – Maurice Dufourmantelle, Etienne Martin Saint-Léon, Georges Blondel, Victor Brants, and Hector Lambrechts – distanced themselves from the methodological individualism of classic liberalism in order to undertake empirical research on the middle class. Their objective was both scientific and political: forging the category of *classe moyenne* meant not only delineating an instrument for diagnosing the ills of industrial society and prescribing the related treatments, but also aimed at encouraging the mobilisation of the intermediate strata to defend a social order marked by growing class conflict and the rise of socialism. In order to counter the Marxist theses that had foreshadowed the demise of the middle class, the new social sciences found it necessary to overcome what was considered a worrying void of conceptualisation and empirical knowledge of social classes and in particular the middle class (See also Halbwachs 1905; Halbwachs 1939; Halbwachs 1955).[31]

This research direction was first undertaken by Victor Brants, a Belgian sociologist and economist, who was very influential in the French debate for having translated the German concept of *Neuer Mittelstand* with the expression *nouvelles couches de classe moyenne*. He explained that the rise of large industry, with the mechanisation of work and the concentration of directive functions, was causing the disappearance of crafts and the affirmation of new types of workers: even if they were 'dependent', engineers and managers, officials and

---

30   Szreter 1993: 305–313.

31   See Mangoni 1985 and Mangoni 1988: 231–252.

employees were not considered *proletaire sans phrase* because they were capable of autonomy due to their income. In this way, Brants grasped the presence of a 'middle class in transformation': from the *classe moyenne vrai* to the *classes moyennes des revenus* (Brants 1902: 1–20, 109). What was important was not so much the use of the term in the plural (which was already used in the past in order to indicate the different figures of the bourgeoisie) as the overcoming of the proprietary and entrepreneurial criteria of the previous century. In light of the transformations that marked work, income defined an unprecedented distinctive character of the middle class because it provided a variable social measure, and therefore was suitable for grasping the changes in the stratification of society, the distribution of wealth, and in consumption habits and expectations. This was also the sense of the distinction that Etienne Martin Saint-Léon introduced in 1910 between *classe moyenne indépendante* and *classe moyenne dépendant* (Saint-Léon 1910: 166–175. See also Hector 1927).[32]

Like other works which analysed the middle class through a new conceptual constellation (income, consumption, professional status), these were not devoid of political significance. This emerged clearly, for example, when Brants invited scholars, intellectuals, and politicians to shift attention from the working class to the middle classes because the possibility of defining the general interest of nations and in this way securing the political stability of the entire continent depended on them. The sociological approach to the definition of the middle class first of all allowed affirming that the *classe moyenne* was not threatened at all by the second industrial revolution and by the growing concentration of wealth, but on the contrary constituted an expanding social class, potentially the most numerous. Even more importantly, it made it possible to escape the *cul de sac* in which the political notion of the middle class had precipitated with the turn-of-the-century crisis of the bourgeoisie. In a context marked by the increasingly influential public presence of the working class, the French social sciences forged a concept that was used to formulate a 'middle-class politics' that distanced itself both from workers' organisations and the economic and financial élites of the large industry: *classe moyenne* became the scientific expression of the potential harmony of a society shaken by growing class conflict and in this sense was publicly used to win the consensus (which was not only electoral) needed to acquire and exercise political force (Brants 1902: 13; Rivière 1910: 3–9; Saint-Léon 1905: 1–2; Lambrechts 1935). This was the goal of the movement of the middle classes supported by the Institute International des classes moyennes, a documentation and research

---

32   Cf. Moulin and Aërt 1954; Gresle 1993. For the Italian debate see: Michels 1909.

centre founded in 1903 in Brussels, from the Congress international des classes moyennes which began meeting in 1903 in various European cities (Brussels, Liege, Vienne, and Monaco), and by the Association de dèfense des classes moyennes established in Paris in 1908.[33]

In the aftermath of World War I, however, this objective seemed distant. A series of essays and articles published in academic journals and the press brought *la grande pitié des classes moyennes* to the fore: sociologists and economists who referred to the republican, conservative, and moderate field, described the consequences of the war economy on the middle classes with concern. The increasing cost of living, indebtedness and decrease in consumption affected their propensity to save, their 'optimism' and 'moral dignity', opening a dangerous rift in the 'political and intellectual greatness' of the French nation: in a way that was similar to the English history of the middle class, it was argued that, faced with the 'conscious and organised' working class that had claimed and obtained wage increases, 'there is no longer a middle class' (Artur 1929: 401–410; de Chilly 1924).[34]

This drastic conclusion not only signaled the growing distance between the residual independent middle class (proprietary and entrepreneurial) and the dependent middle class (identified by income), but also the differences within the latter. While the figures employed at different levels of the public and private bureaucracies were becoming indifferent to property as a factor of economic and moral autonomy, the growing inequality of income prevented them from sharing a general common interest and fueled – above all among middle and lower cadres – the fear of being socially demoted. As demonstrated by the birth of unions that organised professional figures and the growing interest of socialists in the middle classes, these dynamics of social division made clear the now-obsolete character of the liberal representation that had defined the nineteenth-century middle class. If empirical research and sociological studies indicated a growing economic and cultural impoverishment of the subject who had supported and legitimised the Third Republic, what would have become of republican France?[35]

This disturbing question became more and more binding with the *grande dépression* of the 1930s when, with an eye to the worrying spread of anti-Semitic behaviour and the rise of National Socialism in Germany, the French social

---

33   Cf. Sick 1993: 20–30; Crossick 1996; Crossick 1984; Le Béguec 1993; Caroppo 2013.

34   These same arguments were also taken up and discussed by political scientists: Siegfried 1930: 9–16; Fournol 1933: 60–99. And by social scientists: Goblot 1925; Brun 1929.

35   Mouriaux 1989: 32–35; Groppo 1989: 1–3; Ruhlmann 1989: 47–52. On the rise of the cadres, see Boltanski 1987.

sciences questioned the 'lack of solidarity' between different middle-class figures and the consequent dissolution of the historical liberal nexus between
middle class and democracy. In light of Weimar sociology, from which the distinction between *anciennes classes moyennes* and *nouvelles classes moyennes*
derived, scholars such as Henry Laugenburger, Raymond Aron, and Edmond
Vermeil declared that the middle classes no longer embodied the Aristotelian
measure necessary for ensuring the political stability of the republic because
they were associated with the crisis of European democracies. The scientific
problem of elaborating a shared sociological and political conception of the
nouvelles classes moyennes – a problem that remained open throughout the
1930s and was resolved only after World War II thanks to the influence of US
social sciences – was connected to the question of their social and political
behaviour: would the new middle classes follow the economic and cultural
orientation of the *haute bourgeoisie* or the *proletariat*? Above all, would their
values continue to adhere to the democracy of the Third Republic? Since this
literature was developed in continuity with German sociology, it is appropriate
to turn our attention beyond the eastern frontier (Laufenburger 1933; Vermeil
1935; Aron 1936).

3   *Mittelstand* and *Neuer Mittelstand*

For much of the nineteenth century, the German political dictionary featured
the entry *Mittelklassen*. In a similar way to the French and English events, the
German middle class was associated with the success of *Liberalismus*: the unified national state was seen not only as an outcome of the political enterprise
of the 'iron chancellor' of the Reich, Otto von Bismark, but also as a fulfilment
of the Manchesterian liberal vision which had affirmed the ideal of a middle
class that would incorporate an increasing number of property owning individuals, who were thus qualified for political participation. The affirmation of
the term *Mittelstand* instead took place starting above all in the last quarter
of the nineteenth century, during a context of profound social change dic-
tated by the industrial revolution. Wilhelminian Germany was marked by
the decline of small and medium manufacturing and commercial industries,
reduced to being 'indirectly dependent on capital'. At the same time, there was
a sharp increase in the employment not only of industry (especially technicians), but also in commerce, transport, banking, insurance, and other sectors
linked to public and private services. These occupational changes reflected the
economic transformations marked by the rise of what in 1910 the economist
Rudolf Hilferding called *Das Finanz Kapital*: the development of the corporate

form of business with the mechanisation of the productive process, the growing organisation of the market in corporations and the bureaucratization of large companies. In this framework there emerged the figure which would gradually obscure the traditional liberal image of the independent *Mittelklassen*: the figure of the salaried worker, the private and public employee (Hilferding 1910).

Specialised in carrying out commercial functions, the organisation, control, and coordination of the productive process, the employee worked far away from the factories: in the administrative and managing departments of companies, and in public and private bureaucracies. Unlike the worker, the employee mainly performed non-manual work. The most educated and skilled employees especially could count on promotions that allowed them to exercise management faculties by proxy. Furthermore, instead of an hourly and daily wage, they received a salary that was calculated over longer periods (monthly or annually), which was thus determinable in advance, and also in relation to seniority. These objective differences established a subjective perception of superiority over the worker: the awareness of occupying a social position which, although reflecting a strong individual interest in career advancement at the expense of forms of solidarity and collective demands, defined a common sense of belonging outside of work. The highest level of consumption, greater aspirations for education, professional skills, and cultural inclinations all marked a clear distinction between employees and the working class, a distinction which was especially held to in the aftermath of World War I, when further processes of division and the specialisation of work, and the automation and mechanisation of office operations, led to a gradual reduction in career prospects and a progressive decline in salaries. Fear of descending the social ladder to the lowest step occupied by the proletariat fueled a strong sharing among employees of the publicly accepted values of parsimony and diligence, and order and respect for tradition.

This set of economic and social transformations explained the use of *Mittelstand* instead of *Mittelklassen*: both terms indicated a clear separation from the working class, but *Mittelstand* positively recalled the feudal rank-based tradition of the juridical system to consolidate and legitimise a condition of privilege considered indispensible to the mediation of the opposing interests of labour and capital. Starting at the beginning of the twentieth century and in a similar way to the French, the German movement of the middle classes moved in this direction but had a greater involvement of new employee figures that demonstrated a capacity for action such to conquer growing legal protections in the private and public sector. Contracts were successfully claimed that, compared to workers, guaranteed better job security, reduced hours, and specific prerogatives such as holidays, injury and sickness funds, and production bonuses. Moreover, these contractual guarantees found confirmation in legislative measures that favoured employees in the context of social assistance (illness, accidents, old age, maternity). Finally, next to the figure of the worker, the Weimarer Reichsverfassung (1919) not only constitutionally recognised the private and public employee (*Angelstellte* and *Beamten*) as their right to social security, but also constitutionalised the social position of the Selbständinger Mittelstand: the legislative and administrative obligation of promoting the average dependent and independent middle class was assigned to the state, protecting it from the danger of being absorbed into other social classes. All of this contributed to the rise of the German middle class because employees also did not consider themselves workers, much less proletarians, but rather part of a professional class (*Stand*).[36]

Thus, in Germany – this is a distinctive trait compared to England and France – state intervention outlined a legal framework to which to appeal, overcoming the proprietary and income differences. This contributed to the constitution (and constitutionalisation) of a global figure of the middle class insofar as *Mittelstand* could otherwise not have been given on a strictly economic level of employment. The measures in favour of wage labour were also not simply considered as strategic responses to the radicalisation of class conflict. Taken as a whole, they rather represented a political opportunity – offered in particular to specialised workers – to overcome the proletarian condition. They were an institutional expression of the political attempt to form a *mittelständisch* society. The state was not the only actor at stake, however. Within its constitutional horizon, a broad scientific literature acted with considerable influence. This literature attributed a strong public and political meaning to the concept of *Mittelstand*. In order to understand the centrality of the middle class in the German history, it is necessary in this sense to refer to the social sciences, starting from the contribution of the Verein für Sozialpolitik.

Composed of intellectuals and academics who supported Bismark's politics, the Verein took shape at the beginning of the 1870s within a political debate over the social consequences of the second industrial revolution. Since the true polemic object was the role that the state should take in facing the social question, the debate questioned the philosophical and legal convictions of German idealism and its doctrine of the state, opening the doors to economic and sociological disciplines. The new social sciences marked the overcoming of a liberal vision for which society was the rational result of human coexistence orientated according to the entrepreneurial *Weltanschaunng*. Even the

---

36   Kocka 1980: 26–34.

state had to be rethought in light of class conflict with a view to scientifically elaborating the possibility of its governing. The Verein thus intended to put science in the service of politics, legitimising the extension of the functions of the state in an economic and social context: in a moment when *Liberalismus* was cornered by Marxist theoretical and political hypothoses, the social sciences not only had to interpret the world, but also change the liberal order, prescribing forms of social and political organisation capable of facing the danger of socialist revolution. The sociological elaboration of the concept of *Mittelstand* was part of this scientific and political project, particularly in the work of Gustav von Schmoller.[37]

Starting with his inaugural speech at the Verein, Schmoller declared the inadequacy of economic and political liberalism which exclusively paid attention to the 'entrepreneurial class', understanding economic freedom only as 'the freedom of large entrepreneurs, owners of capital, and large companies', i.e., as the 'freedom to exploit'. According to Schmoller, since the economic universe was not dominated by the entrepreneur-individual, but rather by the classes in conflict with each other, it was necessary to define a new subject through which social harmony could be restored. This could not be the aristocracy of feudal society nor the abstract, free, and equal individual of the liberal tradition. Schmoller identified it in the *Mittelstand*: a collective subject that, to the extent that it occupied an intermediate position, would remedy the polarisation of society. If the middle class was initially identified with the artisan, starting from the early twentieth century the economic transformations required a profound rethinking: the political problem posed by the gradual disappearance of the artisan was addressed by coining the concept of the *Neuer Mittelstand*. The new middle class encompassed the broad social formation comprised by the liberal professionals of private and public bureaucracies and the strata of the best-paid workers. The social mediation of the middle class did not fail, but this function was not determined by the intermediate position in society, but rather by technical, administrative, and commercial knowledge which together its figures embodied. In this sense, the *Neuer Mittelstand* was suitable for governing society because it constituted for the state the competent and skilled subject through which to elaborate and implement policies that, while aimed at legally protecting employees and officials, also intended to integrate specialised workers into the institutional framework.[38]

---

37   Gerstenberger 1982: 15–16, 20–23, 25–31; Cavalli 1982: 64–66.
38   See Ricciardi 2013a: 283–300. Cf. Gerstenberger 1982: 28–29; Schiera and Tenbruck (eds) 1989; Gioia 1990; Roversi 1984.

The support of Schmoller and other exponents of the Verein for Bismark's policies went in this direction.[39] In other words, he intended to innovate the German doctrine of the state in light of the different historical context in which society, while being marked by class conflict, found in the formation of the *Neuer Mittelstand* the possibility of its own order. On the one hand, the new middle class expressed the potential continuity of social harmony: it did not represent one class (such as the artisan class) as opposed to the others (entrepreneurial and working class), but rather a collective subject capable of representing the overall interest of the nation. On the other hand, the state guaranteed the orderly existence of society through its constitutionalisation. Schmoller's historical reconstruction of the process of the formation of the (new) middle class coincided in this sense with the writing of a linear and positive national history, which was functional to the legitimisation of the political transition from the Second Reich to the Weimar Republic. Unlike the English experience, the middle class as *Mittelstand* thus assumed an unprecedented centrality in the semantic field of the social sciences. In other words, it acquired a specific scientific content in support of its historical public and political value. This emerged extremely clearly in the work of Schmoller's student Emil Lederer.

His study placed the formation of the middle class on the one hand in the economic dimension marked by the affirmation of a Taylorist model of production, and on the other in the theoretical and political debate within Marxism and German social democracy. In his earliest works on employees in the Wilhelminian period, Lederer argued that the spread of Taylorism was causing the appearance of socially analogous figures: industrial technicians, and employees with commercial and administrative functions. Despite the heterogenous nature of their duties, employees could be classified as *Angelstellte* because the character of their work was neither completely intellectual nor exclusively manual. This not only prevented their classification as workers, but also explained the similar subjective assessment of their social position. Their perception of themselves was not based on tasks actually performed, but rather on the relation that they had with the entrepreneurial and the working class: the unity among employees was not a 'technical, but social unity'. In this sense, although Lederer had doubts about the possibility of globally identifying employees as *Neuer Mittelstand*, he nevertheless believed that they could become 'an increasingly independent group' (Lederer 1937, 1–10).[40]

---

39   De Feo 1992.
40   Kocka 1982.

Lederer was therefore interested in understanding the consequences of Taylorism less on an objective level of the division of work and distribution of income, and more on the subjective level of the perception of social position. In this way he went beyond the quantitative analysis of statistics in order to empirically and theoretically study the psychological dimension as well, introducing a research method which, as we will see, influenced the scientific reflection on the American middle class. In particular, the study of what was called the 'mentality' or 'social mentality' highlighted how employees were still linked to the nineteenth-century imaginary of the independent middle class, even if with a radically different meaning: independence did not derive from possessing the means of production but instead the technical and administrative functions carried out in the productive process. In this way, i.e., by posing the psychological question of mentality, and its continuity and change, Lederer threw a boulder into the stagnant Marxist debate which, through a reflection on the 'destiny' of the new middle classes, saw divergent revolutionary (Karl Kautsky) and revisionist (Eduard Bernstein) political hypotheses, which were however internal to the horizon of a 'historical materialism' that would find fulfilment in socialism. In the wake of Schmoller, Lederer rejected the historical schematism that supported both hypotheses: on the one hand, he did not inscribe employees in the cause of the proletariat, while on the other he intended to show the possibility of their potential social democratic political orientation. In this sense, he considered a different 'historical path' than that outlined by Marxism to be possible. Although employees could not hope to achieve economic independence, their rapid increase in relation to manual labour and their mentality nonetheless devoted to independences made clear the historical tendency towards the neutralisation of 'radicalism' both in the political field and within industrial relations (Lederer 1937: 36–38).[41]

Lederer, who was also engaged in the socialist debate with the role of economic advisor of the Social Democratic Party and the social democratic trade union during the Weimar Republic, intended in this way to emphasise that the spread of salaried labour – dependent, but distinct from wage labour – was creating a set of social figures who presented at their core a different way of thinking, a different cultural disposition. From a scientific point of view, it poses the question of the formation of a new mentality that was still shapeless and indeterminate, but in any case, irreducible to an entrepreneurial or a worker mentality, and thus not predictable in light of the values of the nineteenth-century middle class and not describable with traditional political vocabulary,

41   Cf. Bologna 1977: 81–132, 82–85.

whether Marxist or liberal. It was an unprecedented scientific question that acquired a strong political meaning in the aftermath of World War I, when the transition to democracy raised the decisive question for the Social Democratic Party of whether to remain a worker-based party or whether to seek new consensus among the intermediary groups of society. There was no shortage of significant experiences that hinted at an expansion of the social democratic base, such as those in the first half of the 1920s which saw some of the major employee associations assume a union orientation that included the practice of strikes and collaboration with the workers' movement. This was so much the case that Lederer himself, like others who referred to his school, dissolved the reservations about the future orientation of employees, emphasising that the processes of proletarianisation would push them to the side of the working class. However, these were fragmented and one-time experiences. Employees did not broadly and continuously share the social democratic horizon, and even when this happened, they soon returned to more traditional moderate or conservative positions. In any case, they did not seem to immediately define an 'independent group' capable of expressing its own social and political vision.[42]

As emerged from the studies published in the second half of the 1920s by Lederer, as well as Jacob Marschak and Fritz Croner, the breakup of the independent middle class and the growing number of salaried workers had not led to the formation of a *Neuer Mittelstand* capable of acting as a 'buffer' between labour and capital. The war economy, its subsequent rationalisation, monetary devaluation and inflation imposed an increasing leveling down of their salaries: 'the insecurity of the salaried employee ... thus inflicted the final blow at the initial goal of the middle-class program that aimed to incorporate them into the middle class' (Lederer and Marschak 1937: 1–4, 6–13, 44–45; Croner 1937: 1–10, 12–13). While rumors also reached overseas of the degradation of scientific and professional knowledge that had ensured German national greatness, social harmony appeared as a 'utopic ideal, whose realization ... remains a pious desire' (Ross 1924: 529–538).

These words highlighted the political stalemate of the scientific and political project inaugurated by Schmoller's Verein and continued by Lederer himself in order to give a *mittelständisch* foundation to society. Despite having challenged the different Marxist hypotheses with some success, the sociological study of the middle class had not freed the 'historical path' of the risk of class conflict. As another student of Lederer's, Hans Speier, noted in a 1934 essay, in *Theories*

---

42   On the unionisation of employees in the 1920s, see Croner 1937. Cf. Kocka 1973; Coyner 1977; Winkler 1989; Potthof 1989.

of Surplus Value Marx himself had disproved what he maintained in his writings on the *Class Struggle in France*: 'the growing size of the middle classes' did not change 'the course of bourgeois society' in any way, i.e., it did not resolve the problem of class struggle. In the aftermath of the October Revolution, the aggressiveness of the German workers' and communist movement further raised another question mark: since most of the employees resisted proletarianisation by embracing at first conservative, and then increasingly nationalist and National Socialist positions, would the German middle class remain on the liberal path of democracy? This became the central issue in the years of the *Grosse Depression* which led to the collapse of the Weimar Republic (Speier 1934: 124).[43]

After 1929, many employees lost their jobs, while those who remained employed suffered increasing mechanisation of office operations, overwhelming pressure by employers, and a significant reduction in salary: production bonuses, faculty of direction and organisation of work, career perspectives were all drastically reduced. The depression destroyed the material basis of the *mittelständisch* ideal, fomenting anxieties and fears that fueled a growing skepticism towards the political forces of the constitutional, social democratic, liberal, and Catholic frameworks. Faced with the danger of proletarianisation, public and private employees, like small business owners, developed anti-socialist protest attitudes which contributed to the rise of National Socialism. In this context, the study of the social consequences of the depression was intertwined with the political necessity of explaining the reason why what appeared as an unprecedented crisis of capitalism was causing the rupture of the historical liberal link between the middle class and democracy. This emerged from a broad and widespread literature, which was also of a journalistic nature, and not only German, but that also started from the reflection developed by Theodor Geiger in the essay *Panik in Mittelstand* (1930), published after the elections that marked the unexpected electoral leap of National Socialism (Krakauer 1930; Lederer 1931; Borkenau 1932; Dreyfuss 1933; Speier 1934).[44]

---

43   Cf. Bessner 2018: 15–43.
44   This literature had found a valid anticipation and source in the Italian reflection on fascism: Zibordi 1922; Salvatorelli 1923; Mondolfo 1925. In Notebook VI § 49 (Gramsci 2007), showing that he understood the different cultural and political orientation of the American middle class from the European middle class, Gramsci wrote: 'Babbitt is the philistine of a country on the move; the European petty bourgeois is the philistine of conservative countries that are rotting in the stagnant swamp of cliches about the great tradition and the great culture'.

On the basis of Lederer, Geiger elaborated a method of empirical research that used statistics in order to understand the formation of strata (*Schichten*) of the population on the basis not only of the functions performed in the social division of work, but also of their mentality (*Schichtmentalitäten*). Unlike class and Stand, the concept of strata made it possible to relativise the influence of the economic dimension in favour of the social and cultural sphere. In this sense, a specialised worker could be classified in the middle class, while an employee engaged at the top of the corporate hierarchy was a capitalist. The middle class thus took shape from a set of processes – economic and cultural – which determined the 'social mobility' towards the top or bottom. With these methodological and conceptual premises, Geiger intended to overcome the historical schematism that depicted society as divided between capitalist and proletariat. Since stratification and social mobility denied the presence of two impermeable and counter-posed classes, the theoretical and political conviction that 'class consciousness' was the inevitable consequence of economic condition could be rejected. The mentality could not be deduced exclusively from the function performed in the production process because, as Karl Mannheim maintained in *Ideology and Utopia* (1929) , it was an ideological product, also relevant in the political dimension. On these bases, Geiger not only polemicised with those who, underestimating the rise of National Socialism, continued to identify in proletarianisation the economic data sufficient to believe in the future success of socialism, but was also able to explain the ideological reasons for the National Socialist orientation of the German middle class (Geiger 1930: 637–638, 639, 641, 643–645, 647–649, 651–652).

Mittelstand had not fulfilled the 'socially necessary, dual function' attributed to it by the sociological literature. In other words, it did not function as a transition phase for social ascent, nor as a 'normative area' of mediation between labour and capital. On the contrary, the emergence of intermediate strata had brought about effects of division and marginalisation that found expression in the growing separation between *Alter Mittelstand* (made up of farmers, artisans, and traders) and *Neuer Mittelstand* (made up of salaried workers in the private sector, state functionaries and technicians in charge of production). This conceptualisation, which would influence the academic and public debate on the middle class through the 1930s on the continent and overseas, did not do much to define the 'small-capitalist' nature of the former and the 'objectively proletarian' condition of the latter. Rather, it intended to examine the 'ideological confusion' that marked the intermediate strata. While the old middle class presented a 'historically inadequate' ideology because 'liberal economic idealism' no longer had foundation in the 'impersonal organization of late capitalism', the new middle class expressed a 'socially inadequate' ideology because the social position of employees had collapsed under the weight of the depression. In this perspective, 'there is no doubt that National Socialism owes its electoral success essentially to the old and new middle class'. The constitution (and constitutionalisation) of the *Mittelstand* as a normative area functional to social harmony had failed because a 'collective ideology' adequate to its economic heterogeneity and consistent with democracy was lacking': the fear of losing one's social position pushed the old and new middle class to embrace the 'empty, national-socialistic program', with its anti-elitist, anti-proletarian, and anti-socialist polemics, with its appeal to the racial nation and its mystical and mythic nationalism (Geiger 1930: 643–652; Croner 1937).

4   Crossing the Atlantic

In 1930, Geiger did not see in the Third Reich a strong ideal capable of moving 'mittelstand revolution'. He still believed in the possibility of keeping the intermediate strata within the constitutional horizon of the Weimar Republic. In this sense, he advised the Social Democratic Party not to insist on proletarianisation, not to remain tied to the language of class struggle. In other words, he suggested renouncing a Marxist vision as the official party doctrine in order to consider the widespread nationalist sentiment by referring to the 'classless society' as the national ideal that would unite the German people. In 1933, following Hitler's rise to power, the failure not only of social democracy but also the political project built around the sociological study of the *Mittelstand* could only be registered. In the same year he was forced to take refuge in Denmark, while Lederer, Marschak, and Speier emigrated overseas where they started the experience of the University in Exile within the New School for Social Research in New York City.

    This sociological exodus, part of the broader German intellectual emigration to the United States which also involved the Frankfurt Institut für Sozialforschung, contributed to the Atlantic transmission of methodologies, lines of research, interpretative models, and theoretical suggestions that had been at the centre of the European history of the middle class: its nineteenth-century rise connected to the national and international formation of the liberal order, its support for democratisation, its subsequent social decline and its political dissociation from democracy following the affirmation of fascism and Nazism. In the United States, the spread of this political knowledge did not only occur through informal channels of scientific communication and academic exchanges, but also thanks to the elaboration of specific cultural policies. Between 1937 and 1939 the collaboration between the Department of

Social Welfare of the state of New York, the Columbia University Department of Social Science, and the Works Progress Administration developed by president Franklin D. Roosevelt made it possible to translate a series of monographs – for the most part German, among which are those we have cited – dedicated to the study of the white collar or salaried employee (the English translations of *Angestellte*), social stratification, mobility, and the mentality of the intermediate strata.[45]

The failure of the political project based on the sociological study of the *Mittelstand* therefore did not entail the undoing of its scientific matrix. Weimar sociology and Lederer's school in particular did not simply bequeath an explanation of understanding the rise of National Socialism. They also outlined a hypothesis of empirical research and theoretical reflection aimed at understanding the national and international development (and crisis) of the liberal order in light of a historical account – of the middle class – which, although linked as we have seen to different national histories, assumed a transnational dimension: the scientific hypothesis for which economic transformations imposed by the rise of large industry coincided with social, political, and ideological changes which, not only radically questioned the historical liberal link between middle class and democracy on the European continent, but also projected these tensions overseas, casting shadows on the future of American democracy. At the basis there was therefore a precise political prescription: scientific reflection on the middle class must not only aim at explaining the past, but rather must claim – to use Lederer's words – an 'opinion on the evolution' of the crisis of capitalism in light of the centrality that the middle class had acquired in the Atlantic world as a whole.

This scientific and political hypothesis emerged from Hans Speier's essay, *The Salaried Employee in Modern Society*. Written in Germany where its publication was blocked by the Nazi regime, the essay appeared in an abridged version in January 1934 in the first issue of *Social Research*, a review with which the New School for Social Research intended to make available the literature of the European scholars in exile. In light of the statistics of the International Labour Office related to the Workers and Salaried Employees in Various Countries after the War, Speier identified the growing number of white-collar workers as an 'international tendency' which was undermining the 'sociological basis of political theories'. Although it was linked to the level of economic development, to social legislation and the union and political organisation of different

---

45   Salvati 2000: 1–143; Vidich 1995, in particular the essay of Burris: 15–54. With reference to the Frankfurt School, see the introduction of Laudani et al. 2012.

nations, their rise as a social group led to theoretical and political controversies that fueled an inadequate and fallacious 'international discussion'. Speier not only rejected Marxist theory which had defined white collar workers as a 'new proletariat'. Proletarianisation effectively illustrated the economic transformations of society but did not justify the 'historical prophecies'. The reference to 'false consciousness' did not explain why the majority of employees had refused to deduce socialism from their economic condition. He also distanced himself from his own sociological school: even the theory that had prefigured the formation of a new middle class as 'a guarantee of the continuation of the ruling social order' did not stand up to the test of facts because professional, technical, and administrative skills no longer determined any superiority of the employee. Not unlike workers, employees 'carried out simple, minute parts of a divided work process and could easily be replaced': the administrative functions of industry 'can today be performed by numerous relatively poorly paid and subordinate employees' (Speier 1934: 111–133, 111, 115–116).

Speier did not so much reject the heuristic value of the concept of the middle class as its definition on the basis of employment, education, and income. The middle class had to be reconceptualised in terms of an ideological category. In this sense, he denounced 'the ideological neglect of the salaried worker in the field of political theory' and indicated the possibility of formulating a theory that – similar to liberalism for the nineteenth-century bourgeoisie – would allow the middle class to exercise 'influence and power within capitalist society'. The introduction of the expressions 'social value' and 'social valuation', whose meaning was derived from the Weberian concept of *Soziale Geltung*, went in this direction. It not only served to overcome the economism of the different theories of the middle class, but also intended to show how the perception of the social position derived from the evaluative processes which, not depending exclusively on the work provided, took place by accepting and sharing values: one was not middle class, but wanted to be it. In order to understand how a 'recognized order' became 'predominant', it was necessary to study terms and changes in the process of 'social integration' (Speier 1934: 122–123, 126–129). This was the scientific and political challenge placed on the agenda by the brutal rupture of the historical liberal link between middle class and democracy that the crisis of capitalism had caused: a new theory of the middle class should have filled the ideological void that was bequeathed from the end of liberalism and that the political project developed around the sociological study of the *Mittelstand* had not been able to occupy.

In conclusion, while during the nineteenth century the middle class (as proprietary and entrepreneurial class) had been represented as the historical subject that had supported the processes of industrialisation and democratisation, from the end of the century the different national histories that had legitimised the liberal order on the basis of its centrality were disproved by the economic transformations imposed by the second industrial revolution and by the explosion of the social question.[46] The end of the liberal era coincided with its economic, social, and ideological breakdown. Following the decline of small business and the emergence of dependent but not manual labour, the middle class became the subject of discussion (and conflict) in the broader academic, public, and political debate that rethought liberalism and socialism. Particularly in France and Germany, the concept took on an increasingly marked scientific content. The identification of new classification criteria no longer centred on ownership and independence but rather on education and occupation, income and consumption, the sociological study of the mentality of employees, the quantitative and qualitative analysis of their political behaviour. This set of scientific methods and practices provided new knowledge which, after the collapse of the Weimar Republic, was used to understand the rise of Nazism. Also due to the Atlantic transmission of political knowledge forged by European political theories and social sciences, the laceration between middle class and democracy became a global historical fact: even in the United States it constituted an essential scientific and political challenge. Faced with the economic limit that liberalism and socialism had showed on the European shore, in the face of the political failure of *Mittelstand* sociology, in order to overcome the crisis of capitalism that swept through American democracy, middle class had to be 'invented'[47] as a concept through which to observe and control, according to a specific scientific and political project, the formation of processes of social integration around functions and values capable of involving the intermediary strata of society in a political order that was coherent with democracy. In the next chapter we will thus see that, not unlike the European history, the search for the American middle class also began at the turn of the century, in the progressivist era. However, as demonstrated by the entry for the middle class in the *Encyclopaedia of the Social Sciences* with which we started, it was only during the New Deal that the social sciences placed the middle class not only at the centre of their scientific reflection, but also of US politics.

---

46 See Mann 2012. Cf. Rizas 2018: 28–97; Stearns 1979: 378–387.
47 The reference is to the expression 'invention of the social' (Donzelot 1986), also used by Maier (1988).

The American Middle Class

A Taken-for-Granted History?

From the examination of the nineteenth-century dictionaries, we noted that the term middle class was not part of the US vocabulary, except as a negative reference intended to affirm the non-European, and therefore exceptional, character of a society represented as lacking class distinctions. Over time, this exceptional character has become an element of continuity within US public discourse, especially in the second half of the twentieth century when the middle class constituted the main narrative voice of national history. In the aftermath of World War II, middle class no longer had a negative meaning. On the contrary, the radical alterity of Europe was claimed by positively identifying in the middle class an original subject with a linear evolution and constant value. The progressive imprint of national history, its continuous economic expansion, and the success of the American democratic experiment was attributed to this subject. Not only among the categories employed in the academic context, but also in public discourse, middle class became the key word of the US vocabulary, the master key which allowed one to legitimately be part of the nation, have access to its history, claim its freedoms and enjoy its wellbeing. In this way the sense of exceptionality that since its revolutionary origins had characterised America in front of the mirror of Europe was consolidated.[1]

In a nutshell, this was the historical plot constructed around the middle class by the post-World War II consensus school, as well as the political vision that shaped the social sciences which were committed to defining a model of coexistence in which conflict was represented and legitimated as a struggle for the distribution of resources within a shared framework of middle-class values. Not unlike what happened in European historiographies, US historians have also thus shaped the image of the United States as the middle-class nation par excellence. The continuous reference to the middle class was used to narrate and promulgate a long-term national history, one certainly not free from important caesuras such as the Civil War, but in any case devoid of the abrupt breakdowns of the liberal order which instead marked Europe. A history suited to the present of a nation which, in the framework of the ideological context of

---

1 Bonazzi 2004.

the Cold War, wanted to be consensual because it saw its own liberal tradition as triumphant.

Louis Hartz explained that, although 'profoundly European in substance', the United States had given freedom a 'specifically American' meaning: 'A widespread sense of equality, an individualism not tainted by the old feudal sense of class, a belief in opportunity that was realised here [in the United States] like nowhere else on earth'. This explained not only why the European term bourgeoisie had no place in the US, but also why the term middle class assumed a fully positive meaning which did not allude to class distinctions. On the contrary, it intended to deny them: while on the European continent, liberal culture had historically been associated with the bourgeoisie as an intermediary class between the aristocracy and the plebs, in the US the middle class overcame the class boundary by establishing a common and shared set of values which were a source of national cohesion. At the basis of the United States' exceptionality there was the conviction that 'American democracy and its liberalism' constituted 'a natural phenomenon' that had its historical roots in the 'egalitarian borders within which the life of the middle class unfolded', starting with colonial times: the 1776 Revolution had affirmed the liberal 'mentality' of a 'victorious middle class'. The adherence to middle-class values (individualism, work ethic, equality of opportunity, democracy) appeared so broad and rooted that post-World War II historiography did not feel the need to reconstruct what was defined as the 'backbone of democracy'. The result was to produce a certain image of the United States as 'natural': 'A triumphant middle class ... could be given and taken for granted' (Hartz 1960: 7–8). The consensus school thus elevated the middle class to a subject through which national history is narrated, a source of internal and international legitimation of the nation and its exceptionalism.[2]

In this sense, what middle class defined was not so much a historiographical category aimed at reconstructing the contingent histories of determinant social figures. Rather, it represented a meta-historical concept.[3] It did not indicate a group within social hierarchies – this would have denied the egalitarian character of US society. On the contrary, it defined a timeless foundation of national culture which served to narrate American civilisation, i.e., the linear

---

2 What is understood by 'historiography of consensus' is a tendency of the greater part of postwar US historians, among whom include Louis Hartz, Richard Hofstadter, David Potter, Daniel Boorstin, Oscar Handlin, and Samuel Hays.
3 The reference is to Hayden White's (1973) concept of 'metahistory', which he made to highlight the discursive structure outlined by historiography in order to represent the institutions of the past and historical processes in a coherent narrative form.

and orderly development of national history as opposed to the twisted and disordered history of Europe: the success of the republic in the face of the French revolutionary failure and the precocious affirmation of democracy with respect to the European monarchies, the triumph of the society of abundance and affirmation of a capitalism consistent with democracy because it is not affected by the classist residue of the old world, the specificity of a politics not infected with the ideological germ of European extremism, the global primacy legitimated and supported by a theory of modernisation which had leveraged the potentially universal rise of the middle class. This historical vision had such a profound impact on US political culture that, even when the new historiographies of the 1960s and 1970s (the new social history and labour history) shifted focus from consensus to conflict as the interpretive key of national history by showing the presence of a working class in tension with the values of the liberal tradition, the reference to the middle class still remained essential. Not by chance, even today, middle class constitutes the key word used in scientific literature, public opinion, and political debate in order to understand the nation and its international role.[4]

It is therefore fitting to first discuss the history of the American middle class as an afterthought of the historian: a vision not originally intended by the figures called to the stage in the narrative of national history, but rather subsequently reconstructed in order to affirm the exceptional character of the nation which explained why the twentieth century had become 'The American Century' hoped for by Henry Luce in the famous editorial he published in the February 1941 issue of *Life Magazine*. If the consensus school had preferred – for the sake of the coherence of its own narrative – to take the middle class for granted, subsequent historiography historicised its formation within the field of tensions opened by the second industrial revolution, forging a category that showed how Americans had actually experienced the middle class not as an abstract adherence to the liberal tradition that defined the perimeter of consensus, but rather in the materiality of economic, social, and political relations. However, this historiography has inscribed the different figures examined (professionals, technicians, engineers, experts, civil servants, and public employees) within a historical framework in which the middle class emerged as the subject capable of shaping national history: the gravitational centre of

---

4   Lerner 1957; Schlesinger Jr. 1949; Lipset 1963; Hofstadter 1966; Potter 1954; Galbraith 1958; Rostow 1960. For a critical perspective on US historiography and American civilization, see Bonazzi 1974. See also Lopez and Weinstein 2012: 1–28; Battistini 2015.

society which, by attracting different social forces, ensured the political success of the United States.[5]

1   The Middle Class as a Historiographic Category

'The most valuable class in any community is the middle class, the men of
moderate means, living at the ate of a thousand dollars a year or thereabouts'
(Whitman 1932: 145). With these words, on the eve of the Civil War, Walt
Whitman greeted the entrance of the middle class – male, white, and protestant – onto the scene, a class taking shape in urban and suburban areas. The
reference was not as much to property owners – the farmer, artisan, and busi-
nessman – who were animating westward expansion and the first industrialisation – as it was to employee figures whose success was measured by the
income earned on the market. These were figures who, in increasing numbers,
carried out non-manual labour in different business sectors: clerks, salesmen,
bookkeepers, accountants, and employees in general.
    However, much resonance it received from the pen of the poet who cel-
ebrated American democracy more than any other, in the first half of the
nineteenth century, the words middle class were not widespread at all. They
rarely appeared in the press, where locutions were preferred which alluded
to a condition of social average: 'middle condition of mankind' and 'middling
sort' communicated a sense of revenge with respect to 'lower sort', but presented a negative meaning that referred to the colonial period, when the people of the revolution were divided according to a hierarchical culture of 'rank'
established on the basis of birth ('well-born'), education ('learned man'), and
interests ('landed' and 'mercantile'). It was the national aristocracy of property
owners who emerged victorious from the 1776 Revolution, and not the majoritarian strata of farmers and frontier settlers, and the mechanics and journey-
men of urban areas, who all failed to shake off the sense of inferiority and
deference determined by having to work for subsistence. US society was open
to mobility only with the affirmation of new economic relations linked to the
construction of the national market and the concomitant political democratisation of the first half of the century. From the 1820s to the 1830s, work no
longer appeared to be negative, but on the contrary was accepted as a sign of
autonomy ('self rule') and an instrument for acquiring wealth. The consumption of luxury goods was no longer the prerogative of the superior ranks, but

5   Blumin 1985: 299–338; Bledstein and Johnston 2001.

instead became a symbol of social ascent. The conquest of suffrage and the demand for 'free labor' against slavery also allowed the white and male population to place themselves on a level of moral and political equality with the 'better sort'. Society thus saw the formation of porous social classes within which it was possible to move, rising up or falling down, depending on economic success or failure. Classes thus did not establish a rigid boundary. On the contrary, they coincided with the movement imposed on society by the frontier. They were the expression of individual biographies that followed the market: what was decisive in the perception of oneself was not the republican character of the citizen who is virtuous because he is educated and owns property, but rather his personal or career history as the proof of respectability and morality. This was the meaning that Whitman attributed to the middle class by registering a first partial change in the national vocabulary.[6]

On this basis, historiography has reconstructed the nineteenth-century formation of the middle class through the distinction between manual and intellectual labour ('hand work' and 'brain work'), demonstrating how this distinction reflected and fuelled the new social architecture of urban and suburban areas and the growing divergence in lifestyle between 'worker' and 'employed'. While manual labour, concentrated in poor and dilapidated production districts and dormitories, was provided in exchange for a daily wage that pushed one to accept one's social position with humility and modesty, employees received a salary calculated on a monthly or annual basis which invited the sacrifice of hard work and savings in order to climb the social ladder. Employees worked in clean and elegant environments. Their families resided in urban and suburban neighbourhoods in homes that they owned, where wives and mothers oriented the household budget to consumption, education, and cultural life. Their different lifestyle also emerged in the role that associations – religious, recreational, and philanthropic – had in shaping the national culture, also putting into question the original republican vision of the separate spheres between men and women thanks to the unprecedented public role conquered by middle-class women through their involvement in associations, despite their being denied access to suffrage. This was the middle class in formation that an 1850 *New York Tribune* article exalted in the face of the emergence of the great wealth of business and the strident poverty of the 'laboring class' (Foster 1850). US historiographers thus also portrayed, on the basis of the works of European observers such as Alexis de Tocqueville and Michael Chevalier who had emphasised the industrious character of the American

---

6   Blumin 1989: 1–13. Cf. Appleby 2001; Laurie 2001. On free labor and slavery, see Roediger 1991.

middle class against the indolence of the French bourgeoisie linked to rent (Chevalier 1839: 396–404; de Tocqueville 1839: 209), a middle class that since its nineteenth-century formation distanced itself from the moral debauchery of the rich and the poor.[7]

The distinction between manual and intellectual labour matured in the second half of the century when a specific institutional matrix of social and political behaviour took shape that was based on professionalism. State and federal policies for the development of secondary, higher, and university education no longer aimed at the elitist transmission of knowledge that had characterised the liberal professions of colonial derivation, but rather were oriented towards the production of an empirical knowledge, suitable for the second industrial revolution and the political governing of social transformations that resulted from it. Vocational courses, specialised schools, and research universities shaped a growing number of figures (technicians, engineers, architects, social workers, teachers, lecturers, researchers, scientists, and social scientists) employed in the design, production, and distribution departments of large companies, as well as in the government commissions and agencies that were redesigning the administrative profile of the American state on the basis of the merit system. In this way, the economic and social centrality of technical and scientific instruction was affirmed, establishing the public primacy of specialist skills with respect to economic interests of accumulated wealth and to the partisanship of the traditional party politics denounced as corrupt and patronising. The educated figures were employed not only to identify and overcome obstacles and organisational difficulties in the productive process but were also consulted to understand and resolve the social question that threatened the wellbeing of the nation and the security of property. The educational system performed a constituent function for the middle class because it institutionalised the superiority of intellectual over manual labour as the publicly accepted principle that allowed for differentiation from the worker and identification with the general interest of the nation. The historiographical reconstruction of the formation of the middle class thus defined the salient characteristics of the nation that distinguished US from European history. Middle class entered the narrative of national history as a new subject, according to a script which, by marginalising words considered to be European such as bourgeoisie and proletariat, projected an 'unprecedented enthusiasm' around its values onto the entire society: the moral commitment to sacrifice and savings, to study and work for economic

---

7   Cf. Blumin 1989: 65–95, 240–290; Baritono 2001.

success, equality of opportunity guaranteed by education, career ambition based on merit. On the basis of the historiography of consensus, it was still maintained in the 1970s and 1980s that 'no other national history has been so essentially concerned with this one idea [of the middle class] as America' (Bledstein 1976: IX–XII, 1–8, 13–19, 80–128, 287–331).[8]

Subsequent historiography has identified in the 'new middle class' (nonproprietary) the subject who explained why the turbulence of the second industrialisation did not result in the breakup of the liberal order, but rather in its renewal which coincided with the overcoming of the nineteenth-century laissez-faire in favour of progressivism and the New Deal liberalism of the age of reforms. While on the European side of the Atlantic, employees had been caught in a vortex of social and political decline that prevented the nineteenth-century centrality attributed by classical liberalism to the (proprietary) middle class from updating to the new century, overseas their rise was set exactly between the end of the nineteenth and beginning of the twentieth century, when the United States was also involved in profound transformations that above all concerned the process of work. In the aftermath of the Civil War, the formation of 'trusts' and 'corporations' – in distribution, railway transport, and mechanical, chemical, and food industries – reduced the possibilities of acquiring property and economic independence that had characterised the frontier movement towards the west. The cyclical economic trend with the successive waves of depression of the eighties and nineties made layoffs more frequent, negatively affecting the stability of employment and income. The mechanisation of work based on the exploitation of immigrant labour led to a growing disqualification of workers that, until then, had found in trade the force to affirm the moral principle of 'self-rule', claiming autonomy in labour as well as in politics. The nineteenth-century peculiarities of American democracy – primacy of individual initiative, self-government of one's own person and the local community, economic and political self-determination – were thus undermined by the new entrepreneurial forces of big business which acted on the national scale: the continental construction of railway lines, the emergence of the large department store and the integrated industrial plant, the concentration of financial capital in investment banks, the emergence of joint-stock companies as the prevailing form of business – all of this shattered community life by concentrating population in urban areas and bringing agrarian and populist protests to the attention of government, a disruptive social

---

8   Cf. Dobkin Hall 2010; Testi 2000.

question and unprecedented workers' conflict that also took on a violent streak, as in the tumultuous case of Haymarket Square in Chicago in 1886, the steelworkers' industrial strike in Homestead (Pittsburgh, Pennsylvania) in 1892, and the Pullman Strike which in 1894 blocked railways throughout the country. Not unlike the European situation, this was the 'crisis of authority' that swept through the United States at the end of the century.[9]

The fact that revolts and protests ended with the new century has been traced by historiographies of progressivism to the new middle class made up of employees indifferent to the proprietary and entrepreneurial ideal of the nineteenth-century past, but aware of their own professionalism and capable in this sense of adapting to the changed economic reality.[10] Minorities at the beginning of the nineteenth century, but increasing in the following decades, these figures boasted degrees in engineering, law, economics, statistics, sociology, and psychology. They provided specialist knowledge in mechanical and chemical production. They offered organisational and administrative skills in the private and public sector. Despite the different types of employment and the different level of income, they were therefore united by their absolute confidence in the authority of science. This was not intended as a universal design whose principles must be deduced by a prioristic formulas, but rather as a scientific and experimental method that, due to its objectivity, was considered credible and reliable, and therefore authoritative: a procedure of empirical knowledge through which it was possible to manage the corporate enterprise efficiently, resolving the disputes that tore apart industrial relations, re-knitting the fragmented ranks of the nation by governing a complex and conflictual society. What identified and unified the employees was not the wealth that increasingly was concentrated in the hands of those labelled as 'robber barons'. Nor was it the militancy in mass parties and religious and ethnic affiliations which had characterised the 'free labor' of earlier generations. It was rather the social prestige that derived from their employment, participation in professional and academic associations, and the social and political commitment that was disinterestly claimed as an expert quality. Unlike the nineteenth-century 'middling sort' linked to the local community, these figures expressed a national vocation that renewed the traditional moral and religious worth of American democracy by integrating it with a technical and scientific language aimed at establishing continuity in the face of market discontinuities, regularity in the face of economic uncertainties, and administrative

---

9   Wiebe 1995: 61–85;117–161; Hofstadter 1955. Cf. Haskell 1977; Goodwyn 1976; Kazin 1998; Montgomery 1993; Laurie 1997.
10   Rodgers 1982; McGerr 2005: 43.

conclusions to the social question. In a society shaken by the second industrialisation, the 'search for order' of the new middle class intended to affirm the
original American right to the 'pursuit of happiness' on new scientific bases
(Wiebe 1967: 113–132).

The protagonists of this research were the figures called to manage the managerial revolution of the large company. They were mid-level executives and
managers who made decisions and defined standardised norms of work that
traced the fundamental features of the unprecedented scientific organisation
of production that would take the name of Taylorism and Fordism. They were
technicians and engineers who subtracted the knowledge necessary for work
from trade labourers, preparing rigid scientific tables of tasks and times super-
vised by the new figure of the 'superintendent', who replaced the foreman of
the earliest factories. They were graduates in sociology and psychology who
were recruited, particularly starting from the 1930s, in order to provide programs for improving working conditions and to organise free time outside the
factory with recreational and cultural activities. Since it intended to retain the
worker in the company by integrating him into society with non-bargained
concessions that expanded possibilities of consumption, corporate welfare
took away space from the workers' autonomous initiative that in the years of
progressivism had assumed unprecedented and radical forms of militancy
with the Industrial Workers of the World.

These new employee figures forged a new culture of work suitable and consistent with the spirit of the capitalism of 'big business' because it freed the
Protestant ethic of hard work and personal sacrifice for the economic success
of the proprietary and entrepreneurial ideal in order to link it to the purposes
of consumption. Executives and managers shared management and supervisory responsibilities with technicians and engineers, as well as sociologists
and psychologists, identifying the new American frontier in corporations: the
opportunity to participate in the company that made it possible to develop
one's own skills without exposing oneself to business risk in order to enhance
income on the market. The virtue of consumption (including while in debt)
thus replaced the habit of saving. This renewed sense of autonomy of work and
taste for consumption was transmitted to a growing number of specialised figures (superintendent, skilled worker, and employees in accounting, marketing,
and sales offices) who, although they were lower in the corporate hierarchy,
saw in the second industrialisation a broadening of opportunities for social
mobility and conquest of what, in contrast to the misery of European labour,
was defined as the American standard of living. In 1870 no greater than 1% of
labour-power was employed in office tasks, which grew to 3%, and after forty
years reached 10%, while at the beginning of the 1950s, also considering the

entrance of women onto the labour market and the total number of public administration personnel, it climbed to 37%.[11]

The constant increase of employees who took the name of 'white collar' in order to distinguish themselves from the 'blue collar' of the worker, their growing participation in the corporate organisational process, the increasingly incisive role of their technical and scientific skills in the functioning of the company, and their capacity for consumption allowed historiography to inscribe (and resolve) the class conflict that exploded in the aftermath of the Civil War within the triumphant narrative of American capitalism. Because the employee figures were recruited above all among native and second-generation immigrant working families due to their education rate, the class boundary that had conditioned the nineteenth-century situation of the European bourgeoisie became so porous as to extend the American middle class not only beyond the proprietary margin, but also through the collar line. In the national history of historiography, the middle class was thus removed from the economic and political decline in which the European middle classes had been taken between the end of the nineteenth century and World War I. A particular social relation emerged between (intellectual) labour and capital which did not appear reducible to the hierarchical movement that instead negatively marked manual labour. White-collar workers were not considered subordinate to the impersonal command of the corporate enterprise – their autonomy did not appear to be stifled by corporate bureaucracy. On the contrary, the career opportunities ensured by their skills expressed an emancipatory movement that ensured a community of purpose between (intellectual) labour and capital through consumption. In this sense, their visible hand in the functioning of the company constituted an organisational faculty of society which, accumulating consensus around the new culture of work/consumption, compensated for the tensions arising from the second industrialisation. In this way, the claimed scientific and professional autonomy of the employees fueled a progressive culture transversal to the Republican and Democratic Parties which was therefore capable of activating a broad reforming impulse that ensured the overcoming of the crisis of authority at the end of the century.[12]

According to historiography, the social history of the new middle class was therefore immediately political history because it showed how the middle class had advanced claims that ran through the American state: at the municipal

---

11   Zunz 1990: 130–184; Chandler 1977: 6–12. On the corporate culture of managers, technicians, and employees, see Lears 2009; Sklar 1988. On Taylorism and Fordism, see Nelson 1980; Fasce 1983; Settis 2016.

12   Chandler 1977: 455–501; Zunz 1990: 200–220; Hays 1972; Galambos 1970.

level where the urban areas returned the most eloquent and worrying image of economic inequality and the social question, and on the state and federal level by providing personnel to the government commissions committed to regulating the market and settling the disputes that marked industrial relations. The public staff employed in administration reformed and implemented the government by overcoming the traditional liberal vision of the minimal state, simple in its institutional organisation and limited in its intervention in the economic and social sphere: public servants and officials effectively carried out a government that was broadly and continuously involved with the operations of a society that was different than that of the nineteenth century. It was no longer made up of isolated and autonomous individuals in their proprietary and entrepreneurial realisation, but instead populated by corporations, union organisations, professional associations, and social classes. Since freedom could only be exercised in light of the growing interdependence imposed by the market, society expressed a government that, by means of administrative procedures, was called upon to involve economic and social forces in an institutional confrontation free from the political partisans of the past, and therefore capable of re-establishing harmony and consensus. This made it possible to close the nineteenth century of laissez faire by overcoming the class conflict without questioning the corporate form of business and ensuring continuity to the liberal form of order through its reform. This was ultimately the political ambition of the new middle class that marked the narrative of national history: to conquer the American state and shape its administration in its image with the aim of fulfilling not only its own destiny, but also the future of the nation.[13]

The middle class of historiography is therefore a scientifically impartial, socially and culturally autonomous, and politically authoritative subject who is thus capable of governing, starting from the progressivist era. His professionalism and skills, as well as his needs and values, fueled a reforming impulse aimed at the legitimation of capitalism by expanding opportunities for profit, economic development, and consumption. It was not only the beating heart and mind of progressivism. It was also the hegemonic subject who relegated both the riotous workers' behaviour, as well as the resistance business demonstrated towards the federal state and its reform, to the background. Class conflict was thus erased from national history while the new middle class became the undisputed authority of corporate America: the architect not only of the renewed liberal order after the crisis at the end of the century, but also of the

---

13   Wiebe 1967: 159–170, 222, 293–297; Hofstadter 1955: 215–226.

US international primacy in the post-World War II period, the main inter-preter of the golden age of American capitalism and the democracy of mass consumption.[14]

This historiography has undoubtedly contributed to the comprehension of the American century. It brought to light previously forgotten or underesti-mated figures, carrying out a mirror – and ultimately victorious – operation to what 'labor history' in the 1960s and 1970s had done for the working class. On the basis of the 'consensus school', however, it considered the different biog-raphies of professionals, technicians, engineers, experts, officials, and public employees as exemplifying not only the middle class as a whole, but also the characteristics of the nation: professionalism and work ethic, the scientific organisation of production and corporate form of business, mass consump-tion, progressive culture, and liberalism. The triumphant American middle class emerged in this sense as 'a courtesy of the historian' (Wiebe 1967: 111–112) committed to systematising the unintended consequences of the second industrialisation in national history: economic crises, labour conflicts and social upheavals, political and ideological clashes on both sides of the ocean. These tensions were inscribed in a narrative that did not consider that the dif-ferent employee figures analysed did not have the word middle class in the vocabulary of their time, and therefore could not be identified in a subject that instead was represented as fully aware of his historical formation. This term was not only absent in nineteenth-century dictionaries, or the bearer of a European rather than American meaning. Even in the political and institu-tional language of government, in the technological and social language of economic and professional associations, as well as in the public language of the press and literature, the term was not particularly important. It was thus not as widespread as it appears from historiography and when it was present its meaning was not defined and shared, such that it was communicated with different signifiers that alluded to a collective but indeterminate entity – the public – or it referred to specific occupations or professions.

In the *Report of the Committee of the Senate Upon the Relations between Labor and Capital*, which was published over five volumes in 1885, middle class still indicated proprietary figures – mercantile, artisan, and agrarian – which, unlike in the decade following the long Civil War that concluded with the end of black reconstruction, were subjects to dynamics of impoverishment traced along racial lines. While in the segregated south the formation of a white, pro-prietary middle class took place at the expense of a 'colored people' deprived

---

14   Zunz 1998; Rosenberg 1982.

of 'property and education', in the north the phenomenon of '[concentrat-
ing] many productions in large expensive plants [closed up] avenues of trade
to men of small capital, with a tendency to merge the middle class into the
proletariat'. In particular, in New York and Chicago, the nerve centres of the
national economy, 'the suppression of the middle class' was clear among
mechanics, shoemakers, tailors, blacksmiths, bricklayers, plumbers, transport
workers, bakers, and packing house workers. If until the mid-1870s these figures had managed to accumulate enough money to become owners and have
access to self-employment and economic independence, in the subsequent
decade they found themselves in the situation of any worker (*Report* 1885, vol.
I: 800; vol. IV: 549, 559, 748, 757, 785). When attention shifted onto the new figures of intellectual labour, the term middle class was either not used or used
to denounce the decline of the moral sense of self-determination that had
distinguished nineteenth-century professions. Between the 1880s and 1890s,
Harper's Magazine – the literature, arts, and politics magazine founded in
1850s – dedicated a series of articles to the organisation of employees (book-
keeper, cashier, accountant, stenographer, typist) in customs, post offices,
and the New York chambers of commerce, bringing to light the hierarchical
rigidity that divided their work into increasingly smaller and less autonomous
tasks. Outside of the office, access to consumption and participation in politics did not compensate for the loss of autonomy in labour (Wheatley 1885;
Wheatley 1886; Wheatley 1888; Wheatley 1890a; Wheatley 1890b; Wheatley
1891). At the beginning of the twentieth century, the magazine *McClure's*
published a strong stance against the 'new industrial conspiracy' against the
Chicago middle class. The tough battle (army against army) between labour
and capital had led to forms of arbitration between associations and trade
unions in construction, transport, sewerage, electrical and hydraulic supplies,
clothing, and bread-making and food conservation. The resulting increase in
the cost of living had been to the detriment of 'the professional man, the lec-
turer, the writer, the artist, the farmer, the salaried government employee, and
all the host of men who are not engaged in the actual production or delivery
of necessary material things'. Far from constituting a new authoritative and
conscious middle class, these figures defined a 'defenseless and disorganised
public' that did not find adequate answers in a politics still monopolised by
parties that acted on the belief that the workers' vote constituted an essential
electoral wellspring (Stannard Baker 1903: 451). In this way, in August 1903, the
Independent – the historic abolitionist magazine that supported free labour
against slavery – bitterly registered that 'the middle class is becoming a salaried class, and rapidly losing the economic and moral independence of former days' (The Fate of the Salaried Man 1903: 12).

The proletarianisation of the proprietary middle class, the fragmentation of intellectual labour, the mechanisation of office work, and the impoverishment of employees continued during the years of progressivism. The ordered and orderly presence of the new middle class did not emerge from publications such as those with the title *Labor, Capital and the Public* which gathered editorials from main newspapers throughout the country, interventions from exponents of the business and union world, and scholars and members of academic and professional associations. Rather, they registered the opinion of a public which was resentful and impotent in the face of the constant presence of class conflict. If the 'great mass of honest-hearted, fair-minded people ... who desire to enjoy their rights to life, liberty and the pursuit of happiness' at first looked with empathy on the conditions of blue-collar labour, now the practice of the strike was judged as in conflict with the public ('the strike is against the general public') because it abused the union by violating contracts and using 'physical force, directly or indirectly' (Labor, Capital and the Public 1905: 1–2, 71–78).[15]

Even when the conflict was regulated through industrial relations, the interest of the public was affected by the relation of force between labour and capital which prevented the rise of the middle class advocated for by progressivist politics. Between 1905 and 1906, in different messages to Congress, Theodore Roosevelt denounced the increase in cost of living caused by strikes, claiming that governmental commissions should favour forms of arbitration between companies and the union rather than agreements to the detriment of the public. His politics clearly aimed at the formation of a 'middle class of substantial citizens', with the belief that the 'permanent prosperity of the country' dependent on the 'character of the average American worker ... no matter whether his work be mental or manual, whether he be farmer or wage-worker, business man or professional man' (Roosevelt 1905: 181–189; Roosevelt 1906). However, this goal of harmony and order continually escaped the political grasp of progressivism.

During the war, even after the entrance of women into the labour market, there was a further deterioration of the economic and social condition of intellectual labour, not only the office employee or salesperson, but also those who did more skilled jobs or were engaged in professions enlisted in the 'business machine' (Johnson 1919: 97). In *The Social Unrest: Capital, Labor and Public Turmoil* (1919), a series of interventions by scholars and representatives of professional associations again declared that strikes were causing a general

---

15   In the same volume, see the contributions *Is it the "Trusts" or the Unions?* (71–78); *No Monopoly of Labor. Editorial: Wall Street Journal* (95–96); *Labor's Interest in Law and Order. Editorial: Chicago Chronicle* (174–175); *Enforcement of Law the First Requirement* (195–200).

increase in the cost of living. The high wage level of some categories of workers was judged as disproportionate and unfair compared to the 'our middle intellectual class' composed of 'teachers, bookkeepers, preachers, letter carriers, scientists, and literary workers'. Since the war economy had frustrated the ambitions of intellectual labour, the fear was that of its possible union action (Sprague 1919: 121–128; Komroff 1919: 505–508). The 'public in turmoil' was the symptom of the persistent economic and moral distress of disorganised intermediate figures in the face of persisting social tensions. In the aftermath of World War I, in a national and international context shaken by the communist revolution, while President Woodrow Wilson celebrated America as the nation where progress was not threatened by the 'world problem of the social unrest' because 'labor is not regarded as a commodity', but rather 'as a means of association, the association of physical skill and the enterprise which is managed by those who represent capital', in a *New York Times* article entitled 'The Awakening Middle Class', his vice president Thomas R. Marshall admitted the paradox of a middle class that was publicly invoked but still unable to direct progressivist politics in its own favour. While he recognised that the 'great [American] middle class' was the subject that made it possible to overcome 'the never-ending contest of class against class', he noted that it was 'not organized so as to be heard in the halls of Congress'. Although it was the 'backbone of the Republic', its 'knowledge' did not yet rule the nation. The 'awakening of the middle class', i.e., its conscious and authoritative rise thus expressed a goal to be achieved, it was not the expression of a rediscovered order but rather of a lasting disorder (Marshall 1919: 325–334).[16] In this sense, progressivism did not bring the search for order of the new middle class to an end, but rather revealed its failure. This was so not because the progressivist era signaled the triumph of conservatism, as the revisionist historiography of the consensus school maintained. Rather, it is because the profound social and political transformation that followed the crisis of authority at the end of the century took place under the sign of big business.[17]

I do not intend to deny here the historical function that technicians and engineers exercised in the realisation and scientific direction of the corporate business, as well as the political role experts played in the construction and reform processes of the American state. However, it is historically misleading to represent these figures as the authoritative voice around which a new

---

16   In the same volume, see the contributions by Wilson (385–391), Taft (391–394), and Stoddard (557–569).

17   Balogh 2015: 89–104. Cf. Hofstadter 1955: 225–226; Wiebe 1967: 223; Kolko 1963: 1–10; Sklar 1988: 20–31; Weinstein 1968: VII–XV.

non-proprietary, professional, and employee middle class formed which was capable of mediating the conflict between labour and capital. Not by chance, the word middle class would reappear with greater frequency in the public debate only during the roaring twenties. However, it did so not as a synonym of the success of American capitalism and the nascent democracy of mass consumption, but rather as a cultural symptom of the frustration of white-collar labour. Literature and cinema – Sinclair Lewis' novel *Babbit* (1922) and the screenplays *Safety Last* (1923) and *The Crowd* (1928) – depicted the employee as a helpless subject who was at the mercy of economic events, lost in the crowd of society, disappointed by the career in which he had sought his way for happiness, unable to climb the narrow social ladder except by making a fool of himself in front of the same audience of technicians, engineers, professionals, and experts on which the narrative of the American century was constructed (Ormsbee 1912: 508; The End of the Trail 1923: 30–33; Lewis 1922; Llyod 1923; Vidor 1928).[18]

This strange literary and cinematographic image of the employee is certainly deformed by the artist's hand, but it is undoubtedly dissonant with what has emerged from historiography, as if the goal of the historian was to avoid the historical presence of a lower middle class which, at least in some occupations, acted in solidarity with the workers' movement by using its own union tactics to regulate pay and the working day.[19] The same uncomfortable presence of an inferior middle class which after the crisis of the end of the century overseas, as we saw in chapter one, had prevented the representation of the English middle class as the protagonist of national history. Historiography had put the most educated figures with higher income, qualifications, and skills at the foreground, expanding their values and ambitions to the lower levels of non-manual labour which have remained blurred and in the background, so as to consider the dramatic representations of poverty, the shimmering depictions of wealth, and the worrying centrality of the conflict between labour and capital in the public and political debate as harmful influences of the sensationalist style of the European press and literature.[20] In this sense, what for historiography must be a category of mediation is actually a polemic category, clearly aimed against certain behaviours, and specific social strata and their public representation. Historiography in this sense has denied the polemical outcome of the concept of middle class. It does not simply aim at

---

18   A different depiction of white-collar workers was given in the pages of *Forbes* in 1922: Oakwood 1922. Cf. Davis 2001; Wilson 1992; Blair 2011; Augspurger 2001.

19   Kocka 1980: 54–91, 160–175.

20   Blumin 1989: 287–288. Cf. Vinovskis 1991.

the neutralisation of conflict, but rather at its specific solution which in the progressivist era was impossible due to the too strong presence of workers and big business.

US historiography has therefore projected backwards a consensual image of the middle class by making it the continuous fabric of national history. In this way, not considering that the employee figures did not make use of the word middle class in the vocabulary of their time except in a fragmented and indefinite way, it did not question the marginality of the concept in the semantic field of the social sciences of progressivism. From this perspective, by assuming that constituted by the social sciences, it is then possible to see how between the nineteenth and twentieth centuries the new middle class of historiography takes off the costume of the protagonist of national history in order to wear that of an extra: an appearance without name and script that would enter onto the scene only by expanding the point of observation within production, between the folds of the market, to the margins of society. Not unlike in Europe, in the United States the question of the middle class emerged as a political question which posed the unavoidable problem of attributing to the concept a specific scientific content without which it would never have acquired centrality in society and politics: the history of the American middle class is not to be taken for granted.

2   The Middle Class as a Sociological Problem

Not unlike what happened on the European side of the Atlantic, albeit within the transnational circulation of associative experiences and scientific litera-ture, the decades between the nineteenth and twentieth centuries marked the decisive period in the professionalisation and institutionalisation of the US social sciences. Arising as a social movement linked to the protestant mission based on the 'social gospel', as well as philanthropic associationism and 'social settlement' initiatives in the poorest neighbourhoods of urban areas, where 'social work' combined research and civic engagement, the various scientific disciplines – especially economics and sociology – acquired their position within universities by affirming a reformist vocation that overcame the hege-mony of evolutionism and laissez-faire doctrines that had legitimated the for-mation of corporations after the Civil War. The experience of the American Social Science Association, founded in 1865 on the basis of the British National Association for Promotion of Social Science (1862), was important in this sense not only because it paved the way for the establishment of other aca-demic associations, such as The American Economic Foundation, founded in

1885, the American Political Science Association in 1903, and the American Sociological Association in 1905. It was important above all because it signaled the growing political ambition of scholars and experts who, on the basis of the knowledge and skills they acquired, began to think of themselves as professional compared to the ignorance of mass politics, the corruption of parties, and the conflicting interests of organised labour and big business. In this way a 'community of the competent' took shape: not the new middle class in the search for order by historiography, but a new community of scientific knowledge whose attention was turned to the cyclical economic crises and the consequences of impoverishment and social conflict caused by industrial capital. At the centre of the new social sciences was not the erosion of the proprietary middling sort/rank of nineteenth-century American democracy, nor was it the employee labour of a lower middle class forgotten by historiography, but rather the political question of the conflict between labour and capital or its possible governing through the application of the scientific method in industrial relations and public administration for the improvement of the economic conditions of the poor masses, the social integration of the working class, and the Americanisation of immigrant labour. Science thus legitimated a claim to political authority suitable to the rethinking of a nation that at the end of the century seemed unrecognisable:

> The leading question today has become that of the relations between capital and labour. After the Civil War ... capital was accumulated to an unprecedented degree in the hands of great corporations, and for the first time there appeared in America a true proletariat.
>
> WARD 1908: 446[21]

In the United States, the European crisis of the liberal order took on the appearance of a crisis of the exceptionalism of a nation built on alterity from the old world since its independence. The period that ran from the Civil War to World War I coincided in this way with a radical transformation of society: the productive capacity of 'free labor' and the national wealth produced by small farmers, artisans, and manufacturers became residual with respect to the supply of wage labour, the organisation of production and distribution on a large scale, the concentration of business into trusts and corporations, and the poverty in large urban and industrial centres. However, it was above all the

---

21   On the history of US social sciences, see Bulmer 1984; Haskell 1977; Bernard and Bernard 1943; Goldman 1998; Gunnell 1996.

continental explosion of class conflict that contradicted the exceptionality of the nation, entangling it in the tormented and disordered history of Europe. During the nineteenth century, in George Bancroft's *History of the United States* (1854–1878), as well as Henry C. Carey's (founding economist of the American School of Economics) *The Harmony of Interests* (1851), the novelty of America – with its frontier, its republican experiment and its capitalism, and its democratisation and social mobility – had forged a national culture that relegated European history to the past and freed the American present from the grip of the economic cycle of overpopulation and impoverishment which political economy – particularly that of Thomas Malthus – had identified as the historical problem of capitalism: the un-American spectre of the separation between wage labour and economic independence was removed from the future of the nation. In the turn of the century this vision exploded under the weight of the unexpected presence of a riotous working class that pushed the new social sciences to confront European history. American progress could not be thought apart from the forces which had fueled civilisation overseas. Thus, in dialogue with the European social sciences – from marginalism to the new English liberalism, passing through French sociology and up to the German historical school – which had confronted the crisis of the liberal order by rethinking liberalism in a social key, the new US social sciences took note of the erosion of American novelty by inscribing national history in European history, but also by elaborating theoretical and methodological tools which, in their political vision, would make it possible to reconstitute the exceptionalism through the scientific control of the turbulent change in history and its accommodation with the natural course of American progress.

Unlike the European literature, however, the social sciences of progressivism did not respond to the crisis of the turn of the century by forging a new conception of the middle class based on employee labour. Far from identifying a newfound exceptionality of the nation, in the new economic and sociological disciplines, the middle class appeared internal to European history. Since the middle class had constituted the central subject of the liberal order which at the turn of the century was affected by a profound crisis of legitimation, middle class turned out to be an unusable concept, which was thus useless for reconstituting the exceptionalism. On the one hand, it was exemplified by the civilisation common to both sides of the Atlantic, while on the other, it signalled the historical stalemate from which American should escape.[22]

---

22   Ross 1997: 25–29, 57–59.

This particularly emerged from the polemic between authors of laissez-faire doctrines and the social sciences of progressivism. In various writings published between the nineteenth and twentieth centuries, William Graham Sumner – the leading US proponent of Spencerian evolutionism – described civilisation as the 'history of the struggle of the middle class' to conquer and re-establish political and social power on new foundations. No longer in the name of rank and birth as in the Middle Ages, but rather on the basis of the free contract and the market, namely a 'capitalist system' that defined an order which was ultimately 'free and equal' since it was founded on 'personal right and property' against aristocratic privilege: the evolution coincided with the rise of the middle class and its 'commercial and industrial civilisation'. The historical apex of the 'social movement of the middle class – located on the English side of the Atlantic – also marked, however, the beginning of 'the tendency of all social burdens to crush out the middle class' which followed the formation of social classes: industrial relations had introduced a 'new social question' which made it difficult to 'maintain a middle class on a high stage of civilization' (Sumner 1883: 33, 101–102; Sumner 1914: 36, 72–76, 130; Sumner 1918: 402–403. Cf. George 1879: 528).

In light of this tendency, when Sumner's gaze moved towards the American side of the ocean, middle-class civilisation became uncertain and contradictory. America was no stranger to the historical dynamics activated by the presence of the working class. The social question had induced 'social doctors', 'social philosophers', and 'reformers' to rethink the role of the state in order to improve workers' conditions. The policies of regulating the production and distribution of wealth and the creation of administrative forms of arbitration between the company and union favoured the 'organisation of only two classes, one at each social extreme', destroying the 'whole middle class' which had ensured the wellbeing of the nation. Thus, in his most famous essay, which introduced a term that marked the age of reforms into public and political discourse, the middle class would step back from the role of the protagonist of civilisation in order to take on the guise of the *Forgotten Man* (1883): an indefinite public, an indistinct mass of 'clean, quiet, virtuous' citizens who, without asking for anything and without inciting feelings of rebellion, wanted to obtain a 'contract' to enjoy the fruit of their own work (Sumner 1918: 476–487; Sumner 1883: 120–150; Sumner 1914: 72–76). And yet, adherence to Spencerian evolutionism and confidence in American exceptionalism led Sumner to affirm not only that the words bourgeoisie and proletariat were part of 'the foreign dress of a set of ideas which are not yet naturalized'. Even the word middle class

which had been inherited from European history had lost its political grip and
'has no application to American society' (Sumner 1914: 161, 392).[23]

These uncertainties and contradictions which ran through middle-class
civilisation should not be considered as scientific inconsistences of US evolutionism. Not only because they distinguished the national narrative of the
different European histories in the grip of the crisis of the liberal order, but
also because they were the sign of the 'cultural war' that the explosion of class
conflict had opened on the US public vocabulary, on the words of the nation
and their legitimate or illegitimate meaning. This war, which in the political
sphere involved terms such as anarchism and socialism that were considered
un-American because they were European, was also found in the semantic
field of the social sciences.[24] Although at the turn of the century what Sumner
criticised as the 'paternal theory of government' – judged as extraneous to the
experiment of 'liberal democracy' – acquired scientific legitimacy in universities and political viability in the progressivist experiences of Theodor Roosevelt
and Woodrow Wilson, it happened in the name of an exceptionalism that
needed to be reconstructed (Sumner 1883: 150). Even in a polemic against evolutionism and laissez-faire doctrines, the social sciences of progressivism were
also committed to cleansing the academic disciplines of socialist literature and
liberating the public vocabulary of the influence of European words such as
bourgeoisie and proletariat. In this sense, in the work of the founding fathers
of the new sociology – Lester F. Ward, Albion Small, and Edward A. Ross – the
concept middle class was considered unusable for the purpose of rethinking
the nation because its meaning signalled the stalemate of civilisation, rather
than the possible American overcoming of the limit of European history.

Ward employed middle class as a synonym for business class in order to
indicate the European bourgeoisie or the French Third Estate. If between the
eighteenth and nineteenth centuries their rise coincided with the acquisition of political freedom, the entrance into 'the great millennium of universal prosperity, well-being, and happiness' would be possible only through the
scientific investigation of – and experimental application of the sciences to –
the opposing forces of labour and capital which prevented the affirmation of
'social freedom'. Ward did not deny the presence of the conflict in the name
of exceptionalism, but instead considered it necessary to criticise the historical foundations and contradictory outcomes of evolutionism. If even in the
United States 'the movement that is now agitating society' was no longer that

---

23   Cf. Curtis 1981.
24   Baritono 2018b; Battistini 2018.

of the middle class, but rather the 'coming to consciousness of the proletariat', a new border had to be broken down. No longer the political one of noble rank, but that of the social border of class (Ward 1900: 28, 99). In this perspective, against the backdrop of the agrarian and populist revolts at the end of the century, class distinctions not only had to be rethought in terms of productive ('producer') and non-productive forces ('parasites' of the corporate bureaucracies and government officials), which relegated the middle man dedicated to commercial, mercantile, and financial intermediation to a merely accessory role of production (Ward 1883: 566–586).[25] Government was also no longer considered a 'necessary evil' – or even an 'unnecessary evil' – according to the liberal tradition of common sense which derived from the revolutionary era. On the contrary, the reviled term of the state had to be rehabilitated through science. The state no longer embodied the 'collectivism' which according to Spencer heralded the advent of a new slavery. Rather, it constituted a 'social agency' of the mediation of opposing interests which, operating on a scientific basis, would dissolve the proletariat into a productive force, one inscribed positively 'in the work of civilization' rather than as negation. Since 'collectivism is not therefore the opposite of individualism', but rather constituted its historical and theoretical presupposition, the state was understood as a 'sociological laboratory' for the application of policies aimed at expanding scientific education, the reduction of the working day, the improvement of working conditions, the increase of social wellbeing – 'in short, the organization of human happiness' (Ward 1900: 228–229, 339; Ward 1903: 550–567; Ward 1883: 40–45).[26]

In this new script for American civilisation, on whose trail Albion Small built his sociology of 'associational processes' and Edward Ross his science of 'social control', the middle class lost the role of protagonist which it played overseas. While Ross followed Ward by identifying the middle class with the European bourgeoisie at the top of a 'pyramidal society' which posed a 'severe strain on obedience', Small still used the colonial term 'middle rank' in order to deny the American existence of the 'sharp boundary line' which distinguished the European rich and the middle classes. Deprived of the middle class as subject of civilisation, overseas the liberal order no longer depended on deference towards the nineteenth-century 'morality of gentlemen'. Its reproduction through reforms was entrusted to social scientists – 'professionals specialized in social control', representatives of intellectual and scientific interests ('the

---

25   In this way Ward anticipates Veblen's (1899) *The Theory of the Leisure Class: An Economic Study of Institutions*, a theory to which he would refer in Ward 1900: 336.

26   On government as a necessary evil, see also Small 1905: 253. On the rehabilitation of the state, see Baritono 2013.

intellectual, knowledge interest') who would restore harmony and consensus in society by giving shape to a 'sociocracy': a socially controlled government or a society capable of regulating itself through the state and its social sciences (Ward 1883: 60–62; Ross 1914: 172–173, 237, 362–363; Small 1905: 226–253, 270–301, 390–391; Small 1915: 664).

Middle class therefore remained a European concept and for this reason was unusable for reconstituting American exceptionalism after the crisis at the end of the century. At least until the first postwar period, no scientific literature existed that was specifically dedicated to the middle class, whether it was proprietary or employee. Empirical studies and research were concentrated on the poverty of cities, immigration from southern and eastern Europe, and the condition of the working class.[27] Yet, within the scientific field of the new social sciences and in the sociological laboratory of the American state, there emerged a theoretical and methodological instrumentation which would open national history to the search for a new middle class. The main point of impact of the critique of the progressivist social sciences was in fact the class boundary that had caused the historical stalemate of European civilisation. Their scientific method aimed at the transformation of the class boundary into a new frontier which the sociological and social reform of the American state could make traversable by overcoming the historical limit on which evolutionism and laissez-faire had run aground. Scientific processes in this sense confronted the social problem of the wage, namely its possible solution by means of the definition of consumption as the economic variable for the distribution of wealth. And, consequently, the political presence of the working class, i.e., its sociological decomposition into a plurality of social groups through not only the statistical measurement of their social position (occupation, income, education), but also the application of psychology in order to understand their behaviour. Although middle class was not the subject of theoretical reflection and empirical research, the social sciences of progressivism nevertheless began, without resolving, the search for a new middle class.

It was the new economic sciences – marginalism and the historical school of economics –that identified in consumption the key to reconstruct the exceptionalism of the nation and open national history to the formation of a new middle class. In the decade following the Civil War, on the threshold of the first great depression, Francis A. Walker questioned the natural law of classical economics that fueled the contradictory tendency of European civilisation. In *The Wage Question* (1876) he maintained that since it was making the workers'

---

27   Moskowitz 2012: 75–86.

viewpoint irreconcilable with the entrepreneurial perspective, this law had to change before a history (that of the US) which until then combined democracy and capitalism. Not unlike the critical reflection that overseas found its neoclassical synthesis in the work of Alfred Marshall, Walker's polemical target was Thomas Malthus. Since the author of the *Essay on the Principle of Population* (1826) had flattened natural law onto the cyclical dynamic of overpopulation and impoverishment, it was necessary to update American exceptionalism to the new historical condition that made the possibility of acquiring property through work residual. In other words, it was necessary to reformulate the terms of the relation between labour and capital. Profit was no longer understood as the expropriation of surplus value, but instead as recompense for entrepreneurial skill. In a specular way, the wage was not calculated on the basis of the foundation of fixed capital, but on the overall value expected from the sale of the goods produced. It was the commodity, and therefore its consumption, and not the invested capital, which provided the correct measure of the wage. The resulting conclusion was astonishing because an increase in wages could take place without a loss of profits. However, although Walker saw the possibility of freeing US history from the Malthusian grip, the scientific problem of determining the margin within which the wage increase would be suitable for profit remained open. That margin was not to be left to the free determination of class conflict. The practice of the strike, which for the first time affected the entire national economy, was condemned because it prevented the planning of profit on the basis of the 'efficiency of labor' (Walker 1876: 41–56, 106–107). In this sense, his intuition lacked a rigorous mathematical method which surpassed the crude Malthusian equation. At the beginning of the twentieth century this was the task of US marginalism and its main exponent, John Bates Clark.[28]

Among the founders of the American Economic Association who, following the Verein für Sozialpolitik, intended to affirm a social revision of economic liberalism, Clark was engaged in a scientific effort to politically rehabilitate American capitalism in the face of the challenge of socialism that emerged with the great depression of the late nineteenth century. In order to combine the natural law of the economy and the national history invested with class conflict, it was urgent to rethink the functioning of capitalism in a way that became indisputable or a way that would regain consent after its historical legitimation was questioned by the saturation – officially sanctioned by the closure of the border in 1890 – of the protestant ideal of the acquisition of

---

28   Cf. Ross 1997: 80–85; Dorfman 1966: 749–757.

property through hard work. His study *The Distribution of Wealth* (1899) therefore began with the necessity to absolve capitalism from the charge of the 'exploitation of labor'. If it had been true that labour was 'regularly robbed', 'the zeal of the socialist' expressed an undeniable 'sense of justice'. As Walker had intuited, progress instead made work (at least the most skilled, for the most part provided by white workers) more productive and better paid. In this sense, since the main scientific deduction of classical economics, for which value was the product of labour, had been overturned into a dangerous argument, economic science had to overthrow the point of view by considering the producer in his 'capacity as consumer' (Clark 1902: 4, 160).

With this perspective it was possible to look at production in a different way: man did not acquire independence through work itself, but rather in the consumption of the commodity produced. Consequently, the value of the commodity could be calculated on the basis of the utility of its consumption. The fixed capital invested into the wage was no longer important. Rather, it was necessary to ascertain how many commodities produced should be attributed to a single unity of the labour supplied. It was thus possible to establish the 'specific productivity of labor' and on this basis to calculate the margin within which the increase in wages would not cause a decrease in profit, but rather would lead to a tendential increase. Seen with the eyes of the consumer, production therefore gives a glimpse of an escape from class conflict: although labour and capital constitute opposing forces, their movement was 'interdependent' because neither of the two could act without changing the 'productive power' of the other. If this interdependence fuelled conflict, the continuous improvement of the 'industrial method' with the introduction of the 'mechanical process' made it possible to increase wages which made consumption a terrain of mediation through the distribution of wealth. The 'doctrinarianism' of classical economics which had not been able to avoid the Malthusian historical return of misery was thus overcome with a new economic science for which the natural law was not static, but instead took on a historical character (Clark 1902: 29–31, 48, 69, 282–283). The new 'science of Social and Economic Dynamics' of marginalism recognised the relation between labour and capital as a relation in movement. In this way it shaped the natural law to the 'play of forces' of society so that the wage was not left to the free determination of class conflict, but rather its increase was distributed within a coherent margin that was suitable for the increase in profit (Clark 1902: 373, 406–407):

> The marginal productive power of labor furnishes the standard of wages, and in general this is trending upward ... if, however, labour could instantly get all that a recent improvement enables it to produce, profits

would be annihilated and the incentive to further improvement would
be removed.

CLARK 1903: 130–142, 131

In this way Clark formulated a 'theory of wages' that, within the Atlantic scientific debate that involved the English economist John A. Hobson (Hobson
1903: 143–153), explained the economic crisis not in terms of overproduction,
but rather underconsumption. While classical economics had proposed wage
compression as the only way out of the fall in profits, for marginalism poverty was not considered a function of profit because a high wage guaranteed
more consumption, 'rising comfort', and even 'a modest luxury'. In the volume
Essentials of Economic Theory (1907) which synthesises a decade of studies,
capitalism therefore appeared rehabilitated through the elaboration of the
economic formula that would be identified with Fordism: 'high wages, low
prices' did not only allow a contingent exit from the crisis, but also a definitive
loosening of the Malthusian grip – if necessary, even by resorting to the state.
If organised labour had won wages beyond 'the natural limit set by the specific
product of labor', politics had the duty to intervene through forms of arbitration: an authoritative mode of establishing a 'reasonable' wage. In this sense,
since the scientific determination of the profit margin required a political
sanction in the last instance, the neoclassical synthesis of marginalism opened
the doors of the national economy to the reforms of progressivism. New analytical perspectives and empirical research, particularly with Irving Fisher and
Wesley Mitchell, would concentrate attention on the statistical study of price
trends, the behaviour of markets and fluctuation of consumption, providing
business management, as well as public administration, an instrumentation
suitable to the technical governance of the 'economic cycle' considered impermeable to the harmful influences of class conflict until 1929. Consumption
became a productive variable, the worker was no longer exclusively a cost to
the extent that he acted as a consumer, and the traditional work ethic was integrated into the new morality of consumption (Clark 1918: 455–456, 469–470).[29]

This logical succession made it possible to reconstruct exceptionalism on the
basis of a 'theory of progress' based on the increase of the wage (Clark 1902: 33,
63–69, 72; Clark 1918: 325; Clark 1896. See also Seligman 1903). However, it was
Simon N. Patten who explicitly presented the new economic science as the
foundation of the new American civilisation. While considering marginalism
as nothing more than a mathematical instrument, he used its criticism of the

---

29   Cf. Zunz 1998: 101 and Ross 1997: 175–178.

Malthusian law in order to advance an unprecedented historical interpretation of the national economy: US history no longer appeared entangled in the tumultuous and disordered European history because consumption constituted the cornerstone for not only social and economic progress, but also the moral and political progress of the nation. In his works, the United States was placed in a 'transition stage' from the 'pain economy' – the Malthusian economy of suffering – to the 'pleasure economy': a new economy of pleasure whose traces were sought in the productivity which made 'the harmony of consumption' possible. In *The New Basis of Civilisation* (1907), the end of the first great depression signaled the definitive overcoming of the Malthusian doctrine and the tendential liberation of the national economy from the boundary of class. If the capitalist and labourer were the 'static' product of economic institutions of the past, the expansion of consumption made social classes fluid, bringing the economic ideal of American civilisation to fulfilment. The mathematical method of marginalism thus took on a narrative that identified the new legitimation of capitalism in 'plenty'. In the near future, American democracy would become a social commonwealth or 'the highest stage of civilisation' (Patten 1896: 76–88, 121–140; Patten 1907: 10–11, 69–77, 85, 215).[30]

The social and moral progress that the new economic sciences placed at the basis of American civilisation therefore reconstructed exceptionalism by liberating national history from the European condemnation of misery. In this new telling, however, the middle class played no role except as a reference point to a European history from which the United States claimed to have emancipated itself: middle class still carried a negative meaning of the 'arrogant' individualism of European civilisation. However, the scientific instrumentation provided in particular by marginalism opened US history to the search for a new middle class. This was so not only because consumption was understood as an instrument for governing the conflict between labour and capital by establishing the margin within which the wage could increase without affecting profit. It was also because – as Clark argued – it made it possible to elaborate a science of the 'movements of labour from group to group' (Clark 1902: xvi, 62 ff). In this way, once the social problem of the wage was solved, at least in theory, it was possible to question the political presence of the working class. Its decomposition into social groups that labour could traverse was the task that progressivist sociology took on in dialogue with the new economic sciences: if until the end of the century sociology had tried to establish itself as an autonomous discipline against the academic primacy of classical economics, the rise of

---

30   Cfr. Zunz 1998: 25–46, 73–92; Schulter 1979; Fox 1967; Ross 1997: 216–223.

marginalism made possible a scientific dialogue under the political aegis of the common convergence towards the reforms of progressivism.

This dialogue had begun at the end of the century when, following the publication of *Dynamic Sociology* (1883), Richard Ely invited Ward to a discussion on *Some Social and Economic Paradoxes* that marginalism had introduced into the two disciplines. The discussion started by 'exactly reversing the Malthusian doctrine' that the wage depended on the commodities sold rather than capital. According to Ward, this theoretical innovation caused a double paradox – both economic and social – which affected economic and sociological science: the paradox that 'profits rise with wages' or – in a more exact formula – 'increase of wages results in increased profits'. In light of this, not only did economic science have to subordinate the problem of increasing production to the question of increasing consumption in order to teach the entrepreneur how to overcome his traditional 'mercantile sagacity'. Sociology also had to escape the 'economic myth' that the consumer constituted a class of its own which on the market acquired the commodity produced by the wage earner. In other words, it had to consider the wage earned both as producer and consumer in order to construct a practical science of society on the social relation of consumption. If 'dynamic sociology' defined a 'philosophy of progress' that indicated the final stage of civilisation in social freedom, 'applied sociology' had to formulate the laws and indicate the methods of its historical fulfilment, i.e., the 'perfect distribution of wealth'. In this sense, Ward went beyond the marginalist conception of consumption as 'the dynamic element in political economy' in order to make it into a sociological category: 'sociology has everything to do with consumption'. The transition from the economy of suffering to the economy of pleasure – which Patten had described – was to be achieved by making sociology a 'science of welfare' aimed at overcoming class inequalities. As he wrote, 'we should have but one social class, or rather, we should have no social classes' (Ward 1889: 128; Ward 1883: 25; Ward 1903: 282–285; Ward 1900: 229–234).

This scientific and political objective was first of all pursued by Small in a close confrontation with Marx's work. Small did not deny the debt owed towards the Marxian theory of history. Indeed, he criticised the exceptionalist position of those who denied the existence of the class struggle: it was a fundamental strategic error like the one made during the decade prior to the Civil War when the political discussion of slavery was banned by Congress. However, his scientific effort intended to deny legitimacy to the 'impertinent and inhuman perversity' with which Marx tried to raise the working class as an 'antagonistic interest'. His assertion of class struggle as a 'universal fact' had to be dismantled because it did not consider 'cooperation' as an equally universal fact. The way to do this was to disprove the political assumption that 'the laboring class and the capitalistic class may be sharply distinguished and precisely divided' (Small 1912: 811–815, 819).

In this sense, drawing from George Simmel's sociological reflection on super-ordination and subordination in social groups, Small considered society as a set of social relations that individuals entertained not as members of a class, but rather along ethnic, religious, economic, and political lines. Consequently, sociology had to abandon its 'partisan attitude' in favour of labour or capital in order to become 'a science of men in their associational processes'. With this perspective, Small described a plurality of social groups which, recipro-cally influencing one another, caused convergence or divergence of interests. Society was not lacking conflict, but the phenomenon of the class struggle was increasingly less exorable because the associative process involved a cooper-ative phase that had to be restored to its 'natural' primacy. This was possible through the 'socialization' of interests or the social diffusion of individual and collective behaviours that made class interest no longer antagonistic, but rec-oncilable. If the class struggle had reached the 'extreme point of absolute hos-tility', the social inclination to form groups (vocational groupings) 'would be weakened or even destroyed'. The 'spontaneous and systematic social process' would be blocked and the 'partialness' of labour would burst onto the politi-cal scene. In order to prevent society from taking on a Marxian appearance, sociology must provide politics the knowledge that derives from the 'perpet-ual measuring of strength between the classes'. Knowing the new conditions determined by the conflict would make it possible to trace the line of interven-tion within which 'peaceful cooperation' would proceed through 'mutual con-cession'. Only by considering the state as 'a union of disunions, a conciliation of conflicts, a harmony of discords' would society reprise its natural dynamic of the grouping of groupings and in this way fuel civilization (Small 1905: 205–209, 252–253, 263–269, 300–301, 332, 363; Small 1904: 285–298; Small 1915: 519; Simmel 1896; Simmel 1904) .[31]

The scientific and political objective for the United States to become either a society with only one class or a society without classes was not only pursued by means of a sociological model that enabled 'intellectualizing the conflict', i.e., transforming it into a 'teleological program' in order to integrate the inter-ests of social groups – and the interest of labour in particular – into society (Small 1905: 390–391). In the wake of sociology there also matured a specific scientific attention to the cultural processes that, in addition to the cooper-ation inherent in economic interdependence, allowed the effective moral

---

31   Cf. Page 1964: 116–128 and Ross 1997: 222–229.

connection between individuals and groups. The political problem of break-
ing down the working class into a harmonious society of social groups also
became a psychological question regarding values and their valuation, opinions and their communication. The first important step in this direction was
taken by Edward Ross (Ross 1896a; Ross 1896b; Ross 1900a; Ross 1900b).

In *Social Control*, Ross started from the innovations introduced by the economic and sociological sciences in order to demonstrate how the productivity
that moved industry made it not only possible to increase wages and prosperity through consumption. The moderation of class conflict also passed through
a 'social control' which was spontaneous in the first instance and prevented
the stiffening of contrasts within the industry. Ross re-read Smith's *Theory of
Moral Sentiments* (1759) in order to affirm that a cultural process of sympathy
or evaluation and moral identification was at work in society which, by fuelling a 'feeling of justice' contrary to inequalities, naturally promoted order. This
process had operated and did operate through a multiplicity of forms – from
religion to custom to law and administration – and in industrial society also
assumed the peculiar form of public opinion or the 'control of ideas'. The task
of social science, with its new sociological and psychological instrumentation,
was in this sense to know and reproduce, if necessary, modifying and adapting to the historical time, the value and ideal content of the social ethics that
arose from the control of society. In this way it would be possible to avoid the
'great danger' of a 'resentful proletariat' which could fuel a 'militant' behaviour
capable of paralysing the control that allowed society to progress in an orderly
fashion (Ross 1914: 232–233, 247–249, 314–315, 340–347, 401–403, 418–420).[32]

The political convergence towards progressivist reforms that made the scientific dialogue between economics and sociologists possible thus signalled
a precise analytic convergence. What Small identified as the main 'point of
agreement' in sociology – namely the task to 'discover and to formulate the
laws of those processes of human association' – rendered the disciplinary orientations linked to evolutionism or socialism minoritarian, fuelling multiple
empirical research aimed at achieving the practical result of 'harmonising

---

32   In these same years Charles Cooley (1897) studied the process of 'social change' as a pro-
      cess of 'communication'. Franklin Giddings also moved in a similar direction when he
      spoke of the 'consciousness of kind' in order to indicate 'the perception of resemblance,
      the sympathy, the affection, and the desire for recognition' which made it possible to
      overcome 'the segregation of the population into classes'. In this way, during the 1920s he
      would come to question the existence of a 'psychological middle class' as a class that was
      independent of the 'economic stratification of the people'. See Giddings 1901: 64–65; 99–
      100; 242–243; Giddings 1926: 231–233. Cf. Page 1964: 150–153 and 219–223; Ross 1997: 129–
      130 and 228–229; Lorini 1980: 56–57.

human relations ... and adjusting relations of groups to individuals in the process of securing proportional shares in political, industrial, and social opportunity'. The political question to which the new social sciences intended to answer by also operating through the state was that of measuring 'exactly the kind of quantity of conflict present in society': what was 'the actual division of the people of the United States ... and to what extent is this division the necessary antagonism of the people against each other'? (Small 1905: 373, 723–724; Small 1907: 637; Small: 1906)

The most important answer to this question came from John Commons and his sociological school who studied capitalism from the viewpoint of the working class. An economist by training, Commons entered with a historical perspective into the secret laboratory of production in order to empirically deepen the theoretical intuition with which Clark had defined economic science as the science of movement from one group to another. Commons, who would later be recognised as the founding father of US labour history, revealed the presence of a growing number of new employee figures (from managers to clerks) and the possibility for the workers to become foremen or superintendents. In this sense, the change that swept through industry 'tends toward class solidary ... [and] offers means to circumvent it'. Not only because the employee – at least the highly skilled and specialised employee – did not participate in the workers' demands, but also because the new division of work made a system of promotion possible in which the 'ambitious' worker could climb 'by easy steps all the way to the top': with each step his wage would be increased, and his working conditions would be improved. Industry thus offered a 'great outlet' which substituted the frontier that during the nineteenth century had spread class conflict in space, loosening the grip on society and making possible the narrative of national history that combined capitalism and democracy. If scientifically governed, the organisational dynamics of production would determine a 'steady evaporation of class feeling'. The measurement of the worker's 'individuality' – his skill in terms of 'quality, intelligence, ingenuity, versatility, and interest in his work', as well as his 'consciousness' and propensity for solidarity or competition – would offer knowledge suitable for precluding the collective option of the strike as 'incipient rebellion'. The application of sociology and psychology to industry made it possible to change the meaning of class conflict. It was no longer the expression of an 'apparent' antagonism between entrepreneurial and waged classes. Instead, it signalled a competition among multiple interests that did not lead to the 'explosion' of 'class-consciousness' as had happened in the last quarter of the nineteenth century, because it favoured the formation of a 'non-class', i.e., a class that denied the historical conditions – economic, sociological, and psychological – of the class boundary. Commons did not yet use the concept of middle class, but instead classified these new figures of worker and employee as 'public':

> The great third class, the public, is now beginning to assert its right to hold the balance between two struggling classes ... Class conflict may be growing but it is not inevitable if this third class, which is not a class, is able to determine directly the issues.
>
> COMMONS 1908: 758–761, 764

Despite uncertainties about the public's abilities to determine the final outcome of the conflict between labour and capital, Commons approached the scientific and political objective of a society with only one class or without classes. Although his *History of Labor in the United States* showed the presence of a riotous working class, the US workers' movement was nevertheless presented as historically characterised by the ideal of the middle class, not the 'waged class' as in Europe. Not because between the nineteenth and twentieth centuries workers' mobilisation, which took place mainly in the hands of unskilled figures also started from ethnic and racial solidarity, did not show the border that separated the working class from the small agricultural, mercantile, and manufacturing property that had supported the 'self rule' of American democracy. Instead, it was because the transformation of industry led to the formation of an intermediary stratum (middle stratum) of medium-skilled labourers, specialised mechanical operators, technicians, engineers, and professionals who fueled the middle-class ideal of American labour by updating the traditional ethics of independence and autonomy of labour in the nineteenth century in terms of a new 'philosophy of cooperation' (Commons 1918: 4–5; Commons 1926: 245, 308, 461, 519, 534).[33] The presence of a vast middle class that in the public and political debate was named as the public should have numerically and ideally overcome the two antagonistic classes of labour and capital, influencing 'the politics of the state' in the perspective of 'labor legislation' (Hourwich 1911b: 337).

3   The Middle Class of Progressivism

In the years that marked the political turning point from the progressivism of Theodor Roosevelt's New Nationalism to President Wilson's New Freedom,

---

33   Cf. Ross 1997: 280–281, 290–292.

national history was opened up to the search for a new middle class within the semantic field of the new social sciences. The social sciences of progressivism went beyond the historical limit that evolutionism and the laissez-faire doctrine had shown, tracing the new script of American civilisation after the crisis of the liberal order overseas coincided with the disintegration of the middle class as the subject of civilisation, the protagonist of different national histories. Their theoretical and methodological instrumentation made it possible to think the class boundary as a new frontier which empirical research would make crossable: the science of the movement of labour from one group to another not only resolved the social problem of the wage by means of identifying consumption as an economic variable for distributing wealth and a culture variable to define progress, but also overcame the political presence of the working class through its sociological and psychological decomposition into a plurality of social groups. Even more important was the function attributed to the scientific processes of the knowledge of society that initiated the search for the new middle class: the function of social control.

When the social scientists of progressivism studied society in order to comprehend and exercise control over the individuality of the worker – over his career ambitions within production, his social behaviour as a consumer, the formation of his class consciousness or his association in groups along occupational and racial lines, his Americanisation or his integration according to American values and ideals – they constituted a 'community of the competent' that demanded political authority through the growing role that they were acquiring in governmental commissions, particularly during Wilson's presidency. Although they intended to strengthen the democratic ideal of the nation by advocating for electoral reforms that gave the public a voice through the establishment of the referendum and popular legislative initiative, the political goal of enforcing social control by means of administration involved the constitution of their own space reserved for political action within the state. In this way, by affirming an unprecedented technical character of government, they eroded the 'self-rule' foundations of American democracy. To escape this historical paradox – which historiography has resolved at least in part by narrating national history with the voice of the new middle class as a subject fully aware of its historical formation – the social scientists embarked on the still unexplored path of the search for a new middle class.[34]

In order for their sociocracy not to become a technocracy, i.e., in order not to pervert the democratic ideal of the economy of pleasure and social freedom

---

34   Balogh 2015: 89–101. Cf. Ross 1997: 247–251; Lorini 1980: 27–28, 38–40, 48–49.

into a new 'gentry' of knowledge', it was necessary not to make a 'minority group' of specialised professionals in control of a new natural aristocracy. It was indispensable to socialise their interest for the political application of scientific knowledge with the interests of the broader public of individuals who, by reason of their occupations, constituted a 'social type' with which to share the action of social control. Small and Ross insisted in this sense on the function that the associative process – characterising every area of public and private bureaucracies that provided professional services – had in spreading behaviours that allowed individuals to confirm to the 'ethic standard' of a society in which conflict had to be overcome in more advanced forms of cooperation. Although they did not employ 'middle class' except in its traditional European meaning, they did not exclusively refer to the 'professional spirit' of nineteenth-century liberalism. Nor did they only refer to the 'oversight' exercised by officials and public employees, religious ministers, teachers, engineers, pharmacists, and artists. They also referred to the normative character of 'respect' and 'observance' that emerged with the highly paid worker, the clerk, and in general the salaried employee. The acquisition, through scholastic specialisation or academic study, of a profession or a scientific and technical skill, of a qualification in production and distribution, established an objective function of control in industry and society as a whole. Consequently, the recognition of the social position ('status') of these figures – as Small in particular wrote about, echoing the German experience that he had observed through Gustav Schmoller's work on the *Mittelstand* – was decisive for harmonising the relations between individuals and social groups through the best political, economic, and social opportunities that the progressivist reforms offered. In this specific sense, the neoclassical synthesis of marginalism and progressivist sociology claimed to provide a 'democratic method' that made the state not a 'source', but rather a simple channel of control. The function of social control attributed to professional, skilled, and employee figures operated as a political function of the democratic legitimation of the technical government of the social sciences which, contrary to what Sumner claimed, was not a paternal government because it was democracy itself that took on a 'scientific' character: 'the seat of the common will, then, is no longer the crowd, but the Public' (Small 1905: 723–724; Ross 1914: 80, 82, 23–232, 238).

In this way, although the middle class was not the object of empirical study and theoretical reflection, middle class began to make its appearance among the pages of the scientific, public, and political vocabulary with a different meaning than in Europe. In 1907, as an indication of the historical proof of the overcoming of Malthusian law, Clark indicated the social presence of a 'certain middle class, composed of small employers, salaried men, professional men, and a multitude of highly paid workers': a class which in the majority was composed by a constantly increasing number of individuals who had been lower class and who therefore embodied the progressive nature of the nation. In 1914, in the political pamphlet *Social Justice without Socialism* which revealed his support for the Wilson presidency, Clark appealed to this 'great middle class' in order to support reforms against the revolutionary zeal of the socialist leader Eugene Debs and the Industrial Workers of the World, who threatened to destroy the wealth of industry by reducing working hours and winning higher wages through the unregulated practice of the strike. Consistent with his economic studies, the decrease of the working day and increase in wages had to take place within a margin compatible with the profit ensured by productivity. The middle class was therefore called upon in order to legitimate the progressivist politics of moderation of the social and political demands so that industry was not expropriated and destroyed by a 'revolution', but instead reformed in the direction of making 'higher wages' possible. Only in this way, namely by publicly and politically leveraging the presence of the new middle class, would the 'line of division between labor and capital' no longer constitute a 'sharp boundary': labour and capital would 'more and more merge' by electing the middle class the political subject of the 'New Jerusalem' of scientific democracy (Clark 1914: 14, 16, 19, 25, 32–33, 40, 43; Clark 1918: 328–329).

Nonetheless, the scientific research on the middle class exposed the same tensions that we have seen emerge in the public and political use of the term in the years of the Wilson administration, when his vice president admitted the paradox of a middle class that was publicly invoked but still incapable of determining progressivist politics in its favour in spite of the widespread, but disjointed attempt to organise consumer associations at the local and national level. The lacking fulfilment of the order of the middle class that transpired from the presence of a defenceless and disorganised public, in turmoil but impotent, reflected the economic and political difficulties that the scientists of progressivism encountered in making social control operative through the administrative action of the state.[35]

On the economic level, the forms of arbitration between union and company often collided with the interest of the public as a 'class of consumers': although 'disinterested' in the 'radical' or 'reactionary' politics of classes, the public was interested in 'low prices', it supported regulation in order to reduce the monopoly that corporations exercised on prices but was hostile to a workers' mobilisation for higher wages and less working hours. The difficulty of finding

---

35   Robbins 2017: 18–34.

a just measure between industry regulation on the consumer's behalf and on the worker's behalf rendered the conflict 'more intense and difficult'. On the political level, the prevention of class struggle by administrative means presented the difficulty of legitimising the function of social control. One example was the case of the Commission on Industrial Relations (1912–1915): the most ambitious political attempt that the American state had conducted until then to produce a detailed knowledge of industrial conflict. Established after the bombing attacks on the *Los Angeles Times* building and the massive 1912 strike organised in the Lawrence textile industry by the Industrial Workers of the World, during its three-year of research and hearings, the commission clearly outlined the new explosion of the class struggle, particularly among immigrant and unskilled workers, but did not research any shared conclusion on the political modalities for its solution. As explained by the same Commons who was named in President Wilson's commission, the unresolved tension between the hypothesis of either 'moving the labor movement towards politics' – making the commission a democratic institution that extended the decision-making process to different organisational from those of the political party – or it towards the 'collective bargain' – limiting organised labour to the union dimension in order to safeguard the political space of the social sciences – was the symptom of the growing perplexity that the social sciences were maturing in the face of the democratic method of the public hearing in the commissions which did not seem to transcend, but rather fomented, industrial conflict (Commons 1908: 765; Commons 1905).[36]

Despite the theoretical effort to legitimise the function of social control as democratic by sociologically tracing the presence of a new middle class, the scientific research and consequent elaboration of policies had to be isolated from class conflict in order to be entrusted to the new natural aristocracy of the social sciences: to their political authority which was claimed as impartial because it was scientifically founded on the empirical study of society. Although it was not unanimously shared – especially among reformers and social workers such as Jane Addams and Lilian Wald who asked for and obtained the establishment of the commission to 'resolve the problems of democracy in industrial relations and solve them in democratic ways' – this conviction was strengthened by the role taken on by social scientists, experts, and technicians in planning the war economy. And it would be consolidated with 'the eclipse of progressivism' (Croly 1920) and the affirmation in the following decade of the

---

36   Cf. Weinstein 1968: 172–253, in particular 182 and 202; Eakins 1972; Akin 1967.

associative and technocratic vision of the Secretary of Commerce and future President Herbert Hoover.[37]

The historical moment in which the technical government of the social sciences saw its democratic ideal fade coincided with a polemical return of the middle class on the public and political scene against the continuous and changing presence of a riotous working class that, still in the aftermath of World War I, posed the problem of 'the segregation of social classes occasioned by the industrial revolution' (Ogburn and Peterson 1916). In 1922, while Walter Lippmann – founder of the progressive *The New Republic* together with Herbert Croly and Walter Wey – matured his deep skepticism towards the 'phantom' public to which the social sciences of progressivism had attributed the democratic capacities of social control (Lippmann 1922; Lippmann 1925), the sociologist Franklin Giddings reviewed the volume *The Return of the Middle Class* by the journalist and theatre critic John Corbin in the columns of the *New York Times*, concluding as follows on the parable of the first and unfinished search for the new American middle class:

> The term "middle class" has become one of those phrases that ... are never spoken in good society ... twilight has fallen upon it ... the middle-class voice of common sense is not heard, or if now and then heard is not heeded.
>
> GIDDINGS 1922: 39–40

4   Brain Workers of the World, Unite!

The war years marked the culmination not only of the progressivism that, with the defeat of the Democratic Party in the 1920 presidential elections, was eclipsed by the political normality claimed by the Republican administration against social reform, but also of the first and unfinished scientific search for the middle class. In the aftermath of the war, the social sciences of progressivism exhausted their innovative and reforming impetus in the face of a public and political debate in which the middle class did not emerge as a figure of rediscovered order, but rather of disorder embodied by a disorganised and discontent public. The middle class remained nowhere to be found: dispersed

---

37   On the relationship between social science and democratic theory and the attempt – again in the 1920s – to increase democratic participation even in the context of the technical role taken on by the social sciences, see Baritono 2011b. Cf. Lash 1991. On Hoover's associative and technocratic vision, see Hart 1998; Dempsey and Gruver 2009; Alchon 1985.

between the mechanised organisation of industrial production and the hier-
archal division of office work, separated between the brain work of managers,
professionals, and technicians employed in planning and the white collar workers in charge of business administration, distribution, and sales, hidden in the
folds of a market marked by increasing inflation that was affecting consumption capacities, isolated at the margins of a society again shaken by class struggle. The wave of strikes that up until the two-year red period caused numbers
that were never reached before, the unionisation of immigrant and unskilled
labour-power among the ranks of the Industrial Workers of the World, the consequent reaction of business and the government, the Red Scare provoked by
the Communist Revolution in Russia – all of this did not allow the freeing of
the middle class from the negative meaning it had inherited from European
history. The conflict between labour and capital continuously imposed a class
boundary on society that prevented the social sciences from realising a legitimate and shared function of government through the federal state in the name
of the new middle class. The new script of American civilisation was set in the
'twilight of the middle class': 'Capitalist and laborer everyone knows what they
are. But a twilight has descended upon the most respected of our orders, a
twilight so dark that the one acknowledged virtue of the middle class is under
a cloud' (Corbin 1922: 89).[38]

The image of the middle class obscured by a leaden sky emerged through
pamphlets, books, and articles that referred to it with the rhetorical formula
of 'messages' and 'appeals' in order to favour or to block the consolidation of
what the social sciences had defined – with the pretence of denying – as the
antagonistic interest or militant ethics of the working class. If in 1913 *The North
American Review* had asked what socialism was in light of the 'salaried man'
who expressed 'great discontent' even though they were by education, sobriety, and respectability 'the most conservative element of the body politic', in
1915 in the columns of *The Atlantic Monthly*, in an article reworked in the same
year in the pamphlet *A Message to the Middle Class*, the journalist and writer
Lucien Price – under the pseudonym Seymour Deming – from a socialist viewpoint condemned the position taken against the workers' movement of the
proprietary class and exhorted the new middle class of 'white (collar) slaves' to
'revolt with workers against the capital'. At the beginning of industrialisation,
the 'educated man' had obtained high salaries that allowed him to emancipate
himself from the condition of the waged worker, whereas in the first decade

---

38   On the new cycle of workers' struggles during and after the war, see Green 1998: 89. See
      also Montgomery 1974.

of the twentieth century 'money is no more in the white-collar jobs'. His education and ambition for success did not allow him 'to become capitalist', to be
part of 'the employing and owning class'. The 'wage slavery of 1915' was 'the
slavery of the white collar' (Low 1913: 556–565; Deming 1915: 8–23; 57–61).

Although limited in its spread, this public message signalled, with respect
to the scientific research of the middle class of progressivism, a political
gap that reflected the social process of the unionisation of several groups
of labourers of the lower middle class. Unlike the employee associations
who, in Europe and above all Germany, were claiming the superiority of the
professional groups to distinguish themselves from the worker and ward
off proletarianisation, overseas not only clerks, accountants, stenographers,
insurance and railway employees, but also planners, technicians, teachers,
and public employees demanded the workers' tool of collective bargaining
and union organisation in order to regulate the working day and overtime pay,
and introduce a minimum wage and the adjustment of wages to inflation. In
this way, the term white collar took on political importance but, being associated with the signifier slavery, the traditional perspective of autonomy and
upward social mobility was lacking from its horizon of meaning. Since the
employee became part of the social question, the middle class was drawn into
the polemic field of class conflict from which the social sciences of progressivism had tried in vain to free it.[39]

It is in this sense, i.e., with the objective of preventing the spread of a workers' viewpoint on the middle class, that the 1922 publication of appeals that
express profoundly divergent political orientations must be interpreted. The
sociologist Ross Finney expressed concern over the escalation of class conflict that seemed 'irrepressible' because it was continually fuelled by a workers' movement influenced by socialist and communist forces. The resulting
'polarization of sociality' could not be curbed exclusively through repression,
with arrests or deportations. It was necessary to 'invent a third alternative' or
to undertake 'a middle pathway to justice and peace', the path of 'a gradual
peaceful evolution' against 'a violent, destructive revolution'. This was the task
of the middle class, of those 'who belong on the side neither of labor nor capital' (Finney 1922: 3–5, 38–39).

An Appeal to the Middle Class thus re-proposed the reformist approach of
progressivism, concentrating attention however not on the working class, but
rather on white-collar labour. If the social sciences had identified the causes of
the social question in industry and in this had traced the economic dynamics

---

39   Kocka 1980: 117–126, 136–164; Davis 2001: 201–216.

that made it possible to overcome the iron Malthusian law and circumvent the class conflict by prefiguring the rise of a new middle class, in the first post-war period it was necessary to recognise that 'big business' had transformed American capitalism into an 'oppressive giant', a colossus that had definitively separated ownership and workers by crushing the new middle class towards the poor masses of wage labour. The excessive supply of 'brain work' pushed the average salary to subsistence level, following a direction that had originated with the closure of the frontier, but which ended with the war, when organised labour had increased wages, while capital recuperated the profit through inflation. Since the middle class 'is being gradually eliminated by the growing concentration of wealth' and 'is declining at a rate that encourages the Marxian socialists to hope for its eventual extinction', the social question had to be interpreted as a political question of the middle class (Finney 1922: 32–33, 48–49, 52–62, 82–83, 85–87).

If this appeal called for an 'alliance' between the middle class and working class to free both from the influence of communist and socialist forces by expanding the progressivist program of social reform in order to speak of 'industrial democracy' (Finney 1922: 108–118, 123–129, 136–138, 160–193, 249–269), other appeals and messages instead aimed at distinguishing the middle class from the working class by pointing the finger at progressivism and its social sciences. In the national and local press, as well as in the hearings of congressional commissions, various interventions signalled the presence of associative forms of employees who distanced themselves from the working-class movement by drawing attention to brain workers and white-collar workers as well as to a 'consumer public' on which the wealth of the nation and the virtuosity of the American family with its traditional values of respectability and frugality depended. Among these interventions, the most important was John Corbin's book that was reviewed in the *New York Times* (Meltzer 1919: 225–233; The Great Middle Class Is Beginning to Turn 1920; Incorporate Union of Middle Class 1920; The Short Way Home 1920).[40]

To move away from 'the political peril of revolution' and contrast the 'radical element' imposed on scientific and public discourse by the spread not only of Marxism and communism, but also the middle-class socialism of intellectuals and scholars who drew on Fabianism from across the Atlantic in order to advocate 'industrial democracy', *The Return of the Middle Class* placed the political question of the middle class in the foreground, signalling the urgency of knowing its composition and social condition and understanding its political

---

40   Cf. Robbins 2017: 1–17.

behaviour. The focus was not on the old proprietary and professional middle class, but rather on figures who – regardless of income and occupation – did not carry out manual labour but employed 'their brains in the small business ventures, in the professions, in literature and the arts'. Corbin used the term white collar with caution for the negative meaning it had taken on in socialist publications, where it reflected and invoked the unionisation of white-collar workers. Instead, he preferred brain worker in order to declare the historical decline of their social superiority over manual labour. From the end of the nineteenth century, while constituting the white and protestant brain power of the nation, they had to compete with the immigrant labour force no longer coming from the 'Nordic stock' of north-western Europe. Since the beginning of the twentieth century, especially during the war, millions of them fell into a 'new poverty': the poverty of a middle class conditioned by unstable and poorly paid jobs, rising rent, the cost of clothing and food, incapable of guaranteeing an adequate level of education for children, destined to disappear due to the decline in birth rate that affected the family, also because of 'suffragism' which not only led to the victory of women's suffrage, but had also question the 'reproductive instinct' of the woman (Corbin 1922: 60–70, 110–114, 124–137).

Faced with this 'tragedy of the middle class' represented with a marked racial and patriarchal tone, what worried Corbin most was the absence of a 'class consciousness' capable of determining an autonomous and coherent political behaviour. Although it recorded the response of employees and professionals who founded associations – above all in Chicago and the Midwest – against the strikes that were affecting large industry (especially mining and railways), despite trusting the English experience of the National Union of the Middle Class, he explained that the different figures of brain work were divided between two opposing ideologies: the 'radicalism' of socialism and communism that influenced the unionisation of white collar workers and the 'conservatorism' of capitalism that, while enjoying 'great national belief', was favouring the disappearance of any 'middle-class distinction'. To overcome this political division, it was necessary to valorise that 'between hand worker and brain worker there is an essential and deep-seated opposition'. Unionisation had to be rejected because in the union the employees would be outclassed by the workers, in order to promote 'the movement to organize the middle class' that would affirm the political centrality never achieved with progressivism (Corbin 1922: 25–30, 144–146).

The Return of the Middle Class, then, did not register a historical fact resulting from the newfound normality of republican politics, but rather formulated and spread a message aimed at the 'force of what we vaguely know as middle class'. In other words, it constituted an appeal to a subject still in hibernation that, in order to awaken its own consciousness, would have to close with progressivism and its social sciences. In this sense, Corbin accused 'statesmen and labor leaders, professors of economics and heads of bureaus in Washington' to 'go right on thinking and writing only of labor and capital, capital and labor', ignoring that 'the majority of people' were neither hand workers nor capitalists, but rather brain workers. The middle class had received no comforting words from journalism and advertising. Above all it had been forgotten by universities, where economists and sociologists had studied industrial conflict, the working class, and immigration, ignoring 'the cause of the clerk, the foreman, the manager, the buyer, the seller, the technical executive, the laboratory researcher'. The social scientists of progressivism had not listened at all to the 'voice of middle-class common sense'. They had not been able to see that society was marked by the 'extinction of the best intelligence, the soundest traditions, of American life'. Only Sumner had grasped, by means of his phrase 'the forgotten man', 'the uneasiness of the traditional American, sober and hard-working', without however being able to escape the silence with which he was condemned by 'the dogma that in America there are no classes' (Corbin 1922: 5–22, 30, 46–58, 97–101, 119, 212).

The middle class was a political question because, while labour and capital had a 'class consciousness', the majority of the population had no shared sense of their own social position. They could not name the only word – middle class – through which it would have been possible to acquire an autonomous voice. For this reason, they had not been able to assert any authority over the Wilson administration. In the federal commissions, 'the intermediate salaried folk, though in one sense a group, are not organized and so could not properly be – and at any rate were not – represented'. Unlike unions and associations that spoke in the name of labour and capital, they had not been involved in a decision-making process where the so-called public was not an expression of any organisation, but was made up of political leaders, university executives, presidents of cultural foundations and research institutes, who did not express any specific interest. The lack of a collective name – scientifically forged and publicly recognised – in which it could be identified explained the 'impotence of the public' of progressivism:

> You may search the world in vain for any gathering in which their rights are presented, for any clear definition of them as a class, or for any statement of their present wrongs and their legitimate aims. Capital is organized, class-conscious, and so manages to care for its own. Labor is organized, class-conscious; it takes its own abundantly. But the great

range of fold in between have no organization, no sense of their collective interests, of their relation to the state as a whole. And so they are
forgotten.

CORBIN 1922: 7–8, 218–219

The importance of *The Return of the Middle Class* was therefore not exclusively
in the conservative twist that it imposed on the public and political debate over
the middle class, but also in the urgency it signalled to elaborate, promote, and
disseminate a social science of the middle class for the middle class, i.e., in the
urge to rethink the scientific concept of the middle class by identifying a criterion that, separating it from manual labour, renewed its traditional value and
allowed it to organise its own political behaviour. In the era of large industry,
this criterion could not be 'property', i.e., the presumption of becoming owners
through hard work. Instead, it had to be competence – 'skill' – namely the claim
that education and specialisation gave access to the privileged social position
of the brain worker. If middle-class socialism had elected skill as an indispensable instrument of industrial democracy, if communism – the reference was
to the German and Italian movement of factory councils – intended to use it
to promote revolution and organise production in a socialist state, outside of
these ideologies, social science had to consider skill as the 'dominant factor'
for the formation of the middle class: since 'it could neither be expropriated
[by labour] nor enslaved [by capital]', skill constituted a 'source of power' that,
by restoring the 'middle-class distinction', closed the historical perspective of
industrial democracy in order to open national history to the 'industrial republic'. A republic of the middle class where managers, professionals, technicians,
and superintendents who constituted 'the creative mind and administrative
energy' of the nation would integrate the traditional opinion in favour of individualism with the new organisational function that the government of capital
required in the economy, in society, and the American state. In this way, *The
Return of the Middle Class* did not only intend to legitimate the 'government by
commission' that, in the hands of Secretary of Commerce Hoover, was taking
shape through the exclusion of groups and members considered irreconcilable
with 'the welfare of the nation as a whole' from the decision-making process.
It also offered 'essential materials for sociology' that, while indicating a precise
direction for research, presented a clear political objective: since skill was the
'great resource of the middle class', its public motto must be 'Brain Workers
of the World, Unite!' (Corbin 1922: 92–95, 137, 155–159, 232–233, 218–219, 280,
291–292, 324. Cf. Giddings 1922: 39–40).

Yet, despite the resonance of this conservative appeal in the political and
public debate, the eclipse of progressivism did not coincide with the affirmation

of a specific middle-class movement. Not only because a similar possibility was blocked by the union activism of the lower middle class which however was waning in the second half of the decade. Nor even exclusively because the mobilisation of professional associations and consumer groups against strikes and inflations could not take on a national impact and would end in only a few years. Above all because in the public and political discourse, as well as in scientific literature, the increase in inequalities prevented brain work and white-collar work from keeping together in a new middle class. Although the roaring twenties marked a sharp increase in average income and consumption capacities, as well as an important recovery of employee salary to worker wage due to the weakening of the bargaining strength of the union and the company policies (welfare capitalism) which facilitated the working career and social position of the brain worker, the concentration of wealth and income differences between the two widened. Throughout the entire decade, and not by chance, studies and research still tried, with a reformist accent purged from the political tone of the progressivist social sciences and marked by a strong sense of professionalism, to scientifically define the American standard of living. In other words, they intended to establish a shared measure of 'comfort' on the basis of which to propose policies which, without publicly involving organised labour in the decision-making process, would raise income and consumption of the poor masses, especially manual labour and immigrant labour. Middle class thus again disappeared from the scene: complaints against the erosion of the standard of living of white-collar worker would have been rare as well as the claims of the social superiority of brain work, almost absent would be the reference to the presence of a class intermediate to labour and capital (Oakwood 1922; Living on the Ragged Edge 1925; Comish 1923; Peixotto 1927; Bernard 1928: 190–202; Eliot (ed.) 1931, in particular Rochester 1931, 553–563).[41]

It was therefore not paradoxical that what is now recognised as the first scientific work dedicated specifically to the middle class – *Middle Town: A Study in Modern American Culture* (1929) by Robert S. Lynd and Helen Merrell Lynd – did not present the concept middle class. Despite the nascent mass consumption exercising a specific function of social control, society inexorably appeared as a society divided into two classes: business class and lower class. Even at the beginning of the following decade, before the financial crash of 1929 plunged into a deep economic depression, in the study commissioned by president Hoover on *Recent Social Trends in the Unites States,* the few pages devoted to white-collar workers expressed worry for the negative effect that

---

41   Cf. Kocka 1980: 176–192.

the increase in high school and college graduates had in their employment and modest salary level compared to the worker (Lynd and Lynd 1929; *Recent Social Trends in United States* 1933, in particular Hurlin, Givens, and Lynd).[42] The invocation of a social science of and for the middle class capable of affirming its social and political centrality would only be heard with the New Deal.

---

42   Cf. Tobin 1995: 537–565; Cohen 2003; Jacobs 2005.

The Middle Class as Historical Project

In the March 1932 edition of *Harper's Magazine*, an article was published with the important title 'And If the Revolution Comes ...?'. A little more than two years after the Wall Street crash, George R. Leighton denounced the 'vast economic upheaval' that made 'the word revolution' resound everywhere. What was feared was a revolution different from that 'birthright' which the United States had carried since the war of independence. It was a 'potential revolution' stemming from an unexpected economic depression which politics, business, and the scientific community had been unable to predict, blinded by productivity and average income increases during the roaring '20s. A politics aimed at controlling prices (and wages) in order to ensure widespread consumption had hidden the growing concentration of wealth and the increase in inequalities behind the 'American standard of living' or middle class 'comfort' which purportedly distinguished the United States from postwar Europe. President Hoover, spokespeople for the industrial and financial world, and social scientists that the administration had involved in the Hoover Commission 'predicted eternal prosperity', but after 1929 were 'helpless', entirely incapable of 'admitting their folly'. They continued to utter 'words such as optimism'. At the same time, they denied 'responsibility for the disaster'. Just two weeks prior to the crash, they declared that 'the industrial condition of the United States is absolutely sound, and our credit system is in no way critical'. For two years they continued to present themselves as 'authoritative and serene'. Yet, for the magazine which had first denounced the loss of autonomy and the economic independence of professional and white-collar labour at the end of the nineteenth century, the revolution was just around the corner and found its *raison d'être* in capitalism's crisis of legitimation: while rulers, experts, owners, and business managers had learned no lessons from what happened, the director of the Harvard Business School worried that 'capitalism is on trial and on the issue of this trial may depend the whole future of Western civilisation' (Leighton 1932: 466–468).

What defined the accusation against American capitalism, which the social sciences of progressivism had succeeded rehabilitating in economic theory and in the practice of public and political discourse only through World War I, was the contradictory image of a society of 'producers, fewer and fewer in number, engulfed in goods which they can neither sell nor use, swamped in specie which has no value, while opposed to them is a vast army, laborers, white collars, professional and all, with neither food nor clothing nor the money to pay for them'. Even though not explicitly named, the middle class thus returned in the pages of this and other magazines, but unlike what happened in earlier decades, it was no longer called upon in order to invoke the reforms of progressivism. Conservatives appeared 'too frightened at what the present situation might lead to and frightened still more to the thought of trying any different policies than those which have prevailed in the past'. Liberals were 'as timorous as the conservatives', contemplating any action of reform only timidly: 'at the mere sound they scattered like frightened sheep'. Those who did not find answers in the 'mass meetings of communists and radicals ... asked in vain where the engineers, statisticians, managers, executives, and planners' who had promised prosperity had gone. Who would take command of the revolution? Would it be the gentlemen 'on the right', who were, however, embroiled in the crisis of capitalism, or the gentlemen 'on the left', who looked to Communist Russia and its planning with adoration? Above all, the author concludes, would the mass of white-collar workers and professionals manage to impose an 'American stamp' on the change in society or would it rather be necessary to 'clear from our minds the idea that our system, in itself, is a holy thing to be defended with our lives, our fortunes, and our sacred honor?' (Leighton 1932: 469, 471–476. See also The Plight of the White-Collar Army 1930: 69–70).

These questions remained unresolved for much of the decade, even as President Franklin D. Roosevelt experimented with innovative responses in the New Deal. Faced with unemployment reaching 15 million at the beginning of his Democratic presidency, and with the halving of wages and salaries, the bankruptcy of 85,000 companies, the closure of 5,000 banks, the confiscation of hundreds of thousands of real estate and land holdings, American capitalism was no longer 'triumphant' as it was in the 1920s, losing its 'position of leadership' (Ihlder 1925: 52). In this power vacuum, starting in the 1930s and above all in the latter half of the decade, there was a reprisal of social conflict which traversed not only the various sectors of industrial production. The growing number of strikes and factory occupations, which in 1937 alone saw the participation of more than two million workers, also involved the unemployed and poor who in manufacturing areas demanded assistance and social security, employees and shopkeepers who in urban and suburban areas organised against unemployment and property foreclosure, farmers and agricultural labourers encouraged protests against price collapse and expulsion from land, blacks and other minorities who mobilised against lynching and discrimination, and women who spoke out in and out of the workplace. These mobilisations made the incapacity of business to find its way out of the depression increasingly clear. The forms of entrepreneurial self-regulation, endorsed and directed by the federal government during Hoover's administration and the first two years of Roosevelt's, failed to revive the market. Corporate social responsibility and the corporate policy of welfare capitalism which, by expanding consumption, had supported entrepreneurial leadership in the preceding decade, lost political and cultural hold. While the scientific and public conviction that the American worker (manual and non-manual) did not feel different from his boss because he shared a middle-class ideal with him was brutally disproven by the facts, the working class succeeded – at least in part, above all in the factory – in overcoming the racial, ethnic, and religious lines which had divided it, affirming a sense of solidarity that, especially in large urban centres (less so in the western middle towns), came to involve employee and professional figures. Class solidarity called into question the faith that until that moment, at least the most qualified figures of manual and intellectual labour had placed in the individual career and social mobility, challenging corporate hierarchies, and hindering the orderly functioning of the market.[1]

Despite what was argued by historiography and the social sciences of the latter half of the twentieth century, which had removed social conflict in order to insist on the non-planning character of the New Deal by way of highlighting the experimental and pragmatic nature of its policies, there was no foregone conclusion to the social and political process that had put American capitalism under accusation. On the contrary, the word revolution became increasingly relevant in the second half of the decade when the decline of capitalism was publicly linked to the crisis of the middle class. Middle class returned to the political limelight in the field of tension opened by the class struggle from which the social sciences of progressivism had tried in vain to remove it. In other words, it regained importance as a word through which to explain not only the economic dynamics of impoverishment and proletarianization that swept society, but also to understand the contestation of the traditional democratic vision of the nation and the historical liberal values of individualism, work ethic, and equal opportunity. Since various intellectual, professional, and employee figures embraced (albeit only partially, but not insignificantly) the strike, collective bargaining, and trade unionism, the middle class became the object of a broad polemical confrontation: an ideological battle which was fueled by and in turn fueled social conflict, animating the political positions – liberal and reformist, radical and communist – which supported, criticised, and influenced the New Deal.[2]

---

1   Cf. Freeman 2018; Green 1998: 133–163; Vaudagna 2014: 261–292.
2   Cf. McComb: 2006; Ehrenreich 1989; Baritz 1989.

In this turbulent historical context, the invocation of a social science of and for the middle class (which progressivism had unsuccessfully attempted to find) was finally heard. The middle class became the object of study, empirical research, and theoretical reflection among social scientists who discussed the consequences that economic depression was having for the various figures who comprised it: their proletarianisation and their political and trade union alignment with worker's mobilisation, their impoverishment and the social measures that would have favoured their rise, the cultural and political role they were able to play in society, and their possible organisation and administrative function within business and the nascent welfare state. In this sense, since intellectuals, scholars, and social scientists intervened in the ideological battle over the middle class by contributing to the rethinking of the liberalism of American democracy in light of capitalism's crisis of legitimation, the middle class emerged as an unprecedented scientific and political 'project' which had its origin in a social conflict of uncertain outcome.[3] An unprecedented historical project that the social sciences developed through the state with the aim of obscuring – especially among white America – the collar line that separated intellectual and manual labour, thus integrating large sections of workers into the liberal and democratic logic of the nation in order to reject the advance of European ideologies of fascism and communism. As was written in 1951, in the same monthly periodical which in 1932 had raised the worrying question of revolution, unlike its original European history, the American middle class would become all-embracing by making the United States 'the last country in the world in which the middle class continues to play a strategic role in society' (Hartley 1951: 40, 46).

1   The Demiurge of the Middle Class

The scientific foundations of the historical project of constructing the middle class were laid by statistical science, particularly the statisticians employed by the Census Bureau who worked to classify occupations by forging a new method and vocabulary suitable to the politics of the New Deal. The federal office of the census started as a temporary office that Congress activated every ten years at the Department of the Interior in order to fulfil the constitutional mandate of taking a census of the population to divide the Congressional seats and tax burden among the states of the Union. Since the beginning of

---

3   Ortner 2002: 9–32.

the republic, the office constituted an essential, even if intermittent, mechanism for defining society and the organisation of the federal state. If during
the nineteenth century public statistics had turned its attention above all to
the racial makeup of the population in light of slavery and migration waves,
at the turn of the century the economic upheaval resulting from processes
of industrialisation had induced the academic associations of the new social
sciences to request the establishment of a permanent office which would be
charged with reading demographic change not only through the racial variable, but also through new measurements – employment and unemployment,
employment categories, wage and price trends – whose knowledge was considered indispensable for making government intervention in the economy
possible. As Francis A. Walker, pioneer of US marginalism and president of
the American Economic Association (1885–1892) and American Statistical
Association (1883–1897), wrote at the turn of the century, a permanent statistical office was necessary in order to 'promote general welfare' because it would
allow for the elaboration of 'wise legislation, intelligent administration, and
equitable taxation' (Walker 1888: 148; Walker 1890).[4]

In the months following President Roosevelt's inauguration, against the
backdrop of a depression at its apex, the political necessity to tackle unemployment and poverty required a thorough review of public statistics to meet
policy objectives, not only in terms of administrative implementation, but also
in relation to public communication, namely the language used to attribute a
common sense to the multiple measures that the government promoted. Since
the crisis of capitalism's legitimation had nullified the possibility of taking the
previous dominant form of expression of political and administrative action –
the scientific language of the control of the economic cycle through 'government by commission' – it was necessary to resort to a new vocabulary that was
not only effective in its administrative purposes, but also comprehensible and
publicly shared. In this sense, it was necessary to identify and communicate
with specific figures involved in social conflict for the sake of overcoming the
resistance to reform that came from the business world, while at the same time
containing the tumultuous militancy of the workers within a values framework
in which capitalism could regain its lost leadership. The objective was therefore political because it intended to outline a public discourse which, through
the New Deal, would create the conditions – symbolic as well as material – for
overcoming the field of tension opened by the class struggle.

---

4   See also The Federal Census 1899, particularly William Hunt's essay (466–494). On the his-
    tory of the US census, with particular reference to the racial, ethnic, and sexual classification,
    see Schor 2017.

The new ministers of Labor and Commerce – Frances Perkins and Henry Wallace – on whom the Bureau of Labor Statistics and Census Bureau, respectively, depended – appointed a committee of experts, the Central Statistical Board, to coordinate statistical activities. The directors of the main offices appointed by the previous Republican administration were also replaced with figures from the American Statistical Association chaired by Stuart Rice, who became Assistant Director of the Census Bureau. Sociologists, economists, and mathematicians introduced sample survey techniques and probabilistic calculations in the study of social stratification, redefining the notions of employment and unemployment (active and non-active labour-power) and the occupational categories according to social security policies. The Roosevelt presidency thus profoundly changed the Census Bureau. It removed its intermittent condition and limited constitutional mandate in order to elevate it to a specific function of government: public statistics were called upon not so much to 'tell the truth' or to represent society according to a static image as they were to forecast its change in order to assist the decision-making process by providing projections and solutions. A scientific vocabulary was thus outlined which became publicly important not only because it was used in administrative language, but also because it was employed and developed by the nascent institutes of public opinion research, marketing departments of companies, and advertising agencies which sold services to companies committed to increasing their market shares.[5]

The federal census, statistical surveys, opinion research, and consumption analysis constituted the nation's greatest instrument for self-understanding during the New Deal: an enormous amount of data and information on economic, social, and political life – on the trend in wages and prices, workers' behaviour, and electoral orientation – was used by the government, political parties and trade unions, economic and professional associations, the press and radio, in order to describe the experience of economic depression, to elaborate proposals against its social effects, and to capture the moods and shape the opinions of a disoriented population. In this sense the statistician became a demiurge who influenced political and administrative action, contributing to the transformation of the society he described. A year after Roosevelt took

---

5 Desrosières 1998: 189–207, 330; Didier 2014: 93–102; Conk 1978: 111–130; Conk 1988. On the birth of public opinion research during the New Deal, see Holli 2002. On the role of businesses – as well as social scientists hired by companies and advertising agencies – in developing marketing strategies aimed at identifying different market segments on the basis of occupation and population income, see Fasce 2012: 59–80; Blaszczyk 2000; Robinson 1999.

office, in his inaugural address to the assembly of the academic association of statisticians, Rice pointed out exactly this new function of governing:

> We seek to mobilize the information, the skill, and the talent of our entire professional Association for an appraisal of the statistical requirements of our economic and social situation ... The New Deal represents an attempt to preserve the complexities and hence the standards of our civilization by social control of an economic mechanism that is no longer self-operating.
>
> RICE 1934: 1–10

The figure of the middle-class demiurge in public statistics was embodied by Alba M. Edwards, The Special Agent for Occupation Statistics. Edwards was appointed in 1910 but confirmed in office until the 1940 census. He introduced a new classification of occupations that remained unchanged for much of the second half of the twentieth century, influencing European public statistics during the Cold War.[6] His was obviously not an individual enterprise, but rather a collective work in progress starting in the last quarter of the previous century. From the ninth census of 1870 there was in fact a first, summary revision of registered occupations. The category of the 'mechanic', which since the beginning of the century had defined artisan labour, economically independent as the shop owner, was excluded, while the term 'maker', which had indicated crafts in manufacturing production, was replaced with categories that reflected the mechanisation of industry. This was referred to by terms such as 'operator' and 'worker'. New occupations were introduced – 'professional service', 'clerk' employed in public administration and private office, commerce and distribution, in order to grasp the occupational change determined by the centrality assumed by the corporation and large distribution. These innovations finally provided statistics which, starting from 1890, were no longer organised by county, city, and state, but were instead tabulated on a national basis according to criteria of age, sex, and race. Thus, public statistics reflected – and at the same time supported – the new federal profile that the American state was assuming following the industrialisation process, in this way representing the new 'character' of the nation. As Walker wrote in 1899 in his role of census superintendent:

---

6 Boltanski 1987: 155–236.

> Such an enumeration of occupations ... would convey ... a synopsis of
> the real economical condition of the country, its industrial capacity, and
> even its civilization; for it is in the occupations of the people that we find
> their habits, their tastes, their ruling appetites, their social patterns, and
> their moral standards.
>
> WALKER 1899: 25[7]

Although it remained substantially unchanged until the threshold of the New Deal, this first revision of occupations was refined at the turn of the century by Carroll Wright and William Hunt – the Commissioner of the Bureau of Labor and director of population census, respectively. Wright and Hunt addressed the problem of an increasing immigration population of unskilled workers from southern and eastern Europe. Since the mechanisation of industry eroded craftsmanship by also downgrading manufacturing skills, their statistical science revised the meaning of the generic category of 'laborer' in an attempt to show how labour as a whole 'progressed and has perceptibly risen in the social scale of life'. In this sense, the numerical growth of employee and professional labour was highlighted, and an initial distinction was made between skilled and unskilled manual labour, with the aim of implementing a redistribution of occupations in favour of what, as we saw in the previous chapter, was called the 'public'. Read in a historical key, the census of occupations would thus have shown a social trend towards an increase in intellectual and skilled labour. In the future, manual labour would no longer be in the majority and the future policy of the American state would be determined by 'the vast middle class' or by those who were not 'directly interested in the labor capital matter' (Hunt 1897: 415–420; Hunt 1909: 467–485).[8]

These innovations, not yet systematized within the census, fuelled a scientific debate that considered employment statistics to be not merely an economic index, but also a measure of the 'great body of workers', i.e. an instrument for evaluating social mobility in order to determine whether this happened due to the power acquired by the working class in society or by the orderly development of the market assisted by policies founded scientifically on public statistics. Out of this debate stepped Alba Edwards, who, in view of the 1920 census, took up an in-depth historical study of the *Classification of*

---

7 See also U.S. Bureau of Census 1872: XXXII–XXXIII. Cf. Conk 1988: 7–16; Conk 1978; Blumin 1989: 260–270.

8 The reflections which social scientists of different political orientations (progressive and socialist) carried out in various scientific journals went in this direction: Hourwich 1911a; Hourwich 1911b; Hansen 1920: 423; Sogge 1933. Cf. Conk 1988: 76–78; 1978: 123–124.

Occupations in comparison with European nations. According to the special agent of the census, the categories of owner, employee, skilled and unskilled labour, which were used in the 1910 census, did not adequately reflect the progress of the nation. Instead, they marked the decline of owners and the rise of wage labour, fuelling a distorted image of society and consequently, increasing fears in public opinion. The statistics from overseas were also unsatisfactory. The centrality of mercantilism in defining the European nations' power politics had indeed concentrated scholarly attention 'on the product and not on the producers'. In other words, the classification of occupations took place through categories that divided the worker according to the industry in which they were employed, not according to the work they actually performed. However, Edwards found useful information. The English and French census had introduced a classification that accounted for occupations of non-industrial labour: public, professional, and domestic. Further, despite the confusion between the 'census of industries' and occupations, in Germany a more articulated classification was introduced which divided labour into 'groups' or 'strata' according to the skills of the worker. A social scale was thus outlined which was hierarchically organized by skill: from the 'technically trained officials' to the unskilled worker, passing through the foreman, office employee and 'skilled occupations for which as a rule apprenticeship are necessary'. Although European public statistics were found to be 'inadequate, illogical, and unscientific', their comparative study thus offered valuable indications for overcoming the 'negligent attitude' towards the occupations of US public statistics (Edwards 1911: 618–646, 623–636).

One priority for Edwards was establishing a method that would divide occupations by 'kind of labor' rather than industrial sector. The objective must no longer be – or must no longer only be – establishing the number of agricultural goods packaged, the quantity of minerals extracted, and goods manufactured, the miles of railroad built, the level of imports and exports, according to the mercantilist formula which had distinguished the nineteenth century construction of the state in Europe as well as in the United States. The social question and immigration created the need to develop classifications which accounted for the 'character of service rendered'. In this way, the occupational statistics organised 'on the basis of skill and intelligence' would have returned 'a vivid picture of the occupational position of each and every worker'. In other words, it would make it possible to study their 'social-economic status' and placement in 'social groups' with 'similar conditions of life and work'. Above all, it would have made it possible to grasp oscillations in society which, precisely because it was stratified, appeared mobile. In this way, Edwards approached the main objective which the social sciences of progressivism had only posed in their unfinished research on the middle class: the passage from the census of industries to the classification of occupations which rendered knowable 'the movements of labor from group to group' (Edwards 1911: 618–620, 645).

With this new method, driven by the necessity of addressing the political question of the majoritarian presence of manual labour, in 1917 Edwards presented a new classification which was applied for the first time in the 1920 census. Although considered unsatisfactory, the distinction inherited from previous censuses between hand work and head work was confirmed as an analytic key used, however, in order to advance a different division of labour. Intellectual labour was divided on the basis of professionalism in order to grasp not only the continuous increase in private and public employees, but also the new functions of direction and control of the work process that superintendents performed in mechanised industry. Manual labour was instead classified by skill, depending on the long or short period of training received or apprenticeship. In this way, the generic category of 'laborer' was completely taken apart: combining the semi-skilled, skilled, and unskilled labourer made it possible to isolate a large group potentially distinct from the working class (Edwards 1917: 644–646, 659–660).

Although it departed from European public statistics, particularly the English and French census which took the homogenous presence of the working class as given, the new method was not without contradictions.[9] Faced with the difficulty of determining the level of competence in a hierarchical scale that reflected the labourer's skills, Edwards resorted to his social and cultural location, assuming as determinant his relationship with the head of the family and the community. If a labourer had a skilled or semi-skilled occupation that seemed unusual for their age, sex, or race, the occupational category was changed, and the labourer downgraded. The new classification of occupations thus established a strong relation between identity (racial and sexual) and social and economic status. In this way, a socially nonhomogeneous working class in skill was also divided along the patriarchal and racial lines of society, increasingly considered incapable of undertaking coherent and autonomous action. While it registered that women and minorities populated the majority of unskilled or semi-skilled jobs, the new classification also noted the social tendency towards a decrease – relative, not absolute – in unskilled labour. Still more important, the view it established between manual and intellectual

---

9 A new classification of occupations based on skill was also introduced in Great Britain with the 1921 census. However, this classification did not affect the distinction between the manual labour of the working class and the intellectual labour of the middle class. See Stevenson 1910 and Stevenson 1928. Cf. Szreter 1984; Szreter 1993; Conk 1983.

labour became a scientifically confirmed political axiom. The collar line that separated blue-collar worker and white-collar worker was no longer a 'hard line', but rather constituted a frontier for which the labourer – although pre-dominantly white and native – could move between social groups, elevating all labour upwards.[10]

This radical reform of the classification of occupations took on full political significance only with the New Deal, particular starting with the mid-1930s when, in order to address a social conflict that also involved employ-ees and professionals, it became urgent to define a new scientific vocabulary that would make it possible to represent a society in movement, but not along faults opened by the class struggle. What was important was not only the intro-duction of the term 'gainful worker' in order to identify who was active in the labour market and could thus benefit from government measures, regardless of whether or not they were employed at the moment of the census. Equally rel-evant was the use of 'labor force', because it reflected in the administrative lan-guage the power gained by the working class in society. The decisive factor was above all that the vocabulary of public statistics was rethought around a new conception of the middle class. In a 1934 essay in the *Monthly Labor Review* – published by the Bureau of Labor Statistics – the special agent of the census clarified the meaning of the term 'white-collar worker'. 'Notwithstanding dif-ferences in work and pay, the white-collar workers together do form a group that is in many respects homogenous'. It is a group that, due to the assistance provided to 'managers, officials, and business and professional men', was dis-tinguishable from skilled and unskilled manual labour. What was important, however, was not its occupational specificity and its large growth rate – from 2.9% in 1870 to 16.3% in 1930, with a female composition that reached 40% – but rather the fact that the social question that involved white-collar workers was blocking the rise of what, analysing the *Composition of the Nation's Labor Force*, Edwards called the 'great middle class' (Edwards 1934: 501–505).[11]

In the social and political disorder caused by the unexpected sit-down strike movement – at a time when workers' militancy showed that they were able to overcome the colour line in order to unite skilled and unskilled labour, thus

---

10   Employment statistics from the 1910 census reported that 70.2% of female workers per-formed semi-skilled, manual, or domestic work, while 62.2% of black male workers were manual workers or servants. See Edwards 1911: 652–656. The 1930 census confirmed this data, with exception of the increase of women employed in white-collar work: Edwards 1933: 377–387 and 384–386. See also the official report of the U.S. Department of Commerce 1930. Cf. Conk 1978: 128–130; 135–139; 145–146.

11   Cf. Conk 1988: 24–28; Conk 1978: 114–116.

nullifying the criterion of skill as an individual prerequisite for social mobility –
when white-collar labour also took part in the wave of strikes that moved from
industrial centres towards cities (Can They Unseat the Sitters 1937: 18; Unions
Add White-Collar Members 1937: 39–40; Unions Push White-Collar Drive
1937: 43–44), Edwards raised the classification of occupations to its ultimate
political significance, that of the rupture of class solidarity. To this end, the
new classification method had to be translated into a public discourse that, by
attributing a new meaning to the middle class, challenged the collective form
of expression – and identification – in the working class. Through an exercise
in statistical inference, Edwards emphasised how, following the incessant 'scientific and technological improvements', a 'smaller and smaller proportion of
the Nation's labor force' would be employed in the production of agricultural
and consumer goods, while a 'larger and larger proportion' would be engaged
in distribution and service, 'public service, professional service, and domestic
and personal service'. Consequently, the labour movement would profoundly
change. Faced with the tendential decrease in unskilled work, what was fore-
seen was a marked increase in professional and employee occupations as
well as an increase in semi-skilled labour, particularly the machine operator
required by the complete triumph of the assembly line. In the near future, the
demand for labour 'endowed with intelligence and quick mental reactions
and [workers] who are capable of rapid adjustments to new situations and
to new work conditions' would increase, the 'dividing lines between different
social groups' would be less defined, economic and social status would have
progressed and an increasing percentage of the labour force would abandon
the living conditions of the unskilled labourer. In this way, the social rise of a
middle class was predicted which, by incorporating skilled and semi-skilled
workers, would have erased the tremendous public image that the crisis of capitalism's legitimation was projecting onto society:

> The time will come when it can no longer be correctly represented by
> a pyramid with a large unskilled group as the base and a small profes-
> sional group as the apex. As the unskilled group is gradually displaced
> by the machine, there probably will be a concentration of workers in a
> large middle class, comprising the clerical group, the skilled group, and
> the semiskilled group.
>
> EDWARDS 1936a: 19

The special agent of the federal census thus wore the robe of the demiurge of
a middle class otherwise unable to be found within the space of societal experience. After the inconclusive research of the social sciences of progressivism,

his 'invention' did not take place in the void of history. Not only because it was the fruit of a comparative historical study, but above all because it took on the racial and patriarchal character of society. The scientific foundations of the middle class were laid along the colour line that traversed the traditional terrain of the American family, the breadwinner and his work ethic. A terrain that was made fragile by the erosion of independent, agricultural, and artisan labour. Not unlike manual labour, skilled and unskilled, intellectual labour was entirely dependent on wages and – as Edwards himself admitted – the majority of employees earned a low wage, barely enough to achieve a 'moderate standard of living'. In this sense, the demiurge prescribed the political direction that the New Deal should have pursued. In other words, he identified in the middle class the nerve centre of the social question and the moral imperative of reform policy. Thus, despite the rather worrying presence of a 'great army of the unskilled', increasingly populated by the black labour force,[12] indeed precisely through a racially and sexually connoted conception of the middle class, the New Deal would have given political form to the changing tendency in society, which otherwise could have followed the movement imposed by the workers' mobilisation. The scientific vocabulary of public statistics thus not only defined new terms – 'skill', 'strata', 'social group' – in the dictionary of social sciences and opinion research. It not only supplied the administrative language of the technical terms – 'labor force', 'gainful worker', 'white-collar worker' – that would be employed in federal agency documents and reports. It also outlined a public discourse that inscribed the various policies implemented by the government into a comprehensible and sharable common sense. Middle class did not simply organise a specific scientific semantic (statistical and administrative), but also an unprecedented social and political semantics which, in the present of economic depression, indicated a different future, a horizon of expectation for individual and collective ascent. It constituted a public signifier that – not being partial and potentially partisan like working class, but tendentially universal because even minorities could climb the latter by acquiring new skills – re-signified society by favouring the affirmation of non-antagonistic, collective forms of expression. In the stratified society where labour moved upwards, the middle class became the subject of a discourse that was consensual insofar as it was complementary to the different layers of

---

12   In 1936 Edwards dedicated an essay to the "black" question where, while pointing out 'a gradual and important movement of Negro workers into higher social-economic groups', he found that two thirds of them still performed unskilled labour and asked whether, with the tendential reduction of unskilled occupations, blacks would not replace white workers in this social group (Edwards 1936b). Cf. Lewis 1939.

semi-skilled, skilled, and professional work. Its public communication would have made the rigid boundary between manual and intellectual labour porous and traversable, opening a new historical frontier of American democracy on the collar line (Edwards 1936a: 13–16).

2   The New Deal for the Middle Class

In light of the scientific foundations laid by public statistics, it is thus possible to interpret the New Deal – its policies, its federal agencies, and it political and public discourse – as a historical project of the construction of the middle class. This did not so much emerge from taxation reform, which despite having a progressive character, still provided exemptions for average income. And neither did it emerge only from the measures approved to support credit and real estate. While measures for public housing aimed at workers were only adopted at the end of the decade (and with insignificant results), the Democratic majority in Congress immediately confronted the foreclosure and expropriation of hundreds of thousands of homes by passing laws – the Homeowners Housing Act (1933) and National Housing Act (1934) – which provided financial support for the mortgage loan, in this way consolidating the traditional ownership ideal of the American family.[13] The centrality of the middle class emerged above all from the policies that addressed the question of labour. Legislation on trade union representation, collective bargaining, and the regulation of minimum wages and working hours – the National Labor Relations Act (1935) and the Fair Labor Standards Act (1938) – established the margin within which the working class could exercise power won in the factory, without making any significant distinction between white-collar and blue-collar workers. Other than the sexually and racially connoted domestic and agricultural labour, only the highly skilled labour of engineers and chemists was excluded from the institutional mechanism of union representation. The New Deal thus favoured the convergence of worker wages and employee salary. The same purpose characterised the other fundamental provision of the nascent welfare state, the 1935 Social Security Act. In the report drawn up by the Committee on Social Security, Wladimir S. Woytinsky – an economist originally from Russia who was employed by the Central Statistics Board – explained that, in light of the employment classification in the federal census, the policies of social security – unemployment insurance and social security for the elderly – followed

---

13   Patel 2017: 190–217; Michelmore 2012.

and consolidated the trend towards the middle class, even in its racial and sexual composition. The estimate of the number of persons who would benefit from it excluded the majority of black people and women who were employed in agricultural and domestic labour. The law thus did not establish a right to social security, but rather an entitlement which reflected the position of the labourer in the social stratification and racial and patriarchal hierarchy of society. The New Deal as project for the middle class was an affirmative action for the white American family (Woytinsky 1938: v–xi, 25–40, 266–272).[14]

The measures taken by the government in order to tackle unemployment, especially in the second half of the 1930s, finally paid particular attention to the white-collar worker. In the public lists organized at the local and state level following the May 1933 approval of the Federal Emergency Relief Administration (FERA), employees were underrepresented for reasons of status or because they preferred to resort to private savings rather than public assistance. Their number instead rapidly increased to reach 560,000 units (12% of recipients) in 1935, involving not only clerks or sales staff, but also technicians and chemists, designers and engineers, doctors and nurses, teachers, journalists, and artists. This increase did not only occur because the savings which initially eased the impact of economic depression were no longer there. While the Civil Work Administration (CWA) – an agency active between the fall of 1933 and spring of 1934 – had invested in public work by enlisting labour power without paying particular attention to skills, the Works Progress Administration developed thousands of programs specifically aimed at employees and professionals. Established with the Emergency Relief Appropriation Act (1935), which authorised the largest federal funding in national history and gave the president wide spending discretion, the agency became the largest undertaking of the New Deal. Between 1935 and 1943 it created over eight million jobs, including three million in 1938 alone. Its political importance for the construction of the middle class, however, did not derive from this data, since the problem of unemployment was not resolved for either the employee or worker. Instead, it derived from the quality of its administrative action.[15]

Under the leadership of Harry Hopkins – former director of FERA and SWA, as well as head of public assistance in New York state during Roosevelt's term as governor – the agency operated without fixing strict rules for access to

---

14   See also *National Labor Relation Board Annual Reports* vol. I, 1936: 119; vol. II, 1937: 133; vol.
       III, 1938: 184–188. Cf. Katznelson 2006; Rodgers 2000: 444–445.
15   In 1937, among employees registered on the unemployment list, 26% of women and 28%
       of men were employed in public works. See Burns 1936; Howard 1943: 176ff. Cf. Kocka
       1980: 193–199; Vaudagna 1986: 112–121.

assistance, that is, without the request of information aimed at investigating the poverty level of the white-collar worker. Its officials often approached professional associations directly in order to recruit workers that could be placed into different programs. Furthermore, although the minimum wage of employees varied according to geographical areas in relation to the cost of living and despite being set below the average market wage in order not to compete with private companies, remuneration varied on the social scale established by the classification of occupations, rewarding education and professionalism. Still more importantly, as Hopkins wrote, the Works Progress Administration tried to 'adapt work as nearly as possible to the skills of the available labor on the relief rolls'. The experience of previous agencies had in fact taught that granting direct relief or employing the worker without regard to skills 'destroyed' his self-respect and work ethic. Between 1936 and 1938, programmes aimed at skilled and professional labour thus reached sixteen thousand, although the agency mainly involved unskilled workers who were mostly white (*Report on the Works Program* 1936: 3–5, 18–26; *Inventory* 1938: 4–12, 43–47, 62–66, 70–81).[16] As far as possible – as the director admitted – technicians were employed in public projects for the protection of the environment and architectural heritage, teachers in schools built in the most backward areas hit by the depression, and doctors and nurses in healthcare assistance programs. Actors, artists, and musicians were instead involved in theatrical projects, musical education, and cultural entertainment. Employees catalogued property and expenses, documentation, goods, and books from town halls, archives, museums, and libraries. Statisticians were used to collect data that was useful for the development of federal policies, for the overall evaluation of their economic and social impact. Finally, scholars and graduates carried out historical and scientific research which was considered part of public utility. Among this research was the translation of monographs of European sociology – particularly German – on the middle class, commissioned by the Department of Social Sciences at Columbia University precisely in order to know 'the impact of economic depression on the middle class'.[17]

---

16   See also Ross 1934: 288–294; Wolfson 1948: 23–24. Cf. Fox Schwartz 2014.

17   Project Supervisor. W. R. Dittmar, Ph.D. published by the State Department of Social Welfare and the Department of Social Science, Columbia University, as a report on Project No. 165-97-6999-6027 conducted under the auspices of the Works Progress Administration. Translations are held by Columbia University's Butler Library. In particular, see the preface written by the curator of the project to the most important essay written by Lederer and Jacob.

Hopkins and his collaborators thus aggressively attacked – with only partial success – what they believed to be the social and political waste that unemployment of skilled and professional labour meant for society at large. Their policies did not serve a merely administrative function in order to increase the 'efficiency, accuracy, and accessibility' of the New Deal. They built the social plan which was indispensable to the construction of the middle class. As Hopkins said in a speech delivered in July 1938, the Works Progress Administration preserved the skills and professionalism of US labour, i.e., the work ethic of the entire nation. It was the 'American way' that the government had taken to fill the dangerous power vacuum that capitalism had created by refusing to assume 'responsibility' for its own crisis (Hopkins 1938. See also *Research Work on Projects of the Works Administration* 1938: 3–5).

The powerful director who began his career as a social worker on the streets of New York was not the only New Dealer to publicly enunciate the historical project of the construction of the middle class. In order to respond to the question of revolution that circulated in public opinion, other social scientists used the political semantics of the middle class in order to support the New Deal 'revolution'. In an interview with the *New York Times* on 16 July 1933, Rexford G. Tugwell – Columbia University economist and Assistant Secretary of Agriculture – stated that the buying power of the social groups of agricultural, industrial, and office labour would lead the economy out of misery (Tugwell 1933: 2). In October of the same year, again in the columns of the *New York Daily*, Adolph A. Berle – jurist and author of the volume *The Modern Corporation and Private Property* (1933) – explained that Roosevelt would become 'the greatest president in history' because, against the threats of the 'red revolutionary' and the 'black Fascist' which spanned the Atlantic, he faced economic depression with 'the typical American spirit', that is, by calling on the 'theory of a large middle class'. As he wrote in 1935, in a world of 'easy revolutions', this was the new American revolution: not 'enthroning the proletariat', but 'abolishing it', or rather 'making it wholly unnecessary by lifting it into a different state' (Berle 1935: 37–47; Berle 1933). Stuart Chase – an economist influenced by Fabianism, raised in the technocratic school of the socialist Thorsten Veblen, and fascinated by the Soviet planning experiment – recommended the New Deal as a 'third road' between the 'dictatorship of big business' and the 'dictatorship of the proletariat'. Scientists, technicians, and engineers would take 'control of production' in order to lead a revolution for the 'economy of abundance' in the name of the middle class. As the census statistics showed, this was already a majority and in the near future it would definitely supplant unskilled labour (Chase 1932a: 153–155; Chase 1934: 229–292; Chase 1932b). George Henry Soule

– columnist at *The New Republic* – emphasised the political challenge that awaited Roosevelt:

> The New Deal gives us a foretaste of the rise to power of a new [middle] class ... The virtue of the New Deal will probably be seen, in the light of history, not as successful social planning, but as a step in the educational process which is necessary if the workers, the farmers and the professional and white-collar classes are ever to become sufficiently mobilized and conscious enough of a program so that they can engage in successful social planning.
>
> SOULE 1934a: 207, 278–281[18]

The historic project of the construction of the middle class finally emerged in the very words of the president, even if he did not explicitly name the middle class. In 1932 Roosevelt had organised his electoral campaign around the rhetoric of the forgotten man, using an expression inherited from progressivism, but coined by the evolutionist Charles Sumner at the end of the last century (Roosevelt 1932a: Roosevelt 1932b; Roosevelt 1932c).[19] While the forgotten man referred indefinitely to property-owning people such as consumers, homeowners, farm-owners, shopkeepers, and stockholders, at the beginning of his mandate, in his speeches he named manual worker, brain worker, clerical and professional worker, and white-collar worker. The lexicon of his presidential discourse was therefore enriched, not only to present the measures of his government (particularly the initiatives against unemployment), but above all in order to communicate the political objective of the New Deal to various types of workers who animated social conflict (Roosevelt 1933a; Roosevelt 1933b; Roosevelt 1935a; Roosevelt 1935b; Roosevelt 1935c). On several occasions, speaking on the radio, Roosevelt took positions against the rupture of 'national unity', 'brotherhood', and the 'common good', which the "spirit of class" was causing. In the 1936 presidential campaign, while denouncing the industrial dictatorship that had expropriated men and women of their ability to control wages, hours, and working conditions by imposing a new economic monarchy, Roosevelt stated the following, during the fireside chat before Labor Day:

> There is no cleavage between white-collar workers and manual workers, between artists and artisans, musicians and mechanics, lawyers and

---

18   Cf. Lindley 1974: 23–25, 208–210. On planning between the United States and the Soviet Union, see Cuppini and Ferrari 2020.
19   See also Roosevelt 1934. Cf. Cowie 2016: 91–93.

accountants and architects and minors. Tomorrow, Labor Day, belongs to all of us. Tomorrow, Labor Day, symbolizes the hope of all Americans. Anyone who calls it a class holiday challenges the whole concept of American democracy.

ROOSEVELT 1936a[20]

And yet, two years later, again on the occasion of celebrating Labor Day, aware that the New Deal could not overcome the political margin beyond which capitalism would not be able to regain lost political leadership, the president reacted with these words to the unexpected wave of strikes and occupations which signalled the intensification of workers' militancy in the factories and the broadening of social conflict to employee and professional work despite the policies of his first term:

Class consciousness itself … conceive[s] its interest to be opposed to the interest of all other people, and for this reason a small minority is deliberately trying to create prejudice between this and that group of the common people of America – to create a new class feeling among people like ourselves, who instinctively are not class conscious.

ROOSEVELT 1936b. See also ROOSEVELT 1938

The fact that, again at the beginning of the 1940s, Roosevelt returned to denouncing the 'class feeling' that questioned the orderly functioning of the war economy was exemplary of the fragility of the scientific foundations that public statistics laid in order to initiate the project of the construction of the middle class (Roosevelt 1940; Roosevelt 1942; Roosevelt 1943a; Roosevelt 1943b; Roosevelt 1944). Despite the political commitment of his 'brains trust', government agencies and social scientists who saw in his administration the possibility of social control through planning that had escaped progressivism, for the entire decade the New Deal would act on the unstable ground of class struggle. Its uncertain and experimental character, both innovative and conservative, on which historiography has long debated, thus derived from the contradiction that Roosevelt had to confront: his government of capital in crisis drew strength from the social conflict that from the factory to society exhausted the business world's resistance to change, but it also had to keep its political and administrative action inside a limit compatible with the needs of profit – and therefore the capacity for investment – of companies. In

---

20   On the use of radio in the president's public communication: Frezza 1986; Goodman 2011.

this sense, his 'revolution' was a reform that pursued economic recovery by selectively responding to the demands of society, that is, by identifying and separating social groups in order to institutionally integrate them by means of different methods and intensities which accounted for the skill and professionalism of workers and employees, their economic and social status, and their racial and sexual identity. Although federal agencies operated without any formal discrimination, there were no specific initiatives in favour of non-white labour. Above all, since the implementation of policies took place at the state level, especially in the segregated south, an essential electoral basin of the Democratic Party, claims of black people were downsized, if not completely ignored. With the exception of some unemployment programs initiated mostly by the Works Progress Administration, the labour policies were aimed exclusively at men, while for women – at least until the entrance into the war and again after its conclusion – subsidies were provided which, by favouring their return to the separate sphere of domestic housework, affirmed their role as mothers and wives.[21] In this way, the reform intended to accomplish the mediation between blue-collar and white-collar on the institutional level as an indispensable political condition for the construction of the middle class. Yet, in the middle of the decade, in light of the politicisation of society imposed by the mobilisation of not only blue-collar workers on the shop floor, the project of the New Deal still remained open, contested, and indefinite. The answer to the question of revolution that hung over the future of American democracy was in fact linked to the ideological battle over the middle class, a battle fought between conservative and reactionary forces, on the one hand, and radical and communist forces on the other. At the historical threshold of the social transformation opened by capitalism's crisis of legitimation, 'middle class' was thus not constituted only by the project of the New Deal. It was also the indicator of a social and political clash with an uncertain outcome.[22]

3   The Crisis of the Middle Class

The question of revolution did not find an immediate answer in the historical project of the construction of the middle class elaborated in the first half of the decade. In 1935, the publication of Lewis Corey's *The Crisis of the Middle Class* called into question the scientific semantics and public and political discourse

---

21   Vezzosi 2002: 103–156.
22   Kocka 1980: 234–236, 237–241.

by means of an 'illuminating historical survey', which although written by 'the most important Marxist writer in the United States today', attracted the attention of a wide audience thanks to its 'vocabulary free from official seminar terminology'. Discussed by intellectuals and scholars, reviewed in the main daily and periodical newspapers, both national and local (the *New York Post* advertised its release on the front page) the volume became a best seller, transforming the public debate on economic depression into an ideological battle for the middle class (Hacker 1935: 625–626; Angoff 1935; Chamberlain 1935; Corey Says Middle Class Has Disappeared 1935; Josephson 1936).[23]

An immigrant from the province of Salerno at the end of the nineteenth century, Louis Fraina (this was his first American name) was a militant in the New York section of the Socialist Labor Party, supporting the strikes that the Industrial Workers of the World launched in 1912 in the textile factories of Lawrence, Massachusetts. During the war, this experience led him to distance himself from socialism in order to respond to the call, after 1917, of the new international in support of the Bolshevik revolution. In 1918 he published *Revolutionary Socialism*, which anticipated the interpretive framework that he would use to understand the crisis of the middle class during the depression. The processes of economic and financial concentration had not only rendered the old proprietary middle-class into an 'anachronism' whose final and failed political expression was the agrarian and populist revolt at the end of the nineteenth century. These processes had also caused the emergence of a new middle class of salaried employees, according to the term used by the German scientific literature in order to indicate the subordinate status of employees in private and public bureaucracies. The new middle class was dependent on income, stratified into corporate hierarchies, and composed of managers, superintendents, engineers, technicians, and professionals. Its non-proprietary composition incarnated the transformation of the 'social relationship' of industrial capital which found in progressivism a specific political form that Corey defined as 'state capitalism', a term which was almost unused overseas, in order to indicate the action of the state 'to regulate the rights of labor': regulation through administrative commissions and arbitration courts determined the 'death of democracy'. It not only expressed the complete historical overcoming of the democracy of producers which had animated the nineteenth century experience of the frontier, but also the institutionalisation of the 'right to organize and strike' which, although recognising the social role of the trade union, limited the capacity of autonomous action by a working

23   On Corey: Tait 1973; Kleher 1976; Buhle 1995: 32–86; Pells 1973: 91–99.

class increasingly de-skilled by mechanisation. The liberal and democratic ideal that progressivism had attributed to the new middle class – and which US socialism also embraced – thus carried a 'reactionary factor' with itself: the middle class was an 'obedient vassal' of capital. For this reason, the revolution would have been initiated by the mass action of workers against the bureaucracies of state capitalism that the middle class embodied (Fraina 1918: 38–73, 83–92).[24]

During progressivism Corey had therefore attributed an absolute centrality to the working class composed mostly by an immigrant and black labour force excluded from the union organised on the basis of trade. In the early 1920s, the defeat of the workers' movement and the internal divisions on the communist left convinced him to leave the party in order to become a recognised independent scholar who in the second half of the decade collaborated with the Brookings Institute and the *Encyclopaedia of the Social Sciences* (1931–1934).[25] In this biographical and political context, the economic depression which in May 1927 he predicted on the pages of *The New Republic* – 'Let us produce and accumulate: there are no social problems! But there is an awakening coming' (Corey: 1927: 323) – pushed him to reconsider the middle class. In this sense, *The Decline of American Capitalism* (1934) constituted the final chapter of revolutionary socialism and the first chapter of an appeal to the middle class based on the criticism of the New Deal.[26]

In fact, Corey blamed the depression not only on the 'apologists' of the 'new capitalism' who in the 1920s had propagated the 'myth of prosperity', but also on the 'institutional variety' of the economic science that shaped President Roosevelt's policies by defining the New Deal as an experiment in 'collective democracy' which responded to 'investors, farmers, small capitalists, and lower salary earners' (Commons 1935: 222. See also Soule 1934b: 164; Berle 1934). In light of the inability of capital to restore prosperity, in his view, the Democratic administration did not mark 'the making of a new world', but was the expression of the 'permanent crisis' of capitalism which required a 'government intervention on an unprecedented scale'. This judgment was historically argued in terms of decline: from the epoch of the frontier which had

---

24 On the history of socialism and its rise, decline, and convergence with progressivism, see Testi 1980.

25 The collaboration with the Brookings Institute led to the 1930 publication of *The House of Morgan*, a book that reconstructed the banker's bibliography in order to show how the financial transformation of American capitalism reflected the explosion of class struggle starting in the late nineteenth century. See Buhle 1995: 105–107.

26 Buhle 1995: 122–123.

guaranteed 'an ascending accumulation of capital' to the phase of imperialism which had opened up the foreign market by securing the profit margin
questioned within the national territory, the history of capitalism had been 'a
perpetual struggle against the American dream' which had limited the ideals
of freedom and democracy. If in the 1920s this dream had been perpetuated by
the 'dogma of high wages', the study of statistics showed its absolute ground-
lessness. The so-called 'enlightened employers' did not raise wages 'voluntarily
and constantly'. Their increase took place only between 1921 and 1922 at the
height of the workers' mobilisation in the post-war period. During the remain-
der of the decade their level remained unchanged until the crash in 1929. There
had been no 'policy of high wages', and if anything, the government by commission through price control had diluted their increase over the course of
the decade, limiting them only to technicians, superintendents, and skilled
labourers. Consequently, the social nexus between production and consumption established by economic science appeared marked by a strident contradiction. In spite of the increase in productivity, the capacity to consume was
increasingly less available to the majority of labour. Above all, it was 'labor's
militancy' which imposed the wage increase, the same militancy which the
government had repressed with its 'legal and physical force' (Corey 1934: 10–12,
23–34, 52–53, 76–77, 80–84).[27]

This social and political contradiction provided the interpretative key for
criticising the New Deal. In particular, Corey denounced the National Industrial
Recovery Act (1933) because it accorded government action with entrepreneurial action: the National Labor Board regulated prices in order to favour
the return of inflation, fixed minimum wages that benefitted the skilled part of
labour, and in general determined a 'maximum wage' which compressed the
'average wage'. The final effect was 'a tendency to break down the differentials
between skilled and unskilled and semi-skilled workers not by raising wages,
but by lowering them'. The ultimate goal was 'to discourage, prevent, and settle'
strikes, 'putting unions under the control of the state' through a 'whole network of institutional arrangements' which 'compulsorily' imposed the resolution of 'industrial disputes' and the 'limitation of independent labor action'.
What Corey called 'niraisim', i.e., the New Deal version of state capitalism that
emerged with progressivism, brought American democracy dangerously close
to European fascism because it established an institutional stiffening of social
relations with no precedent (Corey 1934: 97–102, 215, 489–514).[28]

---

27   Cf. Bertram and Lloyd 1926; Lauck 1929; Bonn 1932; Bauer and Gold 1934.
28   Corey cited the study of New York University in the article Labor and NRA 1933: 169.

The scientific commitment to save capitalism from its decline therefore seemed to be completely in vain. Policies were safeguarding profit by controlling production, but in doing so they limited consumption: 'capitalism, the historical creator of abundance, became the enemy of abundance'. The purchasing power which New Dealers considered necessary in order to escape the depression did not increase. A fair 'balance' between wages and profit, which Berle saw as possible through a government that leveraged the alleged independence of the 'professional management' from proprietary interest, was not established. The political intent to pacify society and unify the nation by administrative means was failing because the contradiction between production and consumption did not seem governable through the 'social planning' that Chase advocated in order to abolish poverty. Nor did it seem surmountable in the 'collective planning' that Commons saw as inherent in the supposed middle-class ideal of the workers' movement. Clouded by the 'exceptional' vision presented by progressivist historian Charles Beard in *The Rise of American Civilization* (1927), the social sciences did not consider the strong limitation of democracy that was implied in the unprecedented administrative apparatus. They saw in the New Deal the possibility of realising the historical construction of the middle class but did not grasp its artificial nature or its being a statistical invention which cannot be traced in the experience of society. It can be found only as an index of the crisis of society (Corey 1934: 21, 61, 94, 148, 195, 204 –210, 396–398, 482–487, 564, 567).

The prognosis of the middle class which public statistics had formulated at the hands of its demiurge was thus reversed. It did not seem to grasp a tendency in society, but instead appeared tendentious: a sheer fantasy such as the idea that 'technology is slowly obliterating the proletariat'. There was no upward movement of labour. Without the fictitious category of semi-skilled labour, the census of occupations would have revealed the majority presence of manual labour. Further, early research on the depression – particularly at Columbia University and New York University – registered its devastating impact on employee and professional occupations, showing how the 'wages policy' of the New Deal compressed the 'average salary'. The social and economic degradation which tormented the worker regardless of his skill thus also affected white-collar labour. His proletarianisation made 'class lines become more rigid and class difference more acute'. In this way, 'class struggles would become more violent, and develop new forms and objectives', and would be 'impossible to peacefully adjust' to the 'institutional and ideological' relations. On the eve of the unexpected workers' mobilisation which between 1936–1937 marked industry with unauthorised strikes and factory occupations despite the approval of legislation on union representation and collective bargaining, Corey thus argued that the crisis of capitalism placed society on the threshold of a 'struggle for power' that would open national history onto 'a new American revolution, the coming communist resolution'. His appeal to the middle class to act with the working class went in this direction. This was, in 1935, the political meaning of *The Crisis of the Middle Class* (Corey 1934: 106, 295–297,453–457, 541, 548, 562–564).[29]

The volume, which was preceded by three articles published in *The Nation* (Corey 1935b; Corey 1935c; Corey 1935d), confronted the 'permanent crisis of capitalism' as a 'crisis of the middle class'. The critical analysis of statistics was not abandoned, but served to elaborate a counter-history of the middle class to oppose the narrative of progressivist historiography, confirming the political use of statistics.[30] Corey employed the same story that historians such as Charles Beard (1915), Vernon Parrington (1927), Arthur Schlesinger (1930), and Franklin Palm (1936) were sketching by elevating the middle class to the sole acting protagonist of national history: in the United States just as in Europe, the middle class had played a 'great part in history, creating and realizing the values of capitalist civilisation'. However, he claimed that 'democracy and freedom were not realised': the middle class was not able to combine capitalism and democracy through progressivism and after the 1929 crash was again entangled in the dramatic European history where decline and impoverishment had led to the 'opportunity of fascism' or in any case a 'potentially fascist' mobilisation against the workers. Corey therefore showed a danger in fascism which was not exclusively European: 'state capitalism is no fascism, but fascism necessarily includes state capitalism'. In the United States, what had constituted on the European shores 'the last desperate resource of capitalism in order to save itself' by institutionalising the social serfdom of capital in the 'totalitarian state' appeared as a historical process that was still open. Since dispossessed property owners and salaried workers claimed, 'relief as a right', rejecting the individualism of American democracy, proletarianisation fueled 'confusion' in the middle class between those who 'still cling to capitalism', those who 'flirt with fascism', and those who 'move towards communism'. Historically reconstructing the 'transformation wrought in the composition,

---

29   See also Corey 1935a: 1–8; Debate: "Can Civilization Survive Under Capitalism?" 1935.
30   According to data provided by Corey, since 1929 nearly 600,000 – one in six – industrial, commercial, and professional enterprises had gone bankrupt. In the spring of 1933 around 35% of employees had just lost their jobs and not only in the lower spheres of office work: unemployment climbed to 65% for chemists, 85% for engineers, and over 90% for architects. Those who remained at work suffered a wage decrease between 20 and 30%. See Corey 1992 where his main source is Kuznets 1934.

ideology, and significance of the middle class' thus made it necessary to identify a different political perspective against the state capitalism of the New
Deal (Corey 1992: 10–17, 21–23, 34–35).[31]

Corey started from the historic change in the economic composition of
the middle class. After the Civil War, 'the accumulation of capital inexorably
destroyed the conditions of independent enterprise' and the capitalism of the
'trustification of industry' and the 'large industry' imposed a 'fundamental
structural change' for which independent labour constituted a residual por-
tion of a 'new middle class deprived, like the workers, of independent means
of livelihood'. If salaried employees had found in progressivism a political discourse capable of conveying their interest, the unprecedented role assumed by
government in the regulation of labour outlined an institutional convergence
between state and capital that precluded the middle class from 'controlling capitalism'. Not unlike what happened overseas during the war and the post-war
period, particularly in Germany, the expansion of the administrative functions
of the state and the introduction of new scientific forms of the organisation of
production had caused the new heterogenous composition of the middle class.
While a small, highly skilled and paid group administered the 'managerial and
supervisory functions' of the corporation by acting as an 'institutional capitalist', the 'great masses of lower salaried employees' performed 'routine tasks'
with 'scarce value, privileges, and income'. Their average salary was slightly
more than the average wage, and 'the many union-organized skilled workers
earned more than the great majority of clerical employees'. Furthermore, 'spe-
cialization' and the 'mechanization of labor' had deprived employees of their
skills, transforming the office into a 'white-collar factory' which prevented any
'measure of independence'. The white-collar workers therefore constituted 'a

---

31   Concerning progressive historiography, Corey cited Beard's 1913 *An Economic
      Interpretation of the Constitution of the United States* and 1915 *Economic Origins of
      Jeffersonian Democracy*, as well as Parrington's 1927 *The Colonial Mind*. Other references
      Corey made include Commons 1918; Fish 1927; Schlesinger 1930; and Palm 1936 who pre-
      sented a universal history of the middle class from European feudalism to its American
      triumph. See Corey 1936. In relation to fascism, in addition to Lawrence Dennis, author
      of *Is Capitalism Doomed?* (1932) and *The Coming of American Fascism* (1936), Corey cited
      Speier 1934. Surely, thanks to his work on the *Encyclopaedia*, he had come to know Weimar
      sociology on the *Mittelstand* and its Nazi orientation. On England, he quoted Gretton
      1919. He also reviewed Klingender 1935 in the communist newspaper *New Masses*: Clerck
      become Workers, 7 April 1936. He had also read several articles published in *The New
      Republic* by protestant theologian and future conservative Reinhold Niebuhr (1932 and
      1933). He constructed the chapter 'Fascism and the Middle Class' (1992: 282–308) on these
      sources.

new proletariat' (Corey 1992: 77–94, 113–115, 123–126, 129–143, 154–159, 174–175, 180–185, 249–253, 259).[32]

However, what most interested Corey was showing how this composition of the middle class had profound ideological consequences. The different positions occupied in the corporate hierarchy did not correspond to a 'single clear-cut attitude'. What was defined critically as the myth of the public of progressivism had now vanished. The decline of capitalism made it clear how the middle class expressed only an 'artificial unity'. The proletarianisation of the middle class prevented, in other words, any political and scientific project which relied on its economic constitution. It was not possible to 'restore a middle-class capitalism' because the 'disunity created by diversity of interests is irreconcilable'. On the one hand, the upper strata were 'identified with monopoly capitalism and its reactionary aims', not only for their high income and level of consumption, but also for their 'function of exploiting' which they exercised over manual and non-manual labour. On the other, the lower strata experienced a strident contradiction between their historical middle-class ideal and their social condition which 'drove them in an opposite direction: toward the working class'. The new composition of the middle class therefore posed the question of the 'ideological transformation' or the middle class as a 'split personality' (Corey 1992: 144, 148–153, 160–161, 164, 166–167, 247).

The definition of the 'split personality' referred to the scientific literature, which following the decline of progressivism had rethought the middle class by abstracting from its proprietary and occupational conditions in order to accentuate its psychological character. In the post-war period, the difficulties of grasping an upward movement of labour in society had prompted sociology to privilege the quantitative study of the cultural process of identification which led – or should have led – to the registration of shared values despite diverging economic interests. Although he did not cite Franklin Giddings, the Columbia University sociologist who in 1926 defined the existence of a 'psychological middle class' (Giddings 1926), Corey argued that the internal tensions to the middle class made its personality disorder 'incurable'. This time the reference was not to the restorative cure that New Dealers and social scientists intended to administer to the middle class through regulation and planning. The polemic was directed against the different political positions of the liberal, conservative, and reactionary opposition to the New Deal.

---

32   Corey reported that the number of workers employed had grown from about 600,000 in 1870 to over 4.5 million in 1910, from 5 to 13% of the employed. Professionals, including teachers and technicians, had instead grown from about 410,000 to just over 2 million, i.e. from 3.3 to 5.4%, again in the same period. His sources were Edwards 1933 and Sogge 1933.

It was also against those – such as Walter Lippmann in his *The Method of Freedom* (1934) – who continued to define 'private property' as 'the original source of freedom and its main bulwark' in order to defend capitalism as an 'essentially middle class' phenomenon (Corey 1992: 171, 210–217, 230–233, 241, 254). And above all, the polemic was against those he called 'middle-class demagogues'. Preachers such as Charles E. Coughlin or businessmen like Ogden L. Mills – President Hoover's Secretary of Treasury – who instrumentalised the crash of property-owning and professional status in order to incite 'popular discontent'. Their 'emotional appeal' Defend Property! Against Labor! communicated a 'reactionary content' which reprised the polemic against progressivism that had been fueled by the publication of *The Return of the Middle Class*, the 1922 volume with which John Corbin had imposed a conservative torsion in public discourse on the middle class. His political direction of shaping a 'property consciousness' by leveraging the 'sense of superiority' of intellectual work in order to make it 'a powerful and indispensable ally' of capital was recuperated in order to publicly affirm the middle class as 'the unity of negation … against organised labour'. If this was 'the most significant aspect of the split personality of the middle class', it was necessary to acknowledge that the middle class was not a proprietary class and thus had no interest in the 'struggle for property'. Attention then went to the revolt of the masses of 'lower salaried employees' so that they would distance themselves from ownership and managerial groups by joining forces with 'a new struggle for power' (Corey 1992: 165, 169–170, 230–234, 237–239, 254, 263–265).

In conclusion, Corey argued that New Dealers, liberals, and conservatives ignored 'the great change in the composition of the middle class', thus not understanding that its stratification made it impossible to unify the ownership and managerial figures with the non-ownership and employee masses. The depression had completely deprived the middle class of its capacity to express and affirm an 'independent policy'. Middle class no longer constituted the 'basis of capitalism'. For this reason, facing the prospect that its unity was artificially restored through the state capitalism of the New Deal or through a reactionary antagonism, it was necessary to appeal to it. Although the 'economic barrier' that separated the middle class from the working class no longer existed, an 'ideological barrier' remained strong and needed to be broken down. The political objective of the ideological transformation of the middle class into a new proletariat had to be conquered not only on the economic and political level, namely against state capitalism, but also 'against the dominant culture'. The counter-history of the middle class thus ended with markedly political prose. The 'holy trinity of the American dream' – freedom, equality, and democracy

– was nothing but 'the freedom and equality of starving or going on relief'. It coincided with a 'common servitude to an oligarchy of wholly predatory capitalists'. The opportunity to acquire property and income became 'the opportunity to survive', social mobility became 'mobility downward' and progress became regression. The historical political vision – originally republican, later democratic, and finally progressivist – that the social sciences applied to the project of the construction of the middle class was by now outside of the horizon of the nation:

> The ideals of the American dream trampled upon by capitalist decline and decay. But more: the ideals themselves must be destroyed as *ideals* ... The crisis of the American dream is an ideological expression of the class-economic crisis of the middle class. The dream was its creation, and the dream is now a nightmare. Nightmare of capitalist decline: the alternative to socialism.
>
> COREY 1992: 196–198, 276–277, 218–221, 340–341

The Crisis thus offered an instrument of agitation of the new proletariat of employees, professionals, and intellectuals to 'become part of the workers' movement'. Although aware of the fact that the union had until then ignored the demands of white-collar labour, Corey noted that the economic and ideological crisis of the middle class 'forced' salaried and professional workers to 'adopt proletarian forms of action: unions, strikes and mass demonstrations'. Consequently, the working class was no longer considered the exclusive subject of mass action against capitalism. Not all of the middle class was an 'obedient vassal' of capital, nor was it considered as simply the 'ally of the working class' since it was 'part of the working class and its struggle for socialism'. With this political perspective Corey continued his critique of the New Dealers: economic science was technocratic because it denied the capacity of autonomous working-class action and underestimated the democratic problem posed by private and public bureaucracies, misrepresenting the teaching of its own founder Veblen who had seen in technicians and engineers a possible revolutionary force only if moved by workers' mobilisation. Differently than the 'technocrats' of the New Deal, Corey believed that the road to democracy was not paved with reforms, but that the crossroads was between fascism and socialism. For this reason, the 'upheaval of capitalism' passed through an 'inner struggle in the middle class' which the communists should have led by favouring the mobilisation of white-collar workers into a large working class of manual and intellectual labour. This was the political direction that transformed the public, political, and scientific debate on economic depression into an ideological battle for the middle class (Corey 1992: 260, 266–271, 342–344, 346–347. See also Corey 1935e: 745–756).

4   The Ideological Battle for the Middle Class

Corey's conclusions were thus addressed to the Communist Party of the United States of America (CPUSA). After distancing himself from the Party in the 1920s, he returned to it in 1932 when he signed the *Crisis and Culture* manifesto with which the League of Professional Groups had supported the Communist candidacy of William Z. Foster for President. Although it was not a direct emanation of the Party, but rather an expression of a group of independent intellectuals, the manifesto was signed and distributed among writers, artists, doctors, engineers, scientists, and other professionals. It worked as a first appeal for 'brain work' to unite its own forces with the workers' mobilisation. The League was short lived, however, not only because of the central committee's attempt to reduce its independence, but also because it was signed by the same factions which had divided the Party after the expulsion of Jay Lovestone for his exceptionalist theses which were contrary to the directives of the International. And yet the manifesto indicated a new organised and political perspective which would be pursued above all after the publication of *The Crisis*: for the unionisation of white-collar labour within the broader communist activism in the workers' mobilisation which led to the establishment of the formation of the Congress of Industrial Organization and for the increase in political influence within the popular front, in support of the New Deal, but against the radical positions which intended to exclude communists from the project of the farmer-labour party.[33]

Communist attention on the middle class did not derive exclusively from the publication of *The Crisis*. With the onset of the depression, the two main lines of Party intervention were in the most important textile, mechanical, and mining industries, and in the agricultural labour marked by processes of dispossession of farmers and impoverishment of tenant farmers in the west and south. These lines of intervention characterised the recruitment campaigns of the unemployed and African Americans which were conducted by supporting claims to assistance and by promoting initiatives against lynchings and racial discrimination. Yet in the communist analysis of the depression, attention was

---

33   Buhle 1995: 133–143. Cf. Sylvers 1989: 235–236. On the role of the Communist Party in the mobilisation of the workers and the constitution of the CIO, see Green 1998: 158–164.

also immediately given to different figures of the middle class. If the 'storm of the economic crisis' had brought down the house of cards of exceptionalism by sweeping away 'the opportunist illusions of high wages', what remained was not only misery and unemployment, but also the 'mechanisation of production' and intensification of the rhythms of labour ('speed-up') which leveled down the condition of skilled and semi-skilled labour. The impoverishment also concerned the 'new class' of superintendents and technicians, as well as 'large sections of the middle classes', property-owning and not. If these were the theses of the seventh congress of the Party (1930), during the eighth congress (1934), the central committee declared that 'the overwhelming majority of intellectuals, professionals, teachers, white-collar workers have likewise been cast into poverty' despite President Roosevelt's policies. His 'reformism' had not rendered any New Deal capitalism possible because the National Industrial Recovery Act, while recognising the union of the 'labor aristocracy', offered the institutional tool to administer social conflict by denying the freedom to strike and organise. Before the International had indicated the popular front as a priority, the New Deal was thus not considered a 'progressive regime' but instead criticised as a 'government serving the interests of capital'. The Party's attention was turned less towards the political-institutional framework and more to the social horizon outlined by the 'growing strike movement' which from the manual labour factors should expand to the offices of intellectual labour (*Thesis and Resolutions* 1930: 2, 8–9; *Draft Resolution* 1934: 20–22, 38–39, 44–45).[34]

In this way, there emerged from the Party press an initial interest in the mobilisation of white-collar workers, professionals, and technicians, particularly in the urban and suburban area of New York. The *Daily Workers* and *New Masses* reported on strikes, pickets, and demonstrations by teachers, researchers, and social workers in the public sector, as well as assistants in large department stores in the commercial sector, architects, chemists, and engineers in construction, chemistry, and mechanics. These initiatives, reported by the liberal press with astonishment and by the business press with apprehension, challenged the minimum wages imposed by the National Labor Board and the low impact of the measures adopted by governmental agencies which were set up to tackle unemployment. While warning of the danger represented by the loss of the 'privileged social position' of white-collar workers who for this reason supported the rise of Nazism overseas, the communist press noted favourably how different groups of the middle class made forms of worker

---

34   Cf. Ottanelli 1991: 36–38, 68–69.

organisation their own. The strikes launched in this direction by the Federation of Architects, Chemists, Engineers, and Technicians against the opinion of the 'bureaucrats' of the American Federation of Labor and the constitution of the Inter-Professional Association which brought together various trade unions including the American Newspaper Guild, Typographical Union, and American Federation of Teachers. The presence of communist militants in the new white-collar syndicalism indicated the possibility of allying the middle class with the working class.[35]

This trade union interest became political starting in mid-1935, when the International launched the politics of the popular front. In a series of articles gathered together in the pamphlet *What is Communism?*, the Secretary Earl Browder drew attention to the 'series of intermediary groups' which, although publicly named with the singular signifier of middle class, occupied different positions and performed different functions which rendered an 'identity of interest' impossible. Engineers and technicians, lecturers and teachers, writers and artists were among the most affected by the depression, with many among them not living differently than the proletariat and having no hope to climb the social ladder: 'the economic base of the middle class disintegrated'. Since the United States was no longer the 'middle-class nation', the Party was tasked with preventing middle-class psychology from moving in the direction desired by the 'reactionary middle-class messiah'. It was necessary to promote their alignment with the working class through the work of communication and mobilisation, no longer aimed at the 'revolutionary overthrow of capitalism', but rather at a 'popular government supported by organised masses'. The unionisation of white-collar workers and the extension of their economic demands were inscribed in the politics of the popular front that Browder announced on 3 October 1935 at the public meeting held in Madison Square Garden after the seventh world congress of the communist International. In the latter half of the decade, the recruitment of employees, social workers, teachers, and professionals – which in January 1938 amounted to fourteen thousand members out of about one hundred thousand total – showed the political importance that the middle class had acquired in the Communist Party, in the official resolutions of the central committee and in the propaganda material prepared by the

---

35   Freeman 1933: 3–7; Freeman 1934: 34–36; On the White Collar Front 1934: 9; Seaver 1934: 16–17; Hill 1934: 17–18; Unionization in White Collar 1934: 3–8; The Middle Class Must Choose 1934: 9–13; Unions Back Store Strike in Milwaukee 1934; A Fighting Front in Milwaukee 1935; Minton 1935: 16–18; Haessler 1936: 20. Cf. Unions for Technicians 1934: 295–296; Broun 1935: 420.

Agit-Prop commission (Browder 1935a: 18–19; Browder 1935b: 18–19; Browder 1935c: 9–10).[36]

The battle for the middle class that the Party waged not only responded to the need to reformulate the political judgment on the Democratic administration by emphasising how the same president was going beyond the first New Deal with legislation in 1935. In the 1936 elections, the choice would not have been between the Democratic and Republic Party, but rather between the President Roosevelt supported by the popular front and the Liberty League. The latter was the 'centre of organised reaction' which joined together exponents of business, the Republican and Democratic Parties such as Alfred Smith who rejected the social direction that the president had imposed on liberalism, conservative and liberal intellectuals such as Lippmann who defended property and the free market from government intervention (Editorial Comments 1936: 2–3; War 1936: 5–6; Haessler 1936: 20). The battle for the middle class also responded to the polemic that the Party had to confront from those who intended to exclude communists from the construction of the farmer-labour party, particularly Alfred Bingham, editor of the magazine *Common Sense*, which right from the title advocated for an 'indigenous radicalism' against the communist extremism from Europe. The project of a third party was obviously not new, but in the aftermath of 1929, after the progressivist experiences, it had been relaunched by John Dewey, father of American pragmatism who, in the decade of Republican normality, criticised the growing skepticism towards the public affirmed by Lippmann in the academic and political fields in order to legitimate the role of experts and technicians in the government by commission. According to Dewey, the crisis of capitalism's legitimation reflected the 'disaffection of the masses from politics, their revolt against the political parties as the part of big business'. It would therefore be possible to overcome the 'old political order' through the formation of a new farmer-labour party which would have had to begin from the middle class in order to counter the 'defeatist policy which assumes that there can be no effective radical political action in this country until the majority of the population have sunk into the

---

36   See also Browder 1938, a volume that collects various published writings and speeches delivered between 1936 and 1937, among which we point out 'Our Enemy is Wall Street' (67–69) and 'A Labor Day Message' (76–78). See also *Resolutions of the Ninth Convention of the Communist Party of USA* 1936: 6–33; *Resolutions of the Tenth Convention of the Communist Party 1938*; *Draft Resolution on Browder Report* 1937: 1–5. For enrollment data refer to *Report on Organization* 1938; *Agit-Prop Commission* 1935, 10–12; *The Communists and People of Washington* 1939. Cf. The Crisis of the Middle Class 1935: 6–7; Dimitroff 1935: 8–9, 26–27.

proletariat' (Dewey 1931a: 115–117; Dewey 1931b: 151–152; Dewey 1931c: 178–179; Dewey 1931d: 203–205).[37]

This was the 'central issue' that Alfred Bingham faced in *Insurgent America*, the 1935 book he published against the communist politics about the middle class. According to the author, although the European events demonstrated that fascism and Nazism were 'essentially a popular movement of the middle classes', in the United States 'there is no seriously threatening reactionary Fascist movement'. Despite the presence of fascist voices, only the appearance of 'a threatening working-class movement' could lead to a reactionary outcome. The ideological battle for the middle class was thus fought against the intellectual leadership that the communists exercised in the public debate by emphasising the supposed 'militant proletarian class consciousness'. In this sense, a clear anti-communist position needed to be offered to the 'middle-class public'. The political direction towards planning and collectivism which the New Deal could have taken must not assume the partial character of the working class. Radical political action constituted the only way to prevent 'middle-class revolt' from taking on the 'definite shape' of the communist revolution or fascist reaction. As Dewey had also argued in his *Liberalism and Political Action* (1935), in order to prevent capitalism's legitimation crisis from finding its solution in the crisis of democracy, liberalism had to become radical (Bingham 1935: 5–11, 97–104, 123–124, 165–166, 177–178, 194–195).[38]

Bingham outlined a different 'class-line up' of the nation. Against the 'communist propaganda' which represented a 'weak and vacillating' middle class, economically and morally divided (and thus unable to express an orientation independent from the capital-labor conflict), [Bingham] reaffirmed the 'middle class dominance' in history, society, and politics. Although there was no doubt that the final quarter of the nineteenth century was marked by the unexpected presence of the proletariat, it was equally incontrovertible that its rise had been limited by the formation of a new middle class. As Edwards showed with his new classification of occupations in the federal census, 'the decline of the working class' culminated in the 1920s and 1930s, when white-collar labour

---

37   See also Dewey 1933: 8–9; Dewey 1927; Dewey 1930; Dewey 1935. Cf. Bingham and Rodman 1934, a volume that collected the most important articles published in *Common Sense*, the journal of the 'new American radicalism'. Among the voices of the battle over the middle class, there was also that of American socialism: Thomas 1934: 54–78. For a synthesis of the different socialist and communist positions on the middle class, see Heimann 1938. Pells 1973: 31–51; 91–95; 120–124.

38   Bingham's reading of fascism as a middle-class movement derived from the essay Passos 1935, wherein the diligent student of the Columbia University economist also included the progressivist positions that the third party was proposing within middle-class populism.

became the majority over manual skilled, semi-skilled, and unskilled labour. Moreover, the research that John Commons and Selig Perlman had conducted with their school of labour history demonstrated the bourgeoisification of the working class: due to the conservative parable that unionism had accomplished by accepting the entrepreneurial way of industrial relation and due to the career and consumer opportunities which had weakened a solidarity of a class already strongly hampered by its 'ethnically, linguistically, religiously, and culturally' heterogenous composition. The middle class was thus 'dominant', not only numerically, especially in the large urban and suburban areas, but also for its social role. While economic science emphasised the role engineers, experts, and managers played in directing and administering big business, sociological research showed that the domination of the middle class was also measurably in consumption habits and cultural inclinations. As Robert and Helen Lynd showed in their *Middletown* (1929), although it was not fully developed, but instead becoming increasingly urgent, the study of middle-class psychology hinted at an increasing 'middle-class aspiration', at its security of 'income and employment', its 'social position', and its 'home and family'. For this reason, despite the experiences of unionsation, there was no alignment of professionals and employees with the working class. On the contrary, their historical 'habit of classlessness' seemed to characterise large swaths of industrial labour:

> The working class can no longer lead and dominate a social transformation. Its strength is on the wane ... and it has become increasingly merged with the middle class ... The development of an effective revolutionary proletariat is a remoter possibility in America than elsewhere.
>
> BINGHAM 1935: 19–29, 38–39, 48–63, 73–79, 231–232[39]

Unlike the author of *The Crisis*, Bingham thus made his own prognosis of public statistics and uncritically assumed the narrative of progressivist historiography which had made the middle class the protagonist of the people's struggle against monopolistic capitalism. From his pen, middle class did not emerge as a mark of capitalism's crisis of legitimation. It appeared instead as a socially dominant subject whose political revolt through the farmer-labour party would radicalise the New Deal by removing the danger of fascism and communism from the nation. While critising the measures of the Democratic

---

39   His references also included the works of 'technocrats': Perlman 1928; Chase 1932a; Chase 1933; Chase 1934; Ackerman 1933; Loeb 1933; Rugg 1933.

administration, Bingham maintained that Roosevelt had won the White House
thanks to the votes of the middle class and that the New Deal defined a 'politics
oriented to the middle class'. The political objective was then to overcome the
limit business had placed on its reforming action in order to solve the crucial
issue of the depression: the substitution of the market with a 'planned and
ordered mechanism' of the distribution of wealth. This was the political position of US radicalism against the communist propaganda on the middle class.
The insistence on the 'militant strike action' had to be rejected in order to support a mobilisation of the middle class in an exclusively electoral key or within
a political and institutional horizon that did not sacrifice democracy in any
way but instead radicalised liberalism. The formation of farmer-labour parties in different midwestern states thanks to the initiatives of the progressive
Robert La Follette and the Non-Partisan League linked to various trade unions
of the AFL had to be consolidated on the national level by excluding the communists: the 'historic mission of the working class' had to be overturned into
the mission of a 'specifically American' subject because – as emphasised in a
review of *Insurgent America* which appeared in *The New Republic* – it did not
define a class, but rather a 'state of mind' which denied class struggle (Bingham
1935: 4–5, 182–203, 223–227).[40]

Corey's collaboration with *New Masses* took place in this polemic framework. In the December 1935 issue, the magazine published a long review of
The Crisis. David Ramsey – a writer from the Party's official newspaper, *The
Communist* – recommended the book as essential reading for comprehending
the role of the lower middle class in the crisis of capitalism. Not only because
it provided a 'factual verification' of the Marxist analysis, but also because it
rejected the anti-communist political positions of Dewey and Bingham: class
struggle could not be abolished on paper by appealing to an indeterminate
public. The review was followed by the decision of the Party to distribute the
book in a special issue of *New Masses* edited by a committee chaired by Corey
himself (Ramsey 1935a: 40–42). *Challenge to the Middle Class* – this was the
title of the April 1936 issue – took up themes and arguments from *The Crisis*.
It reconstructed the history of the middle class as a history of its proletarianisation and explained why professionals and white-collar workers went on
strike in different sectors – industrial and commercial, in public service and
culture – with numbers that over the previous two years had resulted in more
than 200 work stoppages involving 32 million workers. It also addressed the

40   On the New Deal as a political program oriented to the middle class, Bingham referred to
      Lindley 1933. Cf. Correspondence: Revolt in the Middle West 1935; Lovett 1936; Against a
      Labor Party, 1936, 716.

'black middle class' by claiming that emancipation from segregation and racism depended on the structural link between capitalism and the colour line. The article signed by Corey, *The Minds of the Middle Class*, finally challenged the national conviction that the United States did not have class consciousness: the supposed 'middle-class mentality' of the nation was a 'myth in decay'. Since the policies of the New Deal favoured the process of economic concentration ('trustification') which destroyed property and small businesses, as they imposed humiliating conditions in order to have access to assistance measures that lowered the standard of living, the only possible alternative was 'the unity of the working class of mental and manual workers' into a new labour party. Only in this perspective would an appeal to the middle class not contribute to the 'tragedy of the New Deal'. In other words, only in this perspective would it be possible to overcome the 'dramatic stalement' of the New Deal: the New Deal 'politically represented the middle class', but the middle class 'psychologically immobilised' the reforming action of the New Deal (Challenge to the Middle Class 1936).[41]

Following this line, until the 1938 mid-term elections, several articles polemicised against Bingham. In a review published in *Marxist Quarterly*, Corey himself criticised his radicalism as a theory of no classes which constituted a 'retreat to reaction'. *New Masses* instead denounced his alarmism, which considered the widespread 'anti-Nazi sentiment' a 'weapon in the hands of the Soviet foreign office'. His idea of production-for-use was also liquidated as an amenity that said nothing about black and white working conditions. The national platform of the famer-labour party approved at the 1935 Chicago conference, from which the Communist Party was excluded, was finally judged vague and senseless, an expression of the desire 'to tear a third party from its working-class base' (Corey 1937: 135; Bingham vs. Common Sense, 1937, 11).[42]

The controversy reached its peak with the 1936 electoral campaign when, at the end of May, the communist secretary Browder was invited to the second conference in Chicago which was deserted by Bingham and the proponents of his project for this reason. However, the outcome of the votes in November made the political clash for a third party pointless because it highlighted the growing difficulties. This was not so much due to divergences between radicals

---

41   The special issue collects various articles, among which we point out Ramsey (10–11); Corey (15–16); Van Kleeck (12, 39–40); Magil (18); Burnshaw (19–20); Miller (20–21); Buchanan (21–22); Gorman (26); Rochester (31–33); Freeman (35–37). Cf. Stolber and Winton 1935: 4–48, 82.

42   See also Ramsey 1935b: 7, 39–40; Editorial 1935: 4; Freeman 1936a: 27–28; Magil 1938a: 10; Magil 1938b: 17. Cf. Buhle 1995: 133–143; Sylvers 1989: 235–236.

and communists as it was due to Roosevelt's overwhelming electoral victory, which reflected a politicisation of society without precedent. The unionisation of employees and professionals could also be considered as a sign of their alignment with the working class, but this did not imply any significant electoral shift. It was rather the Democratic Party which took the institutional position of a Party rooted in the industrial and urban areas of the country, as well as the south. On the one hand, the formation of the new union of the CIO challenged Democrats to nominate strongly liberal candidates, effectively nullifying the hypothesis of a Labour Party. On the other, the conservative reaction and the old-fashioned liberal insisted on the rhetoric of a public shocked by the strikes, fuelling anxieties and divisions in a middle class that could thus not act as a subject of radicalism.[43] If in November 1936 the majority of professionals and low and mid-level employees had voted for Roosevelt in a percentage similar to that of skilled and semi-skilled workers, the intensification of the militant action of the strike, the return of economic depression with the sit-down strike of capital, i.e., with the blocking of investments and the institution of a Congressional Committee on Un-American Activities contributed to a growing sentiment of the 'fear of labor violence': in the 1938 mid-term elections, although it did not overturn the Democratic majority, the Republican Party regained eighty seats in the House, eight in the Senate, and thirteen Governors thanks to the vote of the middle and upper sections of the middle class. Between the end of December and the beginning of the war, the exhaustion of the reforming action of the New Deal coincided with the end of the battle for the middle class. Those who had animated it embraced New Deal liberalism, abandoning not only the hypothesis of a third party, but also their radical or communist rhetoric, in favour of a political discourse in which the middle class no longer referred to a composite and active social force which was politically disputed for this reason.[44]

In August 1937, Bingham signed a *Common Sense* editorial calling on progressivist forces to support Roosevelt as a bloc, rejecting the project of a third party (Bingham 1937).[45] Corey instead distanced himself from the Communist

---

43   The Sit-Down 1937: 343; Is the Sit-Down Unfair? 1937: 32–33; Can They Unseat the Sitters?
       1937: 18; Unions Add White-Collar Members 1937: 39–40; Gallup 1937; Headlines Proclaim
       the Rise of Fascism and Communism in America 1937: 19–26; Lapin 1937: 7; Lerner
       1937: 234–235; Capital's Sit-Down Strike 1937: 59–60; White 1937: 160–162; White-Collar
       Union Drive 1939: 21; White Collar Unions on their Way 1939: 30–31; Magil 1940: 7; White-
       Collar Dilemma 1941: 40.
44   Cf. Lovin 1971; Brinkley 1996: 3–7, 30, 160–163; Vaudagna 1986: 379–380; Leuchtenburg
       1976: 223–250; Ottanelli 1991: 98–129.
45   Cf. Warren 1966.

Party just two months after the publication of *Challenge to the Middle Class*. The decision, probably due to differences with the editors, signalled the mounting disillusionment with a Party that, in his view, despite the politics of the popular front, was unable to embrace democracy and integrate its vision with the various reformist voices of the New Deal. Actually, as a commentator in the *New York Times* had noted, his departure was already filtered through the lines of *The Crisis*, where the transformation of society was connected less to the mass action of the working class and more insistently to the reforming role that progressivist historiography attributed to the middle class. His original Marxism was adapted to the pragmatism that reaffirmed the exceptionality of a historically prosperous and wealthy nation. Although it constituted a new proletariat, professionals, technicians, and employees were nevertheless expressions of collective forms of production and distribution which only the government could have achieved in a 'new social order'. Middle class no longer embodied the private and public bureaucracies of state capitalism, but rather had become 'the great architect of democracy' which allowed the acceptance of the technocratic vision of the social sciences. Consequently, his pen no longer pointed towards the decline of capitalism as a social relation of domination over labour: interpreting capitalism's crisis of legitimation as a crisis of the middle class gradually turned his attention away from the workers' mobilisation. In this way, after the non-aggression pact between Hitler and Stalin which declared the 'end of the American left', Corey entered into the composite group of intellectuals, social scientists, planners, and technocrats engaged in the public work of consolidating the New Deal through its institutional and ideological isolation from the social conflict which had marked the decade (Chamberlain 1935; Lerner 1940: 164–166; Corey 1945).[46]

At the beginning of 1940, following a public and academic debate initiated by an article in which Max Lerner – columnist at *The New Republic* who had worked on the *Encyclopaedia of the Social Sciences* – indicated the underestimation of the 'strength of the middle class' among the 'errors of Marxism', Corey published a series of articles entitled *Marxism Reconsidered*, where he criticised different revolutionary and reformist theories of Marxism for not having understand that their 'emphasis on the proletariat alienated the middle classes' (Lerner 1938: 37–38; Corey 1940a; Corey 1940b; Corey 1940c).[47] Still more

---

46   In 1941, Corey was among the founders of the Union for Democratic Action along with the socialist theologian Reinhold Niebuhr and the union leader Philip Randolph. Cf. Buhle 1995: 127–160; Gillen 1987.

47   Cf. Harris 1939: 328–356. Corey's theses were contested in the columns of the same magazine by the anti-Stalinist Marxist Shachtman 1940a; Shachtman 1940b; Shachtman 1940c; and also on *New Masses*: Landy 1940: 22–26.

122

importantly, in 1941 he contributed to the publication of *Whose Revolution?*, a volume in which intellectuals from different spheres of the socialist, Stalinist, and Trotskyist left closed the polemic between reformism, radicalism, and Marxism by indicating in the 'future course of liberalism' a definitive and unequivocal answer to the question of revolution. The dialogue opened from the political question that James Burnham had announced in *The Managerial Revolution*, the 1941 book which marked the end of his Trotskyist militancy and the beginning of his conservative path. Since the transformation of capitalism into a 'managerial society' implied increasing 'state control' in the hands of administrative groups which precluded the possibility of government both by the masses of people guided by the ideal of classlessness and by the militant proletariat for communism, how would it be possible to preserve democracy in a state that, by integrating the social forces administratively, became tendentially totalitarian'? (Burnham 1941: 188–217)[48]

Those who had animated the battle against the middle class responded in unison to this question. According to Bingham, the answer lay in the 'Technology of Democracy'. If the 'place of experts' in the new 'governmental functions' of social welfare and social security was problematic because the 'cult of a technical elite' fed 'totalitarianism', in order to avoid the 'sacrifice of democracy' it was not enough to appeal to the free exercise of suffrage and freedom of opinion. It was instead necessary to make 'economic planning' a 'democratic method' by integrating the plurality of groups which made up the middle class into the decision-making process of governmental agencies: from commercial and industrial entrepreneurship organisations to worker and employee unions, from agricultural associations to consumer cooperatives. The 'managerial society' of capitalism would thus be compatible with a 'great extension of democracy under the New Deal' (Bingham 1941: 43–45, 56–59, 72).

While Bingham pointed to the future of liberalism in the agreement between the technocracy of the social sciences and middle-class democracy to moderate the potentially conservative note emerging from the managerial society, Corey combined liberalism and democracy in order to institutionally and ideologically reinforce the scientific foundations of the New Deal. Since communism had degenerated into 'its opposite', i.e., 'totalitarianism', and Marxism was 'dead' as a 'progressive social force', the void that the proletariat (as that subject promoting a 'new social order') had left in US history was occupied by a middle class largely immune to syndicalism and socialism. Within the 'great middle class' that public statistics predicted in constant growth, the

---

48   Cf. Borgognone 2000; Borgognone 2015.

groups with 'managerial, technical, and professional competence' not only played a technical function in production, but also a social function of governing: their position being transversal to private and public bureaucracies, they constituted a new 'ruling class' which made it possible to implement a plural, balanced, and moderate politics of planning through the administrative integration of the institutional forces of capital and the union. As a historic project for the middle class, the New Deal constituted a new social pact. It successfully regulated union action in collective bargaining while guaranteeing the autonomy of businesses in the organisation of labour for profit, directed economic collectivism towards 'production for welfare', without sacrificing the free market and free enterprise, balanced production and consumption making abundance possible. Corey ended his initial vision of worker self-action as a key to interpreting and changing US history with these words:

> The workers? The workers remain workers in any conceivable new order of the immediate future ... What workers need is democracy and freedom. They need economic opportunity and security, and abundance of the material things of life, the leisure to cultivate personality. They need a system of universal higher education that will break the monopoly of technical-professional talents ... In the realization of those conditions is the emancipation of the proletariat.
>
> COREY 1941: 249–252, 256–273. See also COREY 1945: 84

The conclusion of the ideological battle for the middle class thus coincided with its change in meaning: middle class no longer indicated a social force to be activated in the workers' mobilisation or in the constitution of a third party for a new social order, whether radical or socialist, but instead became a functional figure to the technical governing of capital. If after the 1929 crash, the middle class had returned to the fore in light of capitalism's crisis of legitimation, and if during the decade it was at the centre of a social and political clash that had followed and fuelled class struggle, during World War II its polemical and contested content would fade and be replaced with politically unequivocal meaning that the social sciences of New Deal liberalism assigned to it. Not only the statistical and economic science which guided the administrative policies and actions, but also the political science of behaviourism called upon in order to shape public opinion. Because it embodied the pragmatic vision of technocracy while conjugating liberalism and democracy in a shared public discourse, middle class would function as a political concept that allowed the social sciences to exercise that governing authority which during progressivism had not found an adequate foundation in the public.

5   The Middle Class as Political Concept

The change in meaning that the middle class took on in the political and public debate was not, however, fulfilled in the alignment of the different voices
of the Left who supported the New Deal. The battle over the middle class
remained open on the terrain of the unionisation of white-collar labour. In
1941 the militant workers of the CIO, among whom Communist influence was
still strong, organised a series of unauthorised production blockages which
questioned the no-strike pledge agreement between the government and
unions in order to safeguard the war economy. The cycle of wildcat strikes in
1943 and 1944 was followed in 1946 with a new strike wave that, while ensuring
a growing share of income for blue-collar labour, led to the approval of the
Taft-Hartley Act (1947) which restricted both the freedom to strike established
by the Wagner Act (1935) and led to an anti-communist campaign that at the
end of the decade led to the expulsion of the communists from the CIO. In this
social framework which was continually driven by the workers' mobilisation,
although the majority of white-collar workers remained excluded, the unionisation of professionals, technicians, and employees continued, particularly
through the United Office and Professional Workers of America, the union
established in 1937 with the fusion of the dozens of white-collar associations,
mostly women employed in the manufacturing, banking, and finance sections,
in several cities but above all the New York area.[49]

The experience of the UOPWA which reached 75,000 members in 1948 before
being expelled by the CIO due to the presence of communist militants was
important not only because for the first time it intended to organise employees
on the national level and not only by sector or profession, but also because it
was considered exemplary of the possibility that the lower middle class could
be unionised with a double perspective: broadening the gains (wage increases,
reduction in working hours, paid holidays, seniority of service) that skilled
and semi-skilled labour had obtained, while also organising a political bloc
against the moderate forces which dominated the Democratic Party during
Truman's presidency. While the business magazines reacted to the 'worry for
the capacity of office workers to stop production' by countering their 'class
prejudice ... the sense of superiority' over manual labour which characterised
the majority of intellectual labour (White-Collar Drive 1944: 104–105; White
Collar Woe 1946: 100–104; A Union Target, 1948, 88–94; Stessin 1946a: 16–18;

---

49   The growth of white-collar unions occurred only during the war and immediately follow-
      ing it. In 1935 and 1939, the percentage of registered employees was 5% and 7% respec-
      tively. In 1948, it climbed to 16%. See Kocka 1980: 206–236.

Stessin 1946b: 19),[50] the president of the UOPWA Lewis Merrill publicly intervened with pamphlets and in columns of *New Masses*. Against the 'reactionary
ballyhoo' of business, he argued that the clash between blue- and white-collar
was overcome by the new working and social conditions of professionals and
employees. Since their work was increasingly 'depersonalised' by the introduction of office machines and the inflationist spiral of the war economy depleted
their wages, the moment was at hand for a 'mass swing by salaried workers to
the labour movement':

> What is the point of speaking these white-collar workers as middle class?
> They are middle class neither by test of income level nor by the much
> more reliable test of their relationship to the means of production. They
> may *think* they are middle class ... but that is a misconception which the
> union should help correct.
>
> MERRILL 1944: 21[51]

This class misunderstanding was at the centre of unprecedented empirical
research in the social sciences which began from the ideological battle Corey
had launched with the publication of *The Crisis*. In 1937 Robert and Helen Lynd
published an updated version of their research which had been carried out in
the mid-1920s in Muncie, Indiana, a manufacturing city considered exemplary
of the national process of industrialisation, particularly in glass processing,
foundries, and parts of the automotive industry. *Middletown in Transition* –
this is the title of the volume – blended statistical analysis with methods of
participatory observation and investigation techniques derived from cultural
anthropology in order to contest the Marxist vision of the proletarianisation
of the middle class. The result of the new research showed how the depression had accelerated the mechanisation of production by replacing the qualifications of mechanic skill with machine operators which erased the distance
between skilled and unskilled labour. Although the federal census considered
these figures as semi-skilled labour, the loss in skill and control of the work
that the assembly line brought intensified competition by pushing down the
average wage. During the depression workers accepted any job under any conditions simply to remained employed. At the same time, the percentage of

---

50   Cf. Shlakman 1951/1952.
51   See also Starch in the White Collar 1943: 20–21; White Collar Problem? 1944: 21; Merrill
     1943: 29; Merrill 1941: 14; Merrill 1944: 9–11; and Merril 1946: 15. Merrill's pamphlets and
     other UOPWA materials and documents can be found at United Office and Professional
     Workers of America Records, Tamiment Library NYU.

the self-employed population dropped drastically, while the number of professionals who distributed their knowledge as salaried employees increased. While it was increasingly difficult for workers to march for promotion, for professionals the opportunity of bossing oneself was disappearing (Lynd and Lynd 1965: 64–72).

Although described in a way not different from *The Crisis*, this economic transformation that led to the formation of an upper class of businessmen was not understood in terms of proletarianisation. While in the first edition of *Middletown*, society appeared dominated by the modern American culture of individualism which found confirmation in the opportunities of 'rising from the bottom' through work ethic and the morality of consumption, the second edition registered a blockage of upward mobility in order to describe which statistical semantics were employed. Middle class appeared to describe the growing tension between a residual ownership class and a new, employee class divided up into highly skilled and paid salary workers and an impoverished lower middle class: because intellectual work was increasingly provided in exchange for salary, the culture of the classless society no longer found correspondence in economic reality. Yet, contrary to what Corey had argued by speaking of the nightmare of the depression, the American dream had 'a much slower course of time'. Even if business had feared 'that union organised labour would enter politics by supporting the Democratic Party *en masse* or by constituting a new party', there was no 'marked sign of crystalizing class status'. The 'personal resentment' had not embraced a 'militant' cause, but on the contrary, it had exacerbated racial and religious divisions which slowed down the threads of class solidarity. The failure of the Muncie workers to act *en masse* against the anti-union, open-shop policy of business, as well as their limited support for a third party in 1936, were proof of this. Above all, the interviews collected between workers and employees showed the solidity of the psychological wall which prevented the identification of the middle class with the working class. Thanks also to the assiduous public commitment of business, which through radio and the press reaffirmed the 'doctrine of opportunity' and the 'faith in the rising standard of living', the average US city remained anchored to the traditional values of the common man: his honesty and kindness, his work ethic and will to succeed, his faith in progress characterising the 'common sense' which saw no divergence in interest between capital and labour: 'capital is simply the accumulated savings of these intelligent and industrious people with foresight'. As an editorial in the local newspaper stated, 'the sovereign authority rested with a great middle class ... the great obstacle to revolution' (Lynd and Lynd 1965: 358–369, 403–410, 446–447, 456–457, 473).

Robert and Helen Lynd thus did not maintain that the middle class was a 'split personality', they did not emphasise its 'psychological alignment' with a working class that appeared endowed with rudimentary class consciousness. Consequently, since no ideological transformation of the middle class into the proletariat was happening, the depression did not entail the decline of capitalism under the gait of class struggle, but rather a 'cultural conflict' engulfing social groups and their values without questioning the economic and political institutions of democracy. The misunderstanding of class was in this sense faced by studying the cultural lag of the middle class, according to the expression coined by the Chicago sociologist William Ogburn (1922). The lack of congruence between mental habit and material condition caused a resistance to institutional change which, without an adequate adjustment of social behaviour, could break the relations that held society together. Lynd – who, like Ogburn distanced himself from the first New Deal because he believed that its policies did not respond to the 'consumer public' – therefore subordinated the social question emerging from the workers' mobilisation to the cultural problem of the middle class, emphasising the moral destruction of its habits. In this way, while it signalled the difficulty of adaptation, the cultural lag indicated the middle road that the social sciences should have taken between the economistic conception of the middle class that fuelled the Marxist vision of proletarianisation and the national culture of the classless society. The future of American democracy obviously did not pass through the revolution of communism, nor even through the planning invoked by radicalism. The new political and administrative structure that the New Deal imposed on democracy needed to be culturally consolidated by shortening 'the distance between the symbolic universe and the pragmatic universe' through the promotion of associative activities aimed at civic education, communitarian organisation, and political participation (Lynd and Lynd 1965: 490, 503–510).[52]

Middletown was the first work of empirical research to employ middle class as an organisation category of sociological analysis in order to moderate the polemical meaning that the public reference to class had assumed with social conflict: the middle class had to be defined outside of the economic data of occupation in order to consider the cultural variables of community, racial,

---

52   Cf. Seidelman 1985: 146–148; Pells 1973: 25–32; Gordon 1958: 63–84. Between 1933 and 1934, Ogburn and Lynd served on the Consumers' Advisory Board of the National Recovery Administration, and then resigned in controversy due to the lack of consumer representation and policies. See the documents, correspondence, and articles collected in the Robert Staughton Lynd Papers, 1933–1945, which are held in the Rare Books & Manuscripts archive of the Butler Library at Columbia University.

and religious belonging. This methodological and interpretive indication was taken up in a series of scientific publications which, however, offered different answers. Even in the first half of the 1940s, the sociological analysis of industrial relations revealed a 'growing class consciousness' which, matured through unions and collective bargaining, changed the social relation underlying the 'democratic process'. Even the research that presented a 'psychological approach' to the study of conflict drawing on the pioneering analyses of worker psychopathologies conducted at the end of the 1920s by Elton Mayo (1933) registered that, while engineers and professionals reacted to the workers' mobilisation by siding with business, teachers, professors, employees, and office workers displayed a favourable attitude towards the union. Although the 'class lines' were by no means 'sharp' as publicly portrayed, labour and capital constituted the 'clearest opposed classes' which attracted different middle-class groups towards opposing poles of society (Kornhauser 1939: 199–264; Bakke 1940: 86–105).

A similar conclusion finally emerged from the monumental research that Lloyd Warner and his study group took up with the Committee of Industrial Physiology at Harvard University, carried out in two different cities, one in New England (Yankee City Series, 1941–1949) and one in the Midwest (Democracy in Jonesville, 1949). In both, it emerged once again how the mechanisation of work obstructed the 'social mobility' which held together 'the very fabric of the American dream'. Differently than Lynd's contention, Warner emphasised the national reach of the workers' mobilisation. In the summary volume published in 1953 with the significant title *American Life: Dream and Reality*, Warner maintained that the 'great faith Americans once had in the leadership of businessmen' had not been completely restored due to the persistent 'worker hostility' witnessed in the significant number of strikes and choice of the union by millions of workers, including employees. If 'social mobility' was the 'motivating force' of the ideal of the classless society, its blockage loosened the work ethic and morality of consumption by fuelling the 'political ideologies of classes' which made it difficult to accommodate labour within the middle class (Warner 1953: 126–127, 130, 141–143, 163–178).

Beyond the different interpretations of the conflict which depended on the nation's composite economic, racial, and religious geography, Warner and his school nevertheless took the middle road Lynd had opened. Social classes – and the middle class in particular – were not to be studied by exclusively classifying the labourer on the basis of property or occupation, income or consumption, education, or neighbourhood of residence. The subjective position of the labourer, i.e. the status that he himself perceived by participating in community life and the status that the community to which he belongs attributed to him, should be grafted onto this objective ground. In this way, it was possible to weaken the perception of the mobility block through interviews and questionnaires, despite the 'caste' of white America rigidly fixing the position of inferiority for the black minority. Recording, analysing, and classifying motivations and behaviours, judgments and values, made it possible to grasp the presence of a plurality of social groups (upper middle, lower middle, and upper lower) which made up a 'symbolic system' in which the middle class appeared as a 'non-economic class' or as a social formation independent of the labour relation, and for this reason capable of overcoming the class boundary that the workers' mobilisation had politicised (Warner 1953: 72–76, 80–90. See also Warner 1936: 234–237; Warner 1937: 278–279).[53]

In the decade between the 1930s and 1940s, empirical research thus shifted from an emphasis on the economy towards a sociological and psychological model of investigation thanks to which a new middle-class science was taking shape which carried out the unfinished research of progressivism. It was not a common and coherent scientific effort. The methodologies were different: the quantitative analysis of economic data which followed the direction of statistical and economic science, the participatory observation deriving from cultural anthropology, the qualitative study of the psychological adaptation of the worker, the social investigation through the instrument of the interview or questionnaire. The criteria of classification were also different – employment and income, education and consumption, community and personal assessment of social position – which led to the elaboration of complex indexes that, taking these dimensions together, moderated or denied the economic determination of class in order to rethink hierarchies of society in terms of standard of living, socioeconomic, social, or psychosocial status. What characterised this set of approaches, however, was not methodological confusion. This was not only because, between the 1940s and 1950s, the recovery of the Weberian separation of the distribution of social power between class, status, and party restored order in empirical research, helping to affirm the sociological study of social stratification as a specific academic discipline. It was also because what ensued was a convergent plural representation of society which took away the polemical content of the public reference to class (Pfautz 1953).[54]

---

53 Several criticisms of Warner were made, such as those by Charles Wright Mills, who denounced his conceptual confusion between class and status, or Lipset and Bendix who criticised the thesis of the block on vertical mobility: unionisation was not the sign of the lack of trust Americans had in the dream of mobility, but instead the possibility of accessing mobility through other means – collective rather than individual. See Mills 1942; Lipset and Bendix 1951. Cf. Gordon 1958: 62–73.

54 Cf. Gordon 1958: 4–15, 406; Grimes 1991: 17–19, 87–96.

When not broken down into the internal groups of upper and lower, classes disappeared from the scientific vocabulary. In the attempt to overcome the fragmentation of empirical research by providing a shared reading of the depression which rejected the Marxist vision of proletarianisation, the analytic approach to social stratification of Talcott Parsons' sociological school banned the term class in order to restore the legitimation of capitalism after its major failure: the term strata conceptually expressed the dissolution of the working class and the adjective social summed up the multidimensional criteria which neutralised the politicisation of society by representing capitalism as an 'evanescent phenomenon', that is, as something deprived of meaning for understanding the power running through society. In this specific sense, in *The Structure of Social Action* (1937), Parsons affirmed the absolute primacy of values over the economic determination of social action. Still more importantly, although the working class vanished in the stratification of roles and functions which reproduced society as an ordered system, the continued presence of hostility in manual and intellectual labour led to the scientific study of the middle class as a political concept: as a 'symbol of identification' which made it possible to culturally translate the hierarchical position determined by the labour relation into a social position that – as Robert Merton effectively synthesised with reference to the empirical research analysed above – rejected a possible 'deviate behaviour' in order to favour adaptable behaviour or behaviour capable of 'transcending class lines' (Merton 1938: 680).[55]

Along the middle road opened with the study of the average US city, through a methodological and conceptual refinement matured in the disciplines of cultural anthropology, social psychology, and systematic sociology, the new science of the middle class thus represented society outside of the uncertain and unstable terrain of class struggle. In this way it provided essential scientific knowledge for carrying out the historic project of the construction of the middle class that statistical and economic science had outlined through quantitative analysis for the elaboration of New Deal policies, without however addressing the cultural problem of its behaviour. The tension existing between the American dream and economic reality was not resolvable exclusively through reforms aimed at increasing opportunities for social mobility, improving working conditions and increasing consumption capacity. It was necessary to resolve the cultural lag of the middle class in order to scrub out the class ideologies from society which prevented the union of liberalism and

---

55   See also Parsons 1937; Parsons 1940; Parsons 1993: 101–130; Parsons 1967: 234; Kingsley and Moore 1945. On the Weberian normalization of the US scientific literature on social classes: Gerth and Mills 1946; Henderson and Parsons 1947. Cf. Brick 2006: 121–145.

democracy: as a political concept, middle class thus had to take on an ideological character which unified and shaped the different types of workers in terms of the legitimation of capitalism and the technical governing of capital.

This perspective clearly emerged in Harold Lasswell's 'policy science for democracy', in his scientific work and his institutional engagement in the federal agencies responsible for public communication during the war. Considered the main proponent of the 'behavioural revolution' that transformed political science into a 'study of power' by affirming a multidisciplinary approach which integrated the traditional science of government with methodologies that analysed the psychopathologies of personality and the propaganda of political elites, Lasswell had begun a theoretical reflection on the middle class in light of the rise of Nazism starting in the early 1930s.[56] In *Psychology of Hitlerism* (1933) and in other essays, he argued that economic depression, the affirmation of the 'upper bourgeois' and the mobilisation of the working class had impoverished the German middle class 'materially' and 'psychologically'. The social groups that made it up had quickly undergone an unexpected process of proletarianisation. The resulting 'personal insecurity' and the fear of the 'dictatorship of the proletariat' had prompted them to embrace the 'symbols of identification' agitated for by Nazi propaganda: nationalism, imperialism, racism, and antisemitism provided a 'social reward' for which 'a lowered standard of living was but a sacrifice to the cause of national resurrection'. A deep connoisseur of German scientific literature for the long period of his doctoral and post-doctoral study in Europe in the 1920s, Lasswell thus recovered the Weimar sociology on the middle class. Although the European spectre of fascism did not seem to have taken hold in the United States, he took up the scientific challenge this research had left as its legacy. Since the *Mittelstand* had not provided adequate knowledge to prevent capitalism from resorting to the order of Nazism, the brutal European rupture of the historical liberal nexus between middle class and democracy was also on the overseas agenda: what would be the 'psychological reaction of the middle classes'? If the proprietary middle class no longer constituted the social foundation of liberalism and the new employee class was contested by the 'world revolutionary propaganda' which insisted on the identification on the proletariat, the demand for equality and the expectation of a communist society without classes, it was urgent to scientifically outline and publicly affirm a new 'ideology' of the middle class

---

56   Easton 1950: 450–477; Eulau 1968; Rogow 1969; McDougal and Reisman 1979; Farr, Hacker and Kazee 2006: 579–587. See also the introductions by Dwaine Marvick to Lasswell's semantic science and Mario Stoppino on the science of power, contained respectively in Lasswell 1977 and Lasswell and Kaplan 1950.

and for the middle class in favour of the democracy of New Deal liberalism (Lasswell 1933a: 374; Lasswell 1933b: 68–93, 78–79; Lasswell 1950: 39–51, 133–137, 255–256).[57]

Convinced that the 'future of Marxism as the principal unifying myth may depend on its capacity to win the middle classes', Lasswell faced this challenge by drawing on statistical semantics and inserting himself into the methodological groove traced by empirical research. In *The Moral Vocation of the Middle-Income Skill Group* (1935), he explained that in the United States the small agricultural, manufacturing, and commercial entrepreneur, the skilled and semi-skilled worker, the public and private employee had historically failed to act and speak as middle class because they had not developed a 'common name'. They were 'tragically fragmented' between proprietary and professional figures who remained 'faithful to the vocabulary of individualism' and 'the new elements ... affiliated with the labor movement'. This cultural lag that historically dated back to the turn of the century had not found a solution in progressivism. Theodore Roosevelt and Woodrow Wilson had failed in their call for unity between brain work and hand work. Their policies had not only consolidated the dependence of the middle class on monopolistic capital. They had also increased an unpopular statist character of American democracy. Even New Dealism would have failed if it had not defined a 'common body' of symbols. The danger was the ideological polarisation of national politics between the worrying spread of 'Marxist symbolism' and the 'waves of indignation' that embraced, also with a 'fascist attitude', the traditional symbols of demand of individual freedom and free enterprise, economic competition, and equality of opportunity. For this reason, the construction of the middle class not only passed through a 'common politics' that facilitated social mobility (Lasswell 1935: 127–137, 128–129; Lasswell 1950: 232–233).[58]

Lasswell explained that the New Deal favoured 'job security' and the 'moderation of income'. Progressive income taxation, the insurance of private savings and the facilitation of access to credit, unemployment and old-age benefits, the planning of public works and other legislative measures were all going in the direction of consolidating confidence in the democracy of 'intermediate groups' because they reduced personal insecurity. Nonetheless, he still considered the 'psychological problem' determined by the absence of a common awareness of their material condition. Lasswell therefore not only recognised the impossibility of the economic unity of the middle class, but also

---

57   Cf. Merriam 1939: 192–193; Pendleton Herring 1940: 48–57; Holcombe 1940.
58   Cf. Stagner 1935: 309–319.

registered its 'split personality' by questioning the consequences on 'national politics': would the middle class acquire political unity and independence? Would social conflict be guided and moderated in this way? Would the workers' mobilisation be led towards democracy, or would it instead fall prey to the ideology of classes? These questions were not answered in society. Although at first he thought of empirically verifying the presence of a 'movement of the middle class', the folder in his research archive dedicated to this question remained empty. The answers were then sought in the possibility of inducing the awareness of being middle class in order to 'psychologically' emancipate the intermediate groups from the 'class politics' of the working class and 'big business' (Lasswell 1937: 298–313, 306–307).

To place the middle class at the centre of national politics, Lasswell shifted attention away from workers and employees and toward the experts who, by virtue of their scientific authority, could assume the responsibility of planning within federal agencies, and organising in public opinion, a message aimed at encouraging a process of identification in the middle class. The future of American democracy did not pass in this sense through civic and community associations or union and party participation. Since these collective forms were not impervious to the class partiality, insecurities, and psychopathologies that destabilised the New Deal had to be resolved by expanding the technical governing of capital beyond the economy. To this end, empirical research also had to be extended beyond the statistical, economic, and sociological study of the working class. The imposing research that Lasswell conducted during the depression on the Communist Party in the Chicago workers' movement – which he considered the *Middletown* of the 'world revolutionary propaganda' – demonstrated that the spread of the 'symbolism of Marxism' had been limited by persistent 'Americanism'. The historical symbolic set of American nationalism was still an expression of the confidence of the population – particularly the rank and file of the middle class – in individualism, market freedom and social mobility, in constitution and the law, in the Republican or Democratic Party, in the plurality of religious and ethnic communities. Nonetheless, although 'communism' did not seem to 'conquer America' through 'one of the most important industrial cities in the world', it was urgent to record, classify, and spread the words that potentially constituted the symbolic equipment that a fully developed 'middle class consciousness' required (Lasswell and Blumenstock 2012: 301–358).

Among these words, the reference to the 'social skill' of the middle class was essential. Skill did not only define the occupational classification criteria that allowed public statistics to elaborate its prognosis, but also provided the 'essential key' for resolving the 'psychological problem' of the middle class because it valued the 'greatest sacrifice middle-income Americans had made'. The social position they gained by studying and working hard did not respond to mere economic interest but carried with it a 'socially useful skill': the ethics of sacrifice should not be considered exclusively functional to personal success because it also constituted a 'moral duty' for which the labourer – whether manual or intellectual – was responsible to society. The economic depression in this sense was represented as a 'crisis of insecurity' determined by the inability of groups to obtain, use, and control their skills. The 'political destiny of the middle class' was therefore to re-moralise society by regaining the initiative for 'social justice' and depriving the proletariat of its historical task. Moralising was not simply what fell to the lot of the middle class, because the ultimate goal of the initiative was to affirm the middle class as destiny of the nation. In this way it would be possible to reconstruct, from the decline of capitalism, a skill society in which the balance between 'hard work' and 'social rewards' would prevent the consolidation of the power of a single social group, the working class or the 'plutocracy' of capital:

> Fully developed skill consciousness requires a common name, a common outlook, a common program. Such symbols would constitute the political mythology of the skill groups: we would call part of it their utopia when they are struggling for control; we would call it their ideology when they are in control.
>
> LASSWELL 1937: 310–312[59]

During the war, Lasswell's institutional engagement in governmental agencies was therefore exemplary of the political goal of the new science of behaviourism: 'reinvigorating the myth of the historic mission of the middle class'. Social scientists and communication experts had to transform the utopia of government control into an ideology functional to the government of the *Democracy Through Public Opinion* (1941a). With this perspective, Lasswell directed the Experimental Division for the Study of War-Time Communications established by President Roosevelt at the Library of Congress. In collaboration with the Office of War Information and other nascent intelligence agencies, his main scientific work on print and radio sources was the *World Attention Survey*: the worldwide analysis of public opinion – including the United States – for the sake of registering and classifying symbols of claim and identification in order to control continuity and discontinuity in the behaviour of

---

59   See also Lasswell 1935: 130–131; Lasswell 1938: 438–439; Lasswell 1947.

populations in light of personal insecurity caused by the depression and the war. The study of internal and international propaganda was not only a pre-requisite to the knowledge of communist and Nazi ideologies in the war of ideas which ran through the second world war. It also served in the elabora-tion of a 'democratic propaganda': to avoid the clash between labour and cap-ital from again putting 'the survival of democracy' at risk, it was necessary to integrate the traditional 'contemplative attitude' of the social sciences with an unprecedented 'manipulative attitude' aimed at 'obtaining transformations in the patterns of reality'. Laswell applied behaviourism to government by prag-matically moving his science from a descriptive method that characterised the study of the propaganda of political elites to a prescriptive approach in the study of power[60] that the scientific elites could achieve by subjecting public opinion to what we could define as a psychological prophylaxis of the middle class: a preventative hygiene with which the political scientists as a 'therapist of politics' intended to cleanse democracy of extremism, although this public work involved its denigration into a political form without participation. In fact, what was at stake was not the mobilisation of the forces of manual and intellectual labour in a 'middle class movement', but rather the possibility of institutionalising a shared set of symbols in public opinion which would orient the population towards identifying in the middle class. The partialities of class were not to have part in the 'defence of democracy' (Lasswell 1941a: 61–70, 132–139, 170–176. See also Lasswell 1943: 43; Lasswell 1937: 4–10).[61]

In this sense, in addition to his institutional engagement, his public role as author and voice at the National Broadcasting Company was particularly important. As he explained in *Radio as an Instrument of Reducing Personal Insecurity* (1941), radio – which in 1940 counted 44 million listeners, mostly middle-income families to whom President Roosevelt spoke in first-person with the fireside chats – constituted an essential technology for democratic propaganda precisely because it allowed the insecurities of the middle class to be reduced. Through conferences and roundtables which guaranteed the democratic principle of free discussion, it was possible to shape and spread opinions by providing analyses aimed at overcoming the fears that troubled the average listener. To overcome the tension between the ideal and reality,

---

60 Ricciardi 2007.
61 The contradiction between scientism and democracy is widely debated in the historiog-raphy of the social sciences, not only in Lasswell: Eulau 1976; Eulau and Emor 1999: 75–89; Seidelman 1985: 134–145; Purcell, Jr. 1973: 189–194, 250–256; Bonazzi 1986; Gunnell 1993: 189–194; Smith 1994: 212–247; Brick 2006: 141–145; Sproule 1997: 178–271; Gary 1999; Haney 2008.

between ambition for success and material condition, it was necessary to appeal to the middle class as 'guardian' of Americanism (Lasswell 1941b).[62] To this end, in a series of radio broadcasts held between the spring of 1939 and winter of 1940, entitled *Human Nature in Action*, in homage to the British political scientist and pioneer of behaviourism Graham Wallas, Lasswell did not only describe the violent and imperialist character of European nationalism by making reference to its racial nature. In addition to this, he also argued that Americanism, as a 'political nationalism' built on the sharing of the universal symbol of freedom, constituted a democratic bulwark against the advance of fascism, Nazism, and communism due to its ascendant middle class. *The Man of the Future* – this was the title of the final episode on 17 December 1940 – would be the 'man of the middle class'. If it was undeniable that the depression had spread disillusion and frustration, public communication had to subvert the perception of reality:

> The world of tomorrow can learn how to run a machine society with regularity ... Then men and women can be less frequently provoked into destructiveness. We can develop new codes of living ... these could be by a great middle class ... the balance wheel of society – neither rich neither poor, but just comfortable, and not jealous of great fortunes and great wealth, nor in fear of poverty.[63]

The middle class was also the protagonist of a second radio series of round-tables. Among these, the most important was that of 18 July 1943, titled *War and Middle Class*, when, together with the democratic politician Walter Johnson and the economist Peter Drucker (considered the theorist of modern corporate management), Lasswell dismantled what he thought was a very widespread conviction, especially in the communist environment, according to which the war would have led to the definitive 'disintegration' of the middle class. The dialogue was constructed to persuade listeners that this conviction was a 'superstitious fallacy' that derived from the 'popular misconception' that matured during the depression about what the middle class was. The participants in the roundtable maintained that in the United States there was no middle class in the European sense of the term, because middle class was not an economic class defined by average income or a set of skilled

---

62   Cf. Goodman 2011.

63   The manuscripts of the radio broadcasts are held in the Harold Dwight Laswell Papers (MS 1043). Manuscripts and Archives, Yale University Library. BOX 109, 109A, 110. For more analysis, see Battistini 2013. Wallas 1908.

occupations. It was rather a 'state of mind', i.e., a democratic mentality that made possible a widespread sentiment of sympathy between individuals and towards the government. This 'psychology of the middle class' updated the Americanism at the time of the New Deal. It combined the traditional symbolism of individualism with a collective responsibility that, safeguarding the value of respect for oneself and others, weakened the political grip of class symbolism by determining a just social balance between capital and labour, government and society, public and private. Lasswell concluded the radio dialogue in this way:

> Gentlemen the most important thing that we have said about the relation between the middle classes and the war is that the war gives an opportunity to strengthen the middle classes ... You have noticed that we have pointed out that America is essentially a middle-class society ... That is the fundamental attitude that we want to maintain.
>
> JOHNSON, LASSWELL and DRUCKER 1943

While starting from the semantics of the occupations that statistical and economic science had developed to shape the New Deal as a historical project of the construction of the middle class, Lasswell thus recognised that the middle class did not exist as a statistical or economic datum deriving from the specific occupational condition determined by the technological development of capitalism. Rather it was to be thought as the historically uncertain result of a scientific and political struggle for democracy. For this reason, by retracing within the ideological battle over the middle class the 'movement of liberalism' from its traditional 'negative' objective to its new 'social' purpose, he considered it necessary to make a cultural advance towards the symbolic set of Rooseveltian 'freedom from want': job security and moderation of income, economic justice and collective responsibility must define the awareness of being middle class. Only in this way would the social conflict that marked the New Deal find its resting point in the ideology of the middle class, that is, through the 'enlightened' enterprise of the policy science of behaviourism. A political science for which communication specialists and experts were 'democratic guardians' of democracy emptied of its participatory character. Although it had deep roots in progressivism, this new science of the middle class for democracy had its historical reason in the intellectual and political urgency of responding to the question of revolution. Only by crossing the fault lines opened by the class struggle during the depression did the middle class become the main term of scientific vocabulary: an indispensable political concept to the definition of the liberal consensual order because it was capable of communicating a common sense of economic growth and civil progress, the possibility of success and social mobility, the affirmation of the public interest in a freely discussed way, of sharing a coherent national narrative of rational conquest of freedom and equality, of media construction of a democratic public opinion (Lasswell 1949, see also Katznelson 2003).

The Rise and Fall of a Fetish

The American middle class as a historical project of the New Deal was there-fore completed with the public affirmation of a policy science for democracy. Unlike what happened in Europe, where the middle classes reacted to the cri-sis of capitalism and the revolutionary pressures of communism by embrac-ing fascism and Nazism, in the United States the social sciences succeeded in the enterprise of renewing and restoring the liberal historical link between the middle class and democracy. While the European scientific literature, particularly in Germany following the collapse of the Weimar Republic, had denounced the lack of a collective ideology adequate to the heterogeneity of the intermediary groups of society, social sciences in the US formulated a sci-entific vocabulary, defined a political semantics and organised a public sym-bolism which, by broadening the base of the middle class, prevented a single social group – worker, employee, or owner – from claiming to be the only true holder of order: middle class presented itself with the persuasive force of a tendentially universal subject, which for this reason was capable of democrat-ically organising society.

   The social sciences of New Deal liberalism not only studied and denounced the precarious material condition of the middle class during the depression in the 1930s, but traced its occupational profile, consumption capacity, psy-chology, and social behaviour. Furthermore, they empirically defined and pub-licly communicated the value it brought, its political and electoral orientation. In this way, unlike the social sciences of progressivism, these social sciences understood that the middle class did not exist ready-made in society.[1] In other words, the middle class did not constitute a historical formation inherent in the presumed exceptionality of the United States over Europe. Nor did it naturally take shape from the organisational and technological specificity of American capitalism. Rather, it had to be socially and ideologically built within the material and symbolic horizon opened by social conflict. Consequently, a new classification of occupations was elaborated which was suitable for the formulation of a politics that arrested its decline and favoured its rise. A map of society increasingly more stratified according to skills, functions, and values, which rendered the social relation of labour indeterminate was not only drawn

---

1   Wacquant 1991.

up. The middle class was also built by means of public opinion, i.e., by defining and communicating an ideology consistent with the economic conditions
following the crisis of capitalism and adequate to the political and administrative structure of the New Deal state. The social sciences in this sense played a
constituent function for the middle class by forging the language of a complex
institutional network of government agencies, public and private universities,
foundations and media, business associations and union organisations. Their
empirical research, sociological and psychological analyses, their theoretical
reflection and their contribution to public communication initiated and nurtured a continuous social process of identification in the middle class which,
from the beginning of the 1940s, was constantly recorded in newspapers of different political orientations (liberal and conservative), and certified by opinion polls and research, and particularly published in the magazines *Fortune*
and *Life* by the great publisher Henry Luce, the voice of American capitalism.
While *The Nation* declared that 'Cold War psychology' favoured middle-class
attitudes even in union leaders, after publicly announcing the crisis of the
middle class, at the beginning of the 1950s *Harper's* magazine claimed that
the United States was back to being 'the last country in the world in which
the middle-class continues to play a strategic role in society' (American Labor
Today, 1955: 492; Hartley 1951: 46).[2]

In this way, the middle class was no longer only a scientific category aimed
at the empirical knowledge of society. As an ideology of the social sciences,
it assumed the role of a fetish which performed a mythopoietic function. In
other words, it constituted a symbolic object of mediation, to which the forces
of manual and intellectual labour attributed a quality – a social skill – which
was not immediately possessed in the labour relation, but which through public opinion offered the opportunity of symbolically dissolving the condition
of wage earners. Identification in the middle class allowed the fulfilment of
the historical democratic ideal of economic independence, social mobility,
and moral and political self-government which however in the capitalism of
the New Deal state was not realised through independent work as an instrument of self-rule, but rather despite its sacrifice. In this sense, after the depression in the 1930s, the middle class did not express the traditional anti-state
culture of national history, but manifested the unprecedented statism of the
government which, technically conducted through the social sciences, was

2 See also Jessup 1943: 105–106; White-Collar Man 1946: 124, 206; One Big Family. A Management
Chart 1949: 65–67; The Rich Middle-Income Class 1954: 98; Middle Class Strengthens
Economic Role 1956; Karsh 1959: 93–96; McGee 1959: 112. On the surveys that identified the
middle class: Centers 1949: 85 ff. On Henry Luce: Baughman 1987.

called to a coherent and continuous intervention in its favour. While statistical and economic science, with their quantitative study of labour, provided a knowledge adequate to the rise of the middle class through administrative action, their semantics of occupations, with which policies were communicated and polls and opinion surveys were conducted, equipped the government with the media instruments which were indispensable for consolidating democracy through public opinion. In particular, behaviourism, with its manipulative inclination, communicated the symbolic rise of the middle class by masking labour, i.e., by abstracting it from the hierarchical conditions that capital imposed. As a fetish, middle class acted in the present as a substitute that filled the social void caused by its historical absence that the crisis of capitalism had made evident. Not being empirically identifiable as a proprietary or professional unit, it existed as a fetish because it publicly provided 'symbolic capital' that performed a double historical function, both scientific and political (Bourdieu 2012).[3]

The scientific function of the fetish was to represent the American middle class as sociologically indeterminate. Unlike the history of the European middle classes, the American middle class did not identify a bourgeois class which embodied a hierarchy based on income secured by industrial, financial, and real estate property or by the status of public servant. Nor was it defined only by the labour relation, i.e., it was not exclusively a new employee class. On the contrary, the middle class indicated a composite social set, but precisely for this reason it was tendentially universal and thus capable of integrating not only small business, entrepreneurs, and professionals, but also those who provided skills and performed roles delegated to business management (manager, heads of departments in corporations, distribution, sales and marketing), those who fell into the lower ranks of office work (employees and assistants), and those who carried out manual, skilled, and semi-skilled labour. The unionised worker who, thanks to his high wage, shared not only an adequate level of income, education, and consumption (the 'American standard of living'), but also a common lifestyle (the 'American way of life') built on the image of the white family who owns a house in the suburbs with a male breadwinner and a woman responsible for the household economy centred on consumption. Through this scientific function of the representation of society, the fetish publicly affirmed the middle class in a politically determinate way. After the ideological battle which had run through it during the New Deal by postponing capitalism's crisis of legitimation until the threshold of the war, the meaning of

---

3   On the historical and political meaning of fetishism, see Mistura 2001.

the middle class could no longer be equivocal in terms of the new proletariat. Its political function was to overturn the perception of the class boundary into a new frontier which smoothed economic divisions and social divergences, even racial tensions, albeit in a way profoundly limited by segregation and racism. As the race riots during and after the war demonstrated, particularly but not only in Detroit, white worker and employee groups rose up against the housing policies with which the government attempted to include black people in the suburban areas of the white middle class. The poverty of the urban ghetto showed that the 'talented tenth' of African Americans had not led to the emancipation of racial communities united on the colour line, but rather to the formation of a black bourgeoisie separated by – and potentially in conflict with – black workers.[4] As a fetish which obfuscated the labour relation and its dependent character, middle class renewed (almost exclusively for the white population) the original American promise of emancipation from European misery, prescribing impartial social behaviour of the labour force, whether manual or intellectual. In this way, above all in 1950s scientific literature and public opinion, US society appeared normalised. Its transformation was not denied, but was deprived of any extreme, non-democratic meaning. In other words, it was assumed as a peculiar progressive character of national history contained in the field of the predictable. The fetishism of the middle class indicated in other words how to be, what to say, what to do to be part of the nation, what was legitimate or not, and what was American or un-American.[5]

With this double scientific and political function, in the postwar period the middle class became the epistemological foundation of the social sciences of Cold War liberalism – the economic, sociological, historical, and political sciences – which measured the exceptional US civilisation in its internal and international frontier. It defined the constitutive parameter of the classless

---

4   On the racial limit of the American middle class and the rise of a black bourgeoisie, at the beginning of the 1960s the African American sociologist Edward F. Frazier referred to the early twentieth century debate between W.E.B. Du Bois and Booker T. Washington on the 'talented tenth'. See Frazier 1962: 62–64. Cf. DuBois 1956. On racial confrontations during and after the war, see Sugrue 2005. As reported by both the African American and other press, class division emerged more and more clearly in the years of black nationalism: California Study Claim Middle-Class Negroes' Discontent Foments Riots 1967: 27; Negro Middle Class 1967; Rostin 1967; Preston 1967; Sloan 1967; Holsendolph 1969. Only at the end of the decade and the beginning of the 1970s, following the political initiative by President Richard Nixon aimed at favouring the formation of a black capitalism against the Black Power movement, did the press and scientific literature register the rise of a new black middle class: The Black Middle Class 1973; America's Rising Black Middle Class, 1974, 25–33; Weems and Randolph 2001.

5   On the promise of America and the progressive character of the nation, see Bonazzi 1974: 41–47.

society, a society in which the articulated social stratification removed conflict in favour of competition between social groups for the acquisition of skills and the distribution of resources within a framework of shared values. It constituted the measure of the liberal consensus which despite the 'paranoid style' of McCarthyism rendered American democracy immune from European extremism. It provided the anti-communist criterion for evaluating the modernisation of the rest of the world on the basis of US hegemony in the West. It indicated the undisputed protagonist of the historiography of consent. In this way, during the Cold War the social sciences claimed to render the power that marked the internal and international order of American capitalism evanescent, representing the middle class as a subject that is real because it is ideal, a figure transparent to the public, and therefore immediately recognisable, which US people reproduced as a national symbol of demand and identification of their personal and collective success. In this specific sense, middle class conferred new legitimacy to American capitalism.[6]

1   The Middle Class of Liberalism

All of this does not mean that the post-war American middle class was only an illusion. Its fetish was constantly producing material effects. Indeed, it was the expression of a historically determinate social formation because it was based on an economic model of production which, although originating in progressivism, was fully realised with the social contract tacitly stipulated by the New Deal between big business, big labour, and big government. From the beginning of the twentieth century, corporations had elaborated company policies which enabled the hiring of an increasing number of employees recruited from social groups – including women, minorities, and immigrants – who had acquired technical and professional skills thanks to reforms in the education system. They had also initiated employment stabilisation programmes, salary increases and a gradual, albeit limited, career option which would also be extended to manual labour, both skilled and semi-skilled. Only with the New Deal, after the anti-union attack in the second half of the 1920s and the depression had shaken the stabilisation that undoubtedly began during progressivism, were these company policies inscribed and refined into programmes that planned organised production on the basis of Taylorism and Fordism in

---

6   Schlesinger Jr. 1949; Bendix and Lipset 1953; Lerner 1957; Lipset 1963; Hofstadter 1966; Rostow 1960. Cf. Hodgson 1976; Mason and Morgan 2017; Pells 1985; Del Pero 2014; Ricciardi 2008.

favour of mass consumption. The reiterated conviction of business, for whom the increase in consumption made it possible to overcome the class boundary around which the social conflict moved, was finally confirmed in the overcoming of the autonomous forms of workers' mobilisation. During and after the war, under the aegis of big government as an indispensable contractor of the social contract, the union was integrated into the plan established by industrial relations. With the merger of the AFL and CIO into a single confederation in 1955, big labour renounced exercising forms of control over the process of work and the decision-making process of corporations, accepting the fact of consumption as the *passe-partout* for opening up worker and employee labour, with a white majority, onto the frontier of the middle class. Thus, a new era of organised labour was inaugurated in which the union leaders were, by their social attitude and lifestyle, members of the middle class. Underpinned in the immediate postwar period by social policies – particularly the Servicemen's Readjustment Act (1944) and Fair Deal (1949) – which favoured education and job training, provided unemployment insurance and healthcare, facilitated mortgages for the purchase of houses in suburban areas, this institutionalised relation between labour and capital materially outlined the social formation which expressed and was the expression of the fetish. The American middle class embodied its own fetish because it was historically determined by the capitalism of the New Deal state. And yet, its fetishism – namely its ideological function of legitimation – was animated by the governing capacity of the social sciences committed to reproducing a historical construction as a natural product because it was considered naturally American. Although it was a social object of government, the middle class was portrayed as a timeless subject of power.[7]

This historical contradiction which marked the rise of the middle class was revealed by the first critical voice of the middle class which emerged in the social sciences of liberalism. In a series of research notes on white-collar labour, published in the spring of 1949 in the columns of *Labor and Nation*, Charles Wright Mills reconsidered the class misunderstanding which had marked the unionisation of employees during the depression and the war. In his view, the sharp increase of white-collar workers constituted 'the most dramatic fact' in the employment structure of US society because, since its status was distinct from the blue-collar worker, it was undeniable that the employee was 'fully classifiable' as a wage worker: numerically significant groups of the

---

7   Zunz 1998: 93–114. On the role of the union after the war: Lichtenstein 1989: 122–152. On the entrepreneurial culture of consumption, see Fasce 2012.

new middle class were increasingly aware that 'the world of the old middle class' of owners and professionals had now been overcome by a 'new society' of dependent work where the employee was caught in 'a struggle between economic reality and anti-union ideology'. After the turning point of 1935, at the end of the 1940s the number of employees registered in unions exceeded 16% but this unionisation should not be interpreted with the 'socialist rhetoric' of the 1930s according to whom labour – the labour of workers organised into the union – indicated the proletariat and middle class indicated white-collar workers who were removed from the control of business. The 'old question of whether white collar workers are a new middle class or a new proletariat' had found an answer in the transformations that ran through working conditions and the union (Mills 1949a: 17–21; Mills 1949b: 17–20).

White-collar workers were not only less middle class and blue-collar workers were not only more middle class than what was represented in public opinion and the scientific literature. Still more important was that this composite social formation existed in a national political economy in which the union extended its 'mass base' only by becoming part of a 'bureaucratic scene'. Within the 'powerful state framework' outlined by the New Deal, where even liberalism had become 'administrative liberalism' deprived of the earlier reforming thrust, labour was a juridically guaranteed 'organized interest', a 'major supporting pillar' of the 'administrative state' which posed a completely different question to the agenda than the one that had marked social conflict during the depression. If the workers' mobilisation was no longer a 'movement' as it was at least in part in the 1930s because it was 'absorbed' into the institutional framework of the social contract of the New Deal, and if democracy was therefore no longer attributable to the autonomous action of the labouring masses, but rather coincided with the regulatory agency of capitalism, had the union perhaps become a watchdog of labour or a guardian called to supervise the overall function of the war economy of the Cold War? (Mills 1949b: 19)

Although he had demonstrated that union leaders were *The New Men of Power* (1948), for Mills this was by no means a rhetorical question. In his view, the institutional change that ran through working conditions and the union did not coincide with the consensus that systematic sociology and the political science of behaviourism described as the incontrovertible horizon of the latter twentieth century. Not unlike the worker, the employee showed a specific disaffection with work. Since this 'routinised' work of the office materially obstructed the opportunity of economic independence and personal realisation, it favoured a relation with the union 'in terms of their instrumental value'. The union could be accepted and rejected but in any case lent itself to being utilised as a 'collective instrument' for acquiring wages. Although part of the

technical governing of capital, its partial use demonstrated the historical contradiction that engulfed the fetish of the middle class. Mills did not indicate
in the grooves of consensus the political presence of a new labour movement.
Indeed, precisely this 'absence' was for him a danger for the 'future of democracy'. However, among the strata that symbolically made up the middle class,
he glimpsed a behaviour of the labour force which rejected the impartiality
prescribed by the fetish. The triumphant middle class that the social sciences
of liberalism had placed at the centre of consensus did not exist without social
conflict. Without a tight clash over wages, no upward mobility, no convergence
between blue- and white-collar, and no identification in the middle class, was
possible (Mills 1949a: 19–20; Mills 1949b: 20).[8]

With this critical perspective, which scholars and union representatives
had rejected by labeling it as socialist in the pages of *Labor and Nation*, in
White Collar: The American Middle Classes (1951) Mills described the alienated
condition of the white-collar worker in order to question the fetishism of the
middle class – namely, its ideological function of legitimation for American
capitalism. As the title itself explicitly stated, no large middle class of workers and employees existed, but rather only separate middle classes. Employees
had undergone the transformation that swept society since progressivism and
with greater intensity during the New Deal. Whatever history they had was a
'history without events', whatever their 'common interest' was did not lead to
any social and political unity, and whatever future they had would not belong
to them: they lived in an 'imaginary society'. This drastic judgment without
appeal that the historian Richard Hoftstadter considered an expression of the
pen, albeit an 'inspired' one, of someone who 'detested white-collar workers ...
perhaps because in some way he identifies with them' marked the beginning
of the volume. According to Mills, although the scientific literature described
a subject which harboured aspirations and advanced claims, despite the
'mass communication' that represented the middle class as an incarnation of
the 'myth' of America which constituted the backbone of the nation, white-
collar labour was fragmented and incapable of speaking with a single voice.
The white-collar worker had never been independent and would always be
the individual of some other: whether the company or the government. Both
the left and right, which during the depression had claimed the representation
of the middle class, had not understood that the problem was not its political
and electoral orientation, but rather its inability to act. As implicitly shown by
public statistics in its attempt to grasp the tendential development of not only

---

8 Mill's thesis of employee dissatisfaction was contested by other research. See Wolfson 1949.

the occupational structure of society, but also the character of manual and intellectual labour, the social position of the white-collar worker could not be understood by looking exclusively at individual labour because it was determined by the 'bureaucratic planning' of capitalism which the New Deal had integrated and consolidated in its administration: the white-collar worker was simultaneously 'a wheel in the gear of the business machine' and a link in the 'big chains of authority that bind society together' through what Mills defined as the 'managerial demiurge' (Mills 2012: IX–XII, XVII–XX, 56–57, 108–109).[9]

The managerial demiurge sociologically described the figure of managerial command of business, union, and government bureaucracies: managers, engineers and foremen, union leaders and public functionaries who allowed the social contract to function materially through company and governmental policies which, by controlling wages and prices, as well as taxation and income, administered who gets what, when and how. Still more importantly, he identified the creative intelligence of the social sciences, human resource experts, and communication specialists who transfigured the image of society within the workplace and in public opinion. However, stratified it was, this could not be represented as a sphere flattened at both ends. Instead, it should be understood as a 'pyramid'. At its base was a complex stratification of those excluded from well-being: African Americans who for the most part constituted the most discriminated social component and those immediately above, Latinos, non-unionised white manual labourers, and new immigrants without skills. At its apex, the economic and political elites who defined an uneasy interlocking device of private and public hierarchies. The intermediary layers were in the central band, which constituted an 'object of management and manipulation' that made it possible to exercise the authority of democracy less and less through coercion and with increasing intensity in 'hidden ways' (Mills 2012: 71–79, 110–111).

Unlike what happened starting in the progressivist era, schools, and universities, as well as research institutes and foundations, were not only aimed at training personnel for social work in urban and industrial areas. In particular, the psychological study of human relations in industry had shifted the sociological attention from the material condition of the labourer to the symbolic level of his 'personality'. Thus, while during the war the attachment to work was ensured by appealing to the nation in its internal and international struggle for democracy, in the postwar period the 'lack of spontaneous will to work',

9 Cf. Kuenzli, Zander and Northrup 1949: 20–23, 32–37. The controversial letter Hofstadter sent to Mills is quoted in Horowitz 1983: 250–252.

exasperated by the further mechanisation and automation of work in factories and offices, made it necessary to train experts who, in departments of human resources at companies, had to nurture the 'morale' of labour, arouse 'happiness' in the labourer. Similarly, the qualified personnel in the 'communication system' – in governmental agencies of communication, large publishers such as Luce, and in the Hollywood film companies – constituted an 'enlightened circle' of specialist employees engaged in the manipulation of public opinion. Their 'mass communication' was not 'autonomous' because it reflected society in a selective way. It generalised certain characteristics – income and skills, consumption and social mobility, values and ideals – of the intermediate layers. Since work was not fulfilling but instead perceived as a 'sacrifice of time, necessary to building a life outside of the factory or the office', in their joint action, social sciences, human resource experts, and communication specialists replaced the traditional work ethic with a public morality of consumption of commodities and symbols that mediate social relations insofar as they interpose between material existence and its 'vision'. The personal 'satisfaction' passed through 'symbols of justification' – of success and the enjoyment of free time dedicated to consumption and entertainment – which did not make any 'symbols to challenge power' available (Mills 2012: 133–134, 218–219, 226–228, 234–238, 333–335).

With this scientific and political critique of the middle class, outlining the interpretative framework of his later works *The Power Elite* (1956) and *The Sociological Imagination* (1959) which would contribute to the intellectual affirmation of the New Left, Mills grasped the historical contradiction that ran through the middle class of liberalism. The fetish was the expression of a composite social formation, but its fetishism depended on the public work of management and manipulation – i.e., the incessant work that social scientists, human resource experts, and communication specialists carried out in the 'bureaucratised society'. *White Collar* certainly corroborated the definition of other-directed 'lonely crowd' with which the sociologist David Riesman approached the notion of totalitarianism that the German sociology of *Mittelstand* and the Frankfurt School had applied to the society of mass consumption after finding refuge in the United States. In the quarter of a century between the 1930s and 1950s, Mills saw a social and political transformation underway in which American democracy, tumultuously animated by the participation in social conflict during the depression, took on the passive character of a technical governing of capital that the power elites conducted by substituting the capacity of the action of labour with an indifferent middle-class public. The public was artificially reduced through a 'statistical ritual' of empirical research, polls and opinion polls that defined communication and opinion through consent. Nonetheless, Mills did not intend to demonstrate the complete absence of 'enthusiasm' in what he defined as the lower middle class of workers and employees (Mills 2006: 71–73, 84–86. See also Mills 1943: 165–180).[10]

In his view, the society of mass consumption did not define a situation that was absolutely 'anomie', nor a condition of total alienation. This was so not only because the fetishism of the middle class appeared unstable and precarious in light of the separate middle classes: white-collar workers did not make up 'one compact horizontal stratum' that carried out a 'single positive social skill'. It was above all because, although 'moral and ideological consensus' characterised American capitalism in the post-WWII period, business could not fail to ensure a 'high material standard of comfort' in order to respond to the persistent 'antagonism' of the forces of labour. In this sense, as would emerge from other critical voices of the middle class in the next decade, the collar line which had divided blue-collar and white-collar work during the depression was actually negotiated in an identification process which changed the perception of society by projecting the image of the middle-class society or the classless society. However, this symbolic negotiation could not materially take place without a 'private' that resisted the public opinion of the managerial demiurge: the middle class did not exist without class struggle. The social contract between big business, big labour, and big government had in the insubordination of labour the very reason of its governing (Mills 2012: 75, 91, 350–351).[11]

2   The Movement against the Middle Class

Although American capitalism appeared unchallenged and indisputable in the 1950s, the rise of the middle-class fetish was contradictory because it implied the possibility of its own decline. Despite the triumph of the notion of consensus particularly in the historical and political sciences, the post-WWII period was characterised by the 'mirage of consensus' (Kirchheimer

---

10   On Mills at the origin of the New Left, see Mattson 2002; Geary 2009. On the category of totalitarianism in the scientific literature of the University in Exile, see Salvati 2000: 65–73; 79–84.

11   Cf. Kirchheimer 1966; Tucker 1968; Nygreen and Schreiber 1970. After celebrating the large blue- and white-collar middle class, in March 1952 *Fortune* reported the white-collar strikes with concern: Labor. The Longest White-Collar Walkout 1952. On worker dissent after World War II, see Bell 1956. See also Romano 1994. Cf. Green 1998: 182–209; Aronowitz 1974: 291–394.

1966: 1–3). Liberalism and its social sciences had acted within capitalism's crisis of legitimation whose political outcome was not immediately obvious. The renewed promise of emancipation through consumption did not exclude dissent, however. Especially in the large manufacturing companies where employees had claimed or accepted the collective bargaining won by the workers' struggles, intransigent strikes or even simply their threat fuelled an increase in wages. The price to pay for the intensification of work rhythms imposed by the productivity needs that the Cold War and US hegemony in the western world demanded was a continuous wage increase that followed inflation and undermined the profit margin. Business thus regained the credit lost during the 1929 crash, and regained autonomy in controlling working conditions and leadership in society but was forced to take on the public responsibility for national well-being.

This new 'social significance' of corporations (Kaysen 1957) emerged in different articles published in magazines such as *Fortune* which, as well as through the big names of the US academy, explained that American capitalism was no longer that of the depression, publicly accused and negatively described in Marxist terms. While it made it possible to prevent workers' claims by means of union increasingly integrated into industrial relations, its managerial transformation implied an irrevocable responsibility towards workers, employees, and consumers. The conflict between labour and capital was not eliminated, but rather understood as a democratic competition between social groups. The expressions used by national propaganda were indicative in this sense – *People's Capitalism* or *Permanent Revolution* – just as those in the historical and economic literature of the post-WWII period – *People of Plenty* (Potter 1954) or *Affluent Society* (Galbraith 1958). These titles not only expressed the triumphant rhetoric of the 'ideologues' of American capitalism, but also called business to the public responsibility it assumed towards the nation. In an essay significantly titled *Abundance for What?*, David Riesman explained that entrepreneurs responded with concern and swiftness to the workers' demands. They were so worried about public relations that in no way did they want to risk being accused of undermining the nation's prosperity: 'in order to avoid rebellions or simply criticism' they were now accustomed to 'paying money' to workers and employees, their unions and their civic associations. Independently from their political orientation – Democratic or Republican – they accepted the social contract inherited from the New Deal as the obligatory way to legitimise capitalism. This was the sacrifice that the fetish demanded, the burden budgeted in calculating profit, the obligation to conduct business which would explode into an ungovernable tension between the 1960s and 1970s, when the revival of the social and labour movement cancelled the magical power of the middle-class fetish as a term of mediation, economic convergence, and symbolic identification (Riesman 1964: 286).[12]

The 1960s and 1970s marked the latest attempt of liberalism to fulfil the scientific and political project of the construction of the middle class. While in opinion polls – carried out in samples where Blacks, Hispanics, women, and the unemployed were underrepresented – the majority of Americans continued to call themselves part of the middle class, in the scientific literature, particularly sociology and economics, middle class showed increasingly more marked signs of economic division and social alienation, cultural anxiety, and political disorientation: it was struck by 'surprising contradictions'. In 1970, in *The Coming Crisis of Western Sociology*, Alvin Gouldner renounced quantitatively measuring the middle class in order to instead reconstruct its history in the semantic field of the social sciences. In this way the contradictions emerged which had run through its rise, preventing its symbolic reproduction as a subject of power. Its social behaviour and political orientation were divided between individualism and 'anomie', personal profit and collective well-being, free market and welfare state. Consequently, despite the end of the federal legal apparatus which had always governed racial segregation in the US South from above, the 'war on poverty', conducted by the Democratic administration of President Lyndon B. Johnson in order to build a great society of the middle class of white and black workers and employees failed to renew the social contract of the New Deal. In Gouldner's sociology, the social process of identification in the middle class was reduced to a 'public charade ... in which people act as if there were no one here except middle-class people'. In Erving Goffman's diagnosis, it had become a suspected pathology (Gouldner 1970: 80–94, 100–101, 107–108, 161–181, 317; Goffman 1963: 162).[13]

Even more important was the silence on the middle class in the work of John K. Gailbraith. Already at the end of the 1950s, the economist par excellence of liberalism had registered that the theoretical effort to consider manual and intellectual labour as labour in general in order to combine wages and profits as a function of consumption had not allowed the grasping of a formation of a 'caste' of individuals distinguished by education and prestige from the middle class prefigured by economic and statistical science. In *The New Industrial*

---

12   See also The Transformation of American Capitalism 1951: 79–83, 154–158; Bell 1952; Bell 1951a; Bell 1951b; Bell 1953; Burck and Parker 1953; The Rich Middle-Income Class 1954: 95–98. On American capitalism's propaganda: The American Round Table. Discussions on People's Capitalism 1956; U.S.A.: The Permanent Revolution 1951; Anti-Americanism and the People's Capitalism Movement, 1957. Cf. Griffith 1983.

13   See also Brooks 1966. Cf. Gambino 1989.

State – a volume published in 1967, when he was president of the political and scientific association Americans for Democratic Action (ADA) which had supported and provided experts for the Kennedy and Johnson administrations – the middle class was leaving the stage for a new 'educational and scientific state'. The growing strategic role that 'knowledge' had for not only the scientific organisation of production (increasingly aimed at the use of services and intangible assets), but also in the administration of new social assistance programs, caused the rise to power of a 'fifth state' that integrated the decision-making processes of public and private: it was this new social class, not unionised labour, that was the shareholder of 'big government' in the new industrial state (Galbraith 1958: 243–254; Galbraith 1998: 268–269, 289–290).[14]

This and other scientific literature, also in the field of historiography, where new research substituted conflict for consensus as an interpretative key of the nation's social and political history, reflected the decline of the fetish of the middle class or the ineffectiveness of its fetishism. In the 1960s, the ideological weave of capitalism's legitimation was torn apart primarily by the civil rights movement and by black nationalism, which demonstrated the racial boundary of a middle class historically built according to the measure of white America. A new social mobilisation further revealed how its frontier was actually punctuated with borders. The student movement rejected a knowledge functional to the national economy centred on the military-industrial complex, the pacifist movement against the Vietnam War showed the imperial nature of liberalism, and the feminist movement criticised the position of women in a society which, while including them in increasing numbers in the labour market with occupations that were inferior to those held by men in terms of income and tasks, relegated them as wives and mothers in the family. Although following different paths, this set of social movements show an 'anti-systemic' outcome because it contested the authority, skills and roles, and symbols and customs which animated the fetish. Towards the end of the decade, in the years of the radicalisation of the student movement that would lead to its division and implosion into collectives which in some cases embraced armed struggle, the secretary of the Students for a Democratic Society, Gregory Calvert, pointed the finger against the liberal reformists who wanted everyone to be 'white, happy, and middle class'. In his view, 'the myth of the great American middle class' had now collapsed under the weight of the 'mass movement' composed of Black and white students, the minority underclass, the working class of traditional industry and the new working class of the professionals of 'advanced

---

14   Cf. Parker 1972: 35–50.

capitalism'. In 1967, the future National Security Advisor of the democratic administration of President Jimmy Carter, the political scientist Zbigniew Brzezinski expressed his concern for what he believed to be 'a rebellion of the middle class against the middle-class society' (Davidson 2011: 11–20; Brzezinski 1970: 88).[15]

The movement against the middle class emerged with particular intensity between the end of the 1960s and the beginning of the 1970s in the most intense cycle of the workers' struggles of the century. This was not only because these struggles demonstrated that the frontier between blue collar and white collar was returning to be a border area: companies circumvented wage gains through inflation which affected the consumption capacity of employees. This was not even only because inflation constituted the question on which protests against taxation and social spending was founded. It was above all because what entrepreneurial press defined as a 'new breed of workers' – mostly made up of young people, not only whites, but also blacks and women, more educated and wealthy than their parents – showed a stubborn character which rejected the discipline of work: they were less inclined to 'obedience and respect', they fomented 'discord in offices and factories', they put pressure on the industrial relations institutionalised after World War II and for this reason represented a 'serious problem for society' (Prosperous ... Restless ... Demanding ... New Breed of Workers 1979: 35–41; Longworth and Neikirk 1979: 1, 18).[16] The 'revolt against work' took place through wildcat strikes, the rejection of stipulated contracts, sabotage of production and insubordination against the very bureaucracies of the union. In this sense, in his speech on Labor Day in 1971, President Richard Nixon claimed that work ethic would be re-established through the shared commitment of government, business, and the union:

> Recently we have seen that work ethic come under attack ... What's happening to the work ethic in America today? What's happening to the willingness for self-sacrifice that enabled us to build a great nature, to the moral code that made self-reliance a part of the American character, to the competitive spirit that made it possible for us to lead the world?
>
> NIXON 1971[17]

---

15   On the racial boundary of the American middle class in the second post world war, see Katznelson 2002. On the movements, see Arrighi et al. 1989; Cartosio 2010. In particular, on the feminist movement, see Baritono 2018a.

16   Cf. Cartosio 1998: 50–51.

17   Between 1966 and 1975, there were over 5,000 strikes per year, with over 2.5 million strikers. See Green 1998: 219–225. On inflation and the mobilisation of the white-collar strata against taxes and social spending, see Jacobs 2002.

3   The New Class of Neoconservatism (and Neoliberalism)

If the sacrifice in work, personal independence, and the spirit of competition defined the moral code of the middle class as the foundation of the nation and its global leadership, its crisis was at the basis of the affirmation of the neoliberal and neoconservative new right. The rise of neoliberalism in the academic world, particularly with the ban on Keynesianism at the hands of the supply-side economy advanced by Milton Friedman and the Chicago School, affirmed a new scientific vocabulary centred on the absolute principle of the market which denied the heuristic capacity of the collective notions of the social sciences. The market became the exclusive matrix of a society in which the language of collective bargaining and full employment, as well as collectivism and social justice, no longer belonged, but instead only freedom as it emerged from the myriad of individual economic actions. Not only was the signifier of class excluded from the semantics of the social sciences, but the scientific and political function of the middle-class fetish was lost. Since society was preordained by the market, it no longer needed any principle or symbol of order: middle class was emptied of its mythological character, i.e., it was deprived of the charm of the managerial demiurge of liberalism. As a result, business could renounce any social and public responsibility. As Friedman claimed, 'the only responsibility [of business] was to increase profits' (Friedman 1970. See also Friedman 1962).[18]

The most evident political sign of the impossibility for the social sciences to update its references to the middle class, however, emerged with the affirmation in public opinion of the polemical notion of the 'new class' in the hands of scholars and intellectuals – particularly Daniel Bell and Irving Kristol – who distanced themselves from the socialist and progressivist left of the New Deal in order to denounce the impasse into which liberalism had fallen.[19] At the beginning of the 1970s, Bell had resorted to the German sociology of the middle class in order to oppose Marxist literature which advanced the thesis of the proletarianisation of intellectual work. In 1979 he admitted that knowledge workers did not constitute a class capable of mediation, but instead embodied and fomented the fractures caused by the politicisation of the university, communities, the factory, and the family because they supported the identity politics of race and sex. At the same time, they expressed the nascent neoliberal vision which refused any mediation in order to entrust the relationship

18   Cf. Rodgers 2011: 15–76.
19   Steinfels 1980: 1–24, 188–213; Hartman 2015: 38–69.

between individual and market to 'meritocracy'. The new class composed of managers, administrators, technicians, and professionals with high-level university and doctoral training, both publicly and privately employed, did not establish a 'code of behaviour' or an 'ideology that provides symbols of recognition', because it exacerbated the racist and sexist tendencies of the white working class and lower middle class. Within these 'cultural contradictions' that ran through the post-industrial transformation of society, a new ideological battle began – not for a new middle class capable of defending a liberal order now in fragments, but rather for the new class to exercise its power in order to move society towards a new order of capitalism (Bell 1976b: 70–71; Bell 1980: 155. See also Bell 1972; Bell 1976a).[20]

With this political objective, in the first half of the 1970s through a series of articles published in *The Public Interest* (a magazine that he founded together with Daniel Bell in 1965), Irving Kristol pointed out the 'extremely precarious' condition of capitalism. The voices of the movements should not be considered 'inarticulate' as the 'sociological and psychological theories' of liberalism had made them in their anxiousness to bring them back to a unity in a newly consensual government of society. Although they seemed to be the result of mental confusion and rooted in nonsense, their political meaning was 'clear enough': the rejection of the 'offer of citizenship' that had been proposed by the policies of the Great Society and the aversion to the 'liberal, individualist, capitalist civilization'. The 'youthful rebels' should not be considered as a 'lunatic fringe'. It was not even useful to explain to them how much progress had been made in 'racial equality' and 'abolishing poverty'. The classical argument of progress, with the promise of the fulfilment of the American ideal, was useless because the object of contestation was not 'America's failure' to realise itself, but American as an 'ideal'. For this reason, as Kristol remarked in his polemical dialogue with Friedman and other authors of neoliberalism, the precariousness of capitalism was not only indicated by the limitation of economic freedom which characterised the 'bureaucratic society', nor was it measurable exclusively through the index of economic growth, because it coincided with the loss of the value horizon of diligence, rectitude, and sobriety. The historical and political task of American business was thus 'the moral reconstruction of society' (Kristol 1970: 8; Kristol 1971: 105. See also Kristol 1973; Kristol 1975a; Kristol 1978: 139–140; Kristol 1979).

---

20   Cf. Cento 2014; Cento 2019: 35–55. For the Marxist literature on the new working class in the United States, see the essays collected in Walker 1979; Johnson 1982. For a reconstruction of the scientific and political debate on the notion of a 'new class', see Bruce-Biggs 1988; Szelény 1988; Kellner 1992; King and Szelény 2004.

Faced with the danger that under the 'banner of equality', different movement experiences could converge, it was not sufficient to mobilise the skilled
and unionised workers, white employees and professionals who still showed
'loyalty to the bourgeois ethos' and 'resistance to radicalism'. It was above all
necessary that business act to prevent the new class from providing an institutional channel of expression for the 'lust for power' of the movements. Like
other politicians, scholars, and intellectuals who took part in the ideological
battle over the new class, such as the Democrat Daniel P. Moynihan, author
of the famous *Report on the Negro Family* (1965),[21] Kristol did not point the
finger generically at the elites who ran public and private bureaucracies, but
specifically against the elites radicalised by the movements which caused what
Samuel Huntington defined as the 'excess of democracy' (Crozier, Huntington
and Watanuki 1975: 59–118).[22] His political discourse did not even implicitly
allude to the extension of political participation. Although it was strategically
aimed at the white working class and lower middle class, thus contributing
to the electoral rise of the 'Middle American Radicals' and the affirmation of
the new Republican majority, he claimed to give voice to a specific part of the
new class. As reported in the memorandum of the US Chamber of Commerce
drawn up by Lewis F. Powell in the summer of 1971 and made known to the
Washington Post the following year when its author became a Supreme Court
judge appointed by President Nixon, capitalism had to overturn the social and
institutional relation with administrators and public officials in its favour, as
well as researchers and professors at universities, and intellectuals and journalists of the media system (Powell Jr. 1971).

This was the political appeal that Kristol launched in the newspaper par
excellence of American capitalism, the *Wall Street Journal*. In 1975, in *Business
and the 'New Class'*, he denounced the harsh 'climate of hostility' towards business lingering in the federal government, in the organs of information and
communication, and in universities. This was a climate resulting from the formation of a 'generation of young people' who, due to the education that they
received, did not know the world of work and fantasised of a world without the
sacrifice of work. Because the new class intended to plan governmental action
in order 'to politicize the economic decision-making process', it was necessary to start its assimilation and integration into the 'business community'.
This was the 'slow and painful business' that awaited the American capitalism: 'an immense educational task' which primarily involved the re-education
of corporate executives and managers who still placed trust and interest in the

---

21   Battistini 2019: 57–77.
22   In the same year, Daniel Bell (1975) posed a similar question. Cf. Cento 2015.

normative framework forged by the social contract inherited from the New Deal. The militant Kristol confronted this collective enterprise in the first person, not only in his academic and journalistic activity, but also as an ideologue of the American Enterprise Institute – the main think tank of the neoliberal and neoconservative right – and the Collegiate Network – the network which financed independent newspapers on campus universities, scholarships, and internships in important national newspapers (Kristol 1978: 25–31; Kristol 1972: 41–47. See also Kristol 1974: 6–7, 27–28; Kristol 1975b: 124–139).[23]

Starting in the 1970s, politicians and intellectuals of the neoliberal and neoconservative new right, as well as executives and managers of corporations, thus found in the polemical notion of the new class a fundamental instrument for analysis and action. In 1978 William E. Simon – Secretary of the Treasury for the Nixon and Ford administrations, together with Kristol, founder of the Collegiate Network – published *A Time For Truth*, a pamphlet where he explained that the 'business community' had to start projects of public education through the mass media, financing universities which agreed on teaching and researching content, investing money into institutional advertising or publicity that advertised not goods, but corporate values. In the same year, Michael Novak published *The American Vision*, a text in which he claimed that business must act on the public and scientific stage imposed by the new class in power, equipping companies with scholars and communication experts to whom would be entrusted the elaboration and dissemination of a public discourse which rejected the 'ideological critics' of alienation and hetero-direction of society. These and other business initiatives successfully pursued the political objective of integrating the new class as a public agent of reaction and transformation of American capitalism (and not only American). While the social scientists and intellectuals of liberalism – such as Gouldner – still believed at the end of the decade that despite its elitist character, the new class constituted 'the most progressive force in modern society and was a centre of whatever human emancipation is possible in the foreseeable future', the founder of the Hudson Institute, Herman Kahn, outlined the new global coordinates of American capitalism, noting with satisfaction that the new class was increasingly respectful of the absolute principle of the market. (Simon 1978: 195–198, 223–234. Novak 1978: 14, 19–59; Gouldner 1979: 93; Kahn 1979: 140–177).[24]

---

23 On Kristol's role in the business ranks, see Steinfels 1980: 81–107. The *Middle American Radical* identified white working class and lower middle-class workers with low to medium income who lacked a college degree and shared a negative attitude against black and poor people. See Warren 1976.

24 Cf. McAdams 2015: 1–27.

As the business ethics economist David Vogel wrote in 1970, in an article significantly titled *Clear as Kristol, Business's 'New Class' Struggle*, the 'new-class doctrine' was having success because it made business aware that it was again possible to join entrepreneurial interest and public interest or to reconcile capitalism and democracy outside of the institutional and symbolic mediation imposed by liberalism and its social sciences. By means of the ideological battle waged within the new class and for a new 'new class', the fetish of the middle class was deprived of its consensual middle reference in order to indicate an elite assimilable to capitalism through a 'public philosophy' which would bring work back to its bourgeois ethical foundation. In particular, Kristol considered the identification of the 'great majority' of US people – above all the white working class – with the middle class as an 'artificial creation' which had to be contested. The consensus in the post-wwii period was therefore not replaced by a new common sense. The new order of American capitalism could not assert itself except through a 'civil war' conducted by other means which prevented the renewal of the middle class because it reflected and reproduced the economic hierarchies, and the cultural and political disorder of society. The 'era of the good feelings' of the middle class ended in a 'new sadism': business had found on the one hand the 'villain' against which white America could be polemically unified in order to reaffirm its own supremacy in a society fractured along lines of race, sex, and class; on the other, it had identified the new subject of power to which to entrust – once educated in the moral, as well as economic, value of the market – the political and scientific direction of globalisation in the last quarter of the twentieth century (Vogel 1979; Kristol 1979: 24; Kristol 1971: 105; Schanberg 1982).[25]

4   The Middle Class as a Figure of the Crisis (in Globalisation)

The ideological battle for the 'new class', which neoconservatism won in dialogue with neoliberalism, reflected – and at the same time fueled – the political response advanced by business on the terrain of production and social reproduction, where not only workers' struggles, but also the mobilisation of white-collar labour were undermining the profit margin of corporations. In the economic conjuncture of stagflation – marked by the financial and economic weakness compared to the European and Japanese economies, the relative success of the Soviet model in the process of decolonisation, and the role of

---

25   On cultural wars and their interpretation as civil war, cf. Hartman 2015; Armitage 2017.

oil-producing countries – *Business Week* and other press close to entrepreneurs linked the growing number of strikes and pressures they exerted on wages to the crises of productivity and competitiveness. They denounced the inflationist vise that was impoverishing the middle class and declared that investments would not be resumed unless conditions changed.[26]

In this way a new entrepreneurial initiative – at once economic, political, and cultural – was announced which, if it had an important precedent in the Boulwarism of the 1950s, became systemic only in the 1970s and 1980s. This was the meaning of the words spoken by the president of the National Association of Manufacturers, Hames B. Henderson in October 1982. When he proclaimed that corporations would return to exert their supremacy in order to change the way in which 'one governs and is governed', he was referring not only to industrial relations, but also to the overall internal and international government of the United States. Henderson considered it indispensable to change the attitude of 'academia, government, and union' so that 'business and the American nation would reach the heights adequate to the national dream' (Henderson quoted in Cartosio 1998: 113).[27]

On the international level, the growth of foreign investments was considered essential to balance the internal fall of the rate of profit.[28] President Nixon responded to the need of business to regain competitiveness over the European and Japanese economies with the devaluation of the dollar. The end of the Bretton Woods agreements, which in the post-wwii period had mediated the US imperative of free trade with the political need to guarantee European nations wide financial margins for reconstruction, spread the fall in corporate profits onto other economies and favoured investments in foreign markets or their transformation into multinational companies. An unprecedented economic regime was forming which outlined globalisation: a political design which, giving a particular shape to the historical processes of the

---

26 Productivity is the Sticking Point 1971: 17–19; Work Rules: The Main Barrier to Productivity 1971: 54–55; Wage Demands Look Explosive 1974: 18–19; The Squeeze on the Middle Class 1975: 52–60; A Boom in White-Collar Salaries, 1978, 50–51; A Warning that Worker Discontent is Rising, 1979, 152–156; The New Industrial Relations 1981: 85–98.

27 'Boulwarism' takes its name from the General Electric personnel director Lemuel L. Boulware, who in the 1950s implemented company policy aimed at undermining the union's hold on workers by preparing companies to escape from the New Deal social contract as soon as possible. See Fasce 2011: 182; Phillips-Fein 2009; Waterhouse 2014; Winkler 2018.

28 For a reconstruction of the long period of relations between the American working class and US foreign investments, see Gambino 1975.

integration of national markets, continued and expanded US global hegemony in different ways after the post-war period.[29]

The United States no longer exported the model of mass production and consumption founded on the Fordist factory. They no longer encouraged the active role of states in the economic sphere and their social intervention in favour of cooperation between entrepreneurial and union interests. They no longer acted as guarantors of Western and global economic growth by means of the export of dollars which had characterised the *New Deal for the World*, from the Marshall Plan to the economic aid policies for modernisation. They no longer assumed the responsibility for exporting the middle class as the subject of power around which to organise the societies that made up the liberal international order. And yet, while the US national market was becoming the largest importer of low-cost goods whose consumption supported the growth of emerging economic regions where formerly internal production processes were outsourced, successive waves of financial deregulation and economic liberalisation assigned to US multinational companies the capacity to lift or depress national economies according to their possibilities of attracting investments: American capitalism was conquering a new global pervasiveness – economic and ideological – which the Soviet system was not capable of handling.[30]

On the internal level, the dream of the global greatness of American business coincided with the emptying of the historic social content of liberalism. The entrepreneurial initiative pointed the finger first of all at the high cost of labour and low productivity. Corporations initiated merger processes and the concentration and diversification of production. They abandoned or reduced their presence in traditional industrial sectors in favour of new economic and financial spheres (microelectronics, information technology, services). They introduced technologies to automate production and save labour costs, particularly professional, skilled, and semi-skilled. The innovation of production transformed the alienation of young people towards the factory and office into precariousness or into part-time jobs which marked a progressive compression of the guarantees of labour and average wages, which was also achieved through the use of de-skilled workers, mostly migrant. The result was the abandonment of the magical formula high wages, low prices which economic science had identified since progressivism and the start of corporate restructuring

---

29   On globalisation as a historical process, see Hopkins 2002. Cf. Bell 2003.

30   Romero 2009: 219–223, 252–266. Cf. Maier 2006: 191–275; Basosi 2006. On globalisation and the transformation of US foreign policy since the 1970s: Sargent 2015. On the New Deal for the World, Baritono 2011a.

which required the end of negotiation habits through outsourcing and union-busting practices that eliminated or prevented the presence or formation of the union in workplaces. State laws which guaranteed the individual right to work outside of union membership also moved in this direction (right-to-work law): politically legitimised by the blatant gesture with which president Ronald Reagan dismissed twelve thousand striking air-traffic controllers *en masse*, these laws gradually came into effect in the majority of states.[31]

The entrepreneurial initiative also involved the undoing of the welfare state which, starting with Nixon and Carter, underwent a violent acceleration with Reagan, when the protest against taxation and social spending became so influential as to be interpreted as a 'revolt of the middle class against the poor': a revolt not of the now-shattered large middle class of liberalism, but rather the upper middle class of the employee and property-owning strata (Kerby 1967). The reaction of white America following the undermining of the federal apparatus which had governed segregation and the policies of affirmative action towards women and minorities – a reaction that marked the implosion of the democratic majority – led to regressive taxation, to the reduction of social assistance for the unemployed and poor, especially women, African Americans, and those with dependent children. To the lament of business against high labour costs, particularly against social subsidies which limited the influx of workers into precarious and poor occupations, Bill Clinton finally responded through a welfare reform which went in the direction of workfare or the reconciliation of the undeserving poor with work considered as moral proof of personal responsibility.[32]

If the globalisation of American capitalism had started between the 1970s and 1980s through the ideological battle of neoconservatism against the new class of liberalism and for a new 'new class' of the business community, if its legitimation had fully taken place between the 1980s and 1990s with the full public affirmation of neoliberalism which deprived the class signifier of its polemical meaning, the entrepreneurial initiative in the field of production and social reproduction radically changed the historical formation which had animated the fetish of the middle class and fostered its fetishism. In scientific literature as well as public opinion, the middle class no longer defined the consensual physiognomy of the post-WWII society, but exemplified the social and cultural disorder that globalisation brought within the nation: middle class did not only become 'one of the most intractable issues' of the social sciences, it

---

31   Cartosio 1998: 41–100, 111–134. On the transformations of production and labour, see Noble 1986; Schor 1992; Fox Piven and Cloward 1982. On Reagan, see Fasce 2008.

32   Cf. Cartosio 1998: 13–40, 135–152; Vezzosi 2002: 183–196; Cooper 2017.

also emerged as a public figure of the crisis of an increasingly fractured society after the social and workers' movement and the political response of business which had swept away liberalism and its social sciences.[33]

Several headlines concerned with the 'contraction' of the middle class, its 'shrinking', or even its 'disappearance' appeared during the Reagan presidency, as different presses declared its economic 'disillusion' and political 'frustration'. Not only was the traditional optimism that middle managers placed in corporate careers and social mobility replaced by a widespread sensation of fear, failure, and depression in the face of the first digital revolution which eliminated superfluous types of white-collar labour. The overall consumption capacity of the middle class – employees and workers – also declined as a result of the negative effects of Reaganomics on income distribution. It was increasingly difficult to access the American dream of homeownership, high instruction, the purchase of a large car as a symbol of elevated social status, except through forms of debt which were becoming the main economic and moral character of the nation (Allis 1981).[34]

The crisis of the American middle class, however, emerged strongly only with the 'new gilded age' of the 1990s, during the Clinton presidency, precisely when the new economy provided increasing results in terms of productivity and profit. In a series of articles published between March 3–6 with the title *The Downsizing of America*, the *New York Times* dramatically recounted the wave of layoffs which were primarily aimed at white-collar labour. The adoption of digital technologies on a large scale made it possible to brutally downsize, after the factories' workshops, even the administrative and technical offices, as well as the design and financial management offices. Not only were low-level employees losing their jobs, but so were those with degrees. Only a third found a job similar in terms of qualification and pay, and the majority had temporary and part-time jobs, with lower wages, in companies that did not offer healthcare and pension plans, while most of the jobs cut were outsourced or moved to areas in the country, particularly in the South of the Sun Belt, where the union was either absent or weak. Thus, although the growing debt consumption made possible by financial deregulation performed the fundamental function of social compensation for economic inequality, the white-collar workers who had defined the American standard of living and

---

33   Wacquant 1991: 39. Cf. Abercrombie and Urry 1983; Wright 1985; Gerteis 1998: 639–666.

34   See also Frustrated Middle Class 1982: 41–42; The Disenchantment of the Middle Class 1983: 82–83; A Work Revolution in U.S. Industry, 1983, 100–110; The Myth of the Vanishing Middle Class 1984: 85–86; Karim 1984; Koepp et al. 1986; Brophy et al. 1986. Cf. Barbagli 1986. On the role of private debt in US history, Hyman 2011.

the American way of life to which workers also had to aspire lost faith in the companies where they had made a career, in which they had identified by consuming their goods, and towards which they had nurtured a patriotic feeling because they brought the greatness of the United States to the world. In other words, there emerged a profound disillusionment with the main value that had held the middle class together: the ethics of hard work as a path to success appeared overturned as entrepreneurial greed. In this sense, the cultural contradictions of capitalism which had fuelled the ideological battle of neoconservatism exploded: the liberalisation of the market, financialisation of the economy and multi-nationalisation of corporations produced wealth only for an elect group, destabilising the ethics of work and savings on which American capitalism (and not only) had built its triumphant historical narrative (Uchitelle and Kleinfield 1996).[35]

This unprecedented distrust of capitalism after its exaltation in the mid-twentieth century was therefore connected to the formation of new elites who, as another article in the series declared, no longer lived in the historical cities of US industry, but in the airplanes of the global economy. In other words, they no longer had any national roots – their horizon had become global. Their choices, just like their salaries and the profits of their companies, were no longer tied to the jobs and incomes of middle-class white America. Their values, ideals, and ambitions no longer coincided with those of a nation led by what intellectuals and scholars, not only of a democratic political orientation, have defined as plutocracy and oligarchy: a caste of managers, technicians, industrial and financial investors, politicians and officials, economists and social scientists who feel themselves as part of a single world indifferent to the national economy, who believe in a single global economy whose functioning and margin for growth is not linked – at least not exclusively – to the consumption capacities of US people, for whom even democracy falls under their management capacity ('managed democracy'). For this plutocracy, the statistics of employment, income, and consumption that had constituted the measure of the great middle class after the post-WWII period no longer enter into the calculation of profit (Bragg 1996; Rimer 1996).[36]

---

35   The Downsizing of America 1996, in particular Uchitelle L and Kleinfield NR, On the Battlefields of Business, Millions of Casualties, *New York Times* 3 March. See also Richman 1990; Richman 1990: 104–113; Rubenstein 1991; Wolfe 1993; Novak 1992; Middle-Class Blues 1994: 14–15; Withheld 1995; Ehrle 1996. On the role of the consumer in the American century and its transformation in the 1980s and 1990s, see Rosenberg 2012. With reference to the economic crisis that exploded in 2008, see Meyer and Sullivan 2013.

36   Cf. Phillips 1992; Formisano 2015; Wolin 2017: 131–210; Crouch 2004: 31–52.

What distinguishes this plutocracy is thus a social irresponsibility that
reflects the profound transformation of American capitalism and business culture. The formation of multinational companies coincided with the overcoming of the historical cooperation/competition between industrial and banking
capital in favour of ownership structures increasingly controlled by financial
institutions and with related ideological changes in management: from a company direction which accepted and organised a certain level of union consulta-
tion and public regulation to a management line centred on the maximisation
of share value in the short-term and the absolute rejection of obligations and
duties towards labour. In this sense, the crisis of the middle class has returned
to the centre of public opinion not so much – or not only – due to the immense
accumulation of wealth that the multinationals have determined, but rather as
above all due to the fact that these have rejected the responsibility for the well-
being of the nation that American capitalism had assumed after World War II,
albeit to a limited extent and reluctantly. In 1991, Robert Reich, an economist
and Labor Minister in the first Clinton administration, wrote:

> As almost every factor of production – money, technology, factories,
> and equipment – moves effortlessly across borders, the very idea of
> an American economy is becoming meaningless, as are the notions of
> an American corporation, American capital, American products, and
> American technology.
>   REICH 1991: 8[37]

The entrepreneurial initiative has therefore brought with it a political change
of American capitalism. Since the beginning of the twentieth century, it had
presented itself as national capitalism, the creator and promotor on an international scale of the fetish of the middle class as the incarnation of Americanism,
an ideal of freedom, democracy, and consumption inseparable from the
exchange value of its commodities. In the last quarter of the century, globalisation had instead led to the end of the Cold War and the triumph of the United
States as the only world power, marking, however, a coincidence between the
dream of business and national greatness that is indifferent to the middle class.
The nation's military strength was not only built on the cuts in social spending.
The supremacy of multinational companies has also nullified the historical
equation between free trade for exports and greater internal well-being. While
in the post-war period US western hegemony had consolidated the social and

37   Cf. Fasce 2006: 371–379; Fasce 1980/1981: 31–35.

ideological rise of the middle class, with globalisation this historical fact disappeared, and economic growth has become an exclusive function of profit, without positive impact on average income. In this way, in an attempt to free itself from the power of labour, business has deprived American capitalism of its own historical source of legitimation. When in the 1990s, after economically downsizing and politically defeating and obfuscating the working class in the previous decade, the entrepreneurial initiative was extended to employees, the middle class definitively lost the orderly and reassuring guise that liberalism and its social sciences had sewn on.

Middle class appeared as a naked, anxious, and disturbing figure of the crisis determined by the concentration of wealth and the increase in inequalities, the polarisation of the labour market with the reduction of skilled and semi-skilled jobs, the disintegration of the welfare state through 'workfare' policies. Although globalisation had stripped the middle-class fetish of his material historical basis by imposing a new work regime onto US society, its fetishism remains as an ideological anachronism. Still today, despite the fact that the financial and economic crisis which exploded in 2008 has further reduced and impoverished its ranks, the middle class is not considered as a social formation of an outdated past. It continues to be perceived as the national symbol that, however aleatory, ideologically rewards white America despite the separation of labour from the opportunity of economic independence, social mobility, moral and political self-government. The social sciences of liberalism have in this sense been successful in their public work of abstraction of the middle class: from a historically contested social force in the field of tension opened by class conflict during the depression to a symbolic object of mediation for the consensus of democracy in the post-WWII period. However, its consequent change of meaning in public opinion – from its class content (inseparable from labour) to its political and cultural identity (with racial connotations) – still has profound negative consequences on the possibility of rethinking labour – its general impoverishment, the hierarchical conditions it imposes, the sexual and racial differences that cross through it – in light of the economic, social, and political conditions affirmed by globalisation.[38]

In the new century the middle class exemplifies a crisis that is not only economic and social, but also cultural and political. An unprecedented crisis, not so much because of the continuous recessions that have followed one after the other since the 1970s. And not only because the terms of its overcoming are not yet decipherable. This crisis is unprecedented because, being congenital to the

---

38   Walkowitz 1999: 303–307; Roediger D 2020.

disorder of globalisation, it poses an unprecedented problem of legitimation that, unlike what happened in the 1930s, can hardly be resolved on the same national and international scale. US people are not faced with the failure of their business and thus cannot simply call the federal state back to its historic function of social reform. In the same way, they can hardly appeal to a new 'New Deal for the World' in the face of the economic, political, and ideological disintegration which runs through the contemporary global world. The question of the legitimation of capitalism thus does not concern business itself, but rather the overall governance of US society in globalisation. The historical liberal link between the middle class and democracy no longer assures the success of capitalism through mass consumption or the expansion of well-being. On the contrary, as the enormous amount of empirical research, scientific literature, and journalist investigations which have flooded public and political debate in the last decade testifies, the crisis of the middle class affects the very historical conditions of possibility of democracy to the extent that it does not appear capable of governing globalisation. While progressively oriented economists and sociologists see in the global protests of new middle-class generations impoverished by neoliberal policies the possibility of restoring the trusting relationship between the middle class and democracy, Francis Fukuyama, who in 1989 had enthusiastically celebrated the end of history with the triumph of liberal capitalism, questions whether democracy can survive the death of the American (and not only the American) middle class. Even the historical studies which reflect the growing gap between capitalism and democracy, using notions such as 'plutocracy' and 'oligarchy', actually show how unlikely it is that a new middle can be glimpsed around which to rethink the liberalism of the American century, at least in the immediate future (Fukuyama 1992; Sassen 2013; Krugman 2014).[39]

Its social sciences do not exclusively forge the fetish of the middle class by placing it at the foundation of the legitimation of capitalism. Its fetishism was also closely connected – in a scientifically stringent, but historically contingent way – to the social contract between big business, big labour, big government in which the New Deal state was the guarantor and manager of the public responsibility of business for the well-being of the nation. Since globalisation has declassified the state as the agency of the global market and its reform as an international rating factor in order to attract investments from multinational companies, the social science of the middle class that I have

---

39   Also of note is National Public Radio's special series, *The New Middle* 2016. On the transformations of the state in the light of globalization: Ricciardi 2013b: 75–93.

reconstructed from progressivism to the post-WWII period does not seem capable of renewing itself and renewing the social content of liberalism. It is its own 'anxiety' for order' (Wolin 1960: 315–325, 338–339) – the anxiety which induces liberalism to rhetorically re-propose the classic motif of the middle class as the irreplaceable subject of the power of democracy – that makes its stalemate evident. Its political and scientific culture has so internalised the neoliberalism of globalisation that, when it has shown that it can culturally integrate racial and gender differences by distancing itself from neoconservatism, its ideologues have maintained that labour as a social relation mediated by the wage no longer constitutes a matter of discussion: since middle class is reduced to a rhetorical figure of an American identity that manages to be universal only by ignoring its class content, the different partialities of labour that conflict with the new hierarchies caused by globalisation do not find a political discourse in liberalism that is adequate to their social position. Freed from its fetishism and restored to its inescapable historicity, the middle class provides in this sense an instrument to reflect on the global making of American capitalism which has shaped the world of our present. A political indicator of its legitimation, an economic and symbolic measure that establishes the historical limit of its capacity for production and ruling, the effectiveness of its political and scientific cultures, the social and ideological frontier beyond which its order is suspended by the bursting onto the public scene of masses whose social and political articulation is not sociologically and historically attributable to the post-WWII large middle class and its historical democratic function of legitimation (Therborn 2012).

References

A Boom in White-Collar Salaries (1978) *Business Week* 11 September: 50–51.

A Union Target: The White-Collar Worker (1948) *Business Week* 7 February: 88–94.

A Warning that Worker Discontent is Rising (1979) *Business Week* 4 June: 152, 156.

A Work Revolution in U.S. Industry. More Flexible Rules on the Job are Boosting Productivity (1983) *Business Week* 16 May: 100–110.

Abercrombie N and Urry J (1983) *Capital, Labour and Middle Classes*. London: Allen & Unwin.

Ackerman FL (1933) *Facts Behind Technocracy*. New York: Continental Committee on Technocracy.

Adelman P (1984) *Victorian Radicalism. The Middle-Class Experience (1830–1914)*. London: Longman.

Against a Labor Party (1936) *The Nation* 12 December: 716.

Agit-Prop Commission: Discussion on the Decisions of the Seventh World Congress of the Communist International. The Struggle for Peace and Against Imperialist War (1935) In: CPUSA Records: Series I, Tamiment Library NYU, BOX 257, Folder 7.

Akin WE (1967) Arbitration and Labor Conflict: The Middle-Class Panacea 1886–1900. *The Historian* vol 4(29): 565–583.

Alchon G (1985) *The Invisible Hand of Planning. Capitalism, Social Science, and the State in the 1920s*. Princeton: Princeton University Press.

Allis S (1981) Era of Middle Class Has Arrived, but It's Hard to Say Who's in It. *Wall Street Journal*, 10 February.

America's Rising Black Middle Class (1974) *Time* 17 June: 25–33.

American Labor Today (1955). *The Nation* 10 December: 489–511.

Angoff A (1935) The Past, Present and Future of the Middle Class. *Boston Evening Transcript*, 30 November.

Anti-Americanism and the People's Capitalism Movement, addressed by T.S. Repplier, President (1957) San Francisco: The Advertising Council at a Luncheon of the Commonwealth Club of California, September 20.

Appleby J (2001) The Social Consequences of American Revolutionary Ideals in the Early Republic. In: Bledstein BJ and Johnston RD (eds) *The Middling Sorts. Explorations in the History of the American Middle Class*. New York: Routledge, 31–49.

Armitage D (2017). *Civil War: A History in Ideas*. New York: Knopf.

Aron A (1936) Une révolution antiprolétarienne: idéologie et réalité du national-socialisme. In: Halévy E et al. *Inventaires: la crise sociale et les idéologies nationales*. Paris: Félix Alcan, 24–55.

Aronowitz S (1974) *False Promises: The Shaping of American Working-Class Consciousness*. New York: McGraw-Hill.

Arrighi G et al. (1989) *Anti-Systemic Movements*. London: Verso.

Artur J (1929) Le sort des classes moyennes dans l'état social actuel. *Revue internatio-nale de sociologie*: 401–410.

Augspurger M (2001) Sinclair Lewis' Primers for the Professional Managerial Class: Babbitt, Arrowsmith, and Dodsworth. *The Journal of the Midwest Modern Language Association* vol. 34(2): 73–97.

Bakke EW (1940) *Citizens Without Work. A Study of the Effects of Unemployment upon the Workers Social Relations and Practices*. New Haven: Yale University Press.

Balogh B (2015) *The Associational State. American Governance in the Twentieth Century*. Philadelphia: University of Pennsylvania Press.

Barbagli M (1986) Si sta contraendo la classe media americana? *La rivista il Mulino* (3): 382–403.

Baritono R (1993) *Oltre la politica: la crisi politico-istituzionale negli Stati Uniti fra Otto e Novecento*. Bologna: il Mulino.

Baritono R (ed.) (2001) *Il sentimento delle libertà: la dichiarazione di Seneca Falls e il dibattito sui diritti delle donne negli Stati Uniti di metà Ottocento*. Torino: La Rosa.

Baritono R (2011a) "A New Deal for the World": liberalism e internazionalismo negli Stati Uniti post-1945. In: Cau M (ed.), *L'Europa di De Gasperi e Adenauer. La sfida della ricostruzione (1945–1951)*. Bologna: il Mulino, 231–250.

Baritono R (2011b) *La Democrazia vissuta. Individualismo e pluralismo nel pensiero di Mary Parket Follet*. Torino: La Rosa.

Baritono R (2013) Ripensare lo Stato: scienze sociali e crisi politica negli Stati Uniti fra Otto e Novecento. *Ricerche di Storia Politica* vol 12(3): 301–318.

Baritono R (2018a) "Dare conto dell'incandescenza". Uno sguardo transatlantico (e oltre) ai femminismi del lungo '68. *Scienza & Politica* vol 30(59): 17–40.

Baritono R (2018b) Politics has always been a rough and tumble business: le campagne presidenziali statunitensi (1896-1980). In: Cammarano F and Cavazza S (eds) *La delegittimazione politica nell'età contemporanea. 3. Conflitto politico e propaganda elettorale in Europa e negli Stati Uniti (1861–1989)*. Roma: Viella, 203–223.

Baritz L (1989) *The Good Life: The Meaning of Success for the American Middle Class*. New York: Knopf.

Bartlett JR (ed.) (1848) *Dictionary of Americanisms. A Glossary of Words and Phrases, usually regarded as peculiar to the United States*. Barlett & Welford: New York.

Basosi D (2006) *Il governo del dollaro. Interdipendenza economica e potere statunitense negli anni di Richard Nixon*. Firenze: Polistampa.

Battistini M (2012) Un mondo in disordine. Le diverse storie dell'Atlantico. *Ricerche di Storia Politica* vol 15(2): 173–188.

Battistini M (2013) Harold Lasswell, the "problem of World Order," and the Historic Mission of the American Middle Class. In: Fasce F et al. (eds) *Beyond the*

Nation: Pushing the Boundaries of U.S. History from a Transatlantic Perspective. Torino: Otto, 225–254.

Battistini M (2015) Il declino della classe media americana. *La rivista il Mulino* (3): 564–573.

Battistini M (2018) L'instabile ordine della politica middle-class: le campagne elettorali di New York e California. In: Cammarano F and Cavazza S (eds) *La delegittimazione politica nell'età contemporanea. 3. Conflitto politico e propaganda elettorale in Europa e negli Stati Uniti (1861–1989)*. Roma: Viella, 203–223.

Battistini M (2019) La New Class del neoconservatorismo e la de/legittimazione del capitalismo americano. *Scienza & Politica* vol 31(61): 57–77.

Bauer J and Gold N (1934) *Permanent Prosperity.* New York: Harper & Bros.

Baughman JL (1987) *Henry R. Luce and the Rise of the American News Media.* Baltimore: Johns Hopkins University Press.

Beard CA (1913) *An Economic Interpretation of the Constitution of the United States.* New York: Macmillan.

Beard CA (1915) *Economic Origins of Jeffersonian Democracy.* New York: Macmillan.

Beck U and Grande E (2010) Beyond Methodological Nationalism: Non-European and European Variations of the Second Modernity. *Soziale Welt* vol 61(3): 329–331.

Bell D (1951a) Do Unions Raise Wages? The Illusion of the Wage-Price Spiral. *Fortune* January: 65–66.

Bell D (1951b) Labor's Coming of Middle Age. *Fortune* October: 144–145.

Bell D (1952) The Prospects of American Capitalism. *Commentary* (6): 603–612.

Bell D (1953) The Next American Labor Movement. *Fortune* April: 120–121.

Bell D (1956) *Work and Its Discontents. The Cult of Efficiency in America.* Boston: Beacon Press.

Bell D (1972) The Cultural Contradictions of Capitalism. *Journal of Aesthetic Education* vol 6(1–2): 11–38.

Bell D (1975) The Revolution of Rising Entitlements. *Fortune* April: 98–103.

Bell D (1976a) *The Coming of Post-Industrial Society: A Venture in Social Forecasting.* Harmondsworth: Penguin Books.

Bell D (1976b) *The Cultural Contradictions of Capitalism.* New York: Basic Books.

Bell D (1980 [1979]) The New Class: A Muddled Concept. In: Bell D *The Winding Passage. Essays and Sociological Journeys (1960-1980)*. Cambridge: ABT Books, 144–164.

Bell DSA (2003) History and Globalization: Reflections on Temporality. *International Affairs* vol 79(4): 801–814.

Bendix R and Lipset SM (eds.) (1953) *Class, Status and Power. Social Stratification in Comparative Perspective.* London: Routledge & Kegan.

Berle AA (1933) The Social Economics of the New Deal: Berle Interprets the Philosophy of the New Deal. *New York Times* 29 October, p.4.

Berle AA (1934) Lewis Corey Examines American Capitalism. *The Nation* 12 September.

Berle AA (1935) The New Deal and Economic Liberty. *The Annals of the American Academy of Political and Social Science* vol 178(1): 37–47.

Bernard LL (1928) Standards of Living and Planes of Living *Social Forces* vol 7(2): 190–202.

Bernard LL and Bernard J (1943) *Origins of American Sociology: The Social Science Movement in the US*. New York: Cromwell Company.

Bertram A and Lloyd WF (1926) *The Secret of High Wages*. London: Unwin.

Bessner D (2018) *Democracy in Exile. Hans Speier and the Rise of the Defence Intellectual*. Ithaca: Cornell University Press.

Bingham A (1935) *Insurgent America. Revolt of the Middle Class*. New York: Harper & Bros.

Bingham A and Rodman S. (eds.) (1934) *Challenge to the New Deal*. New York: Falcon Press.

Bingham vs. Common Sense (1937). *New Masses* 11 May: 11.

Bingham A (1937) New Deal or New Party. *Common Sense* August 6(9): 3.

Bingham A (1941) The Technology of Democracy. In: DeWitt Talmadge I (ed.) *Whose Revolution? A Study of the Future Course of Liberalism in the United States*. New York: Howell, 43–72.

Blair A (2011) *Reading Up: Middle Class Readers and the Culture of Success in the Early Twentieth-Century United States*. Philadelphia: Temple University Press.

Blaszczyk RL (2000) *Imagining Consumers. Design and Innovation from Wedgwood to Corning*. Baltimore: Johns Hopkins University Press.

Bledstein BJ (1976) *The Culture of Professionalism. The Middle Class and the Development of Higher Education in America*. New York: Norton.

Bledstein BJ and Johnston RD (eds) (2001). *The Middling Sorts. Explorations in the History of the American Middle Class*. New York: Routledge.

Blumin SM (1985) The Hypothesis of Middle-Class Formation in Nineteenth-Century America. A Critique and Some Proposals. *The American Historical Review* vol 90(2): 299–338.

Blumin SM (1989) *The Emergence of the Middle Class. Social Experience in the American City (1760-1900)*. Cambridge: Cambridge University Press.

Bologna S. (1977) Per un'antropologia del lavoratore autonomo. In: Bologna S. and Fumagalli A (eds) *Il lavoro autonomo di seconda generazione. Scenari del postfordismo in Italia*. Milano: Feltrinelli, 81–132.

Boltanski L (1987 [1982]) *The Making of a Class. Cadres in French Society*. Cambridge: Cambridge University Press.

Bonazzi T (1974) *Struttura e metamorfosi della civiltà progressista americana. Saggi di storia e sulla storia*. Padova: Marsilio.

Bonazzi T (ed.) (1982) *Potere e nuova razionalità. Alle origini delle scienze e della società e dello stato in Germania e negli Stati Uniti*. Bologna: Clueb.

Bonazzi T (1986) Il New Deal e il Leviatano: la cultura politica della tradizione rifor-matrice americana. In: Bonazzi T and Vaudagna M (eds) *Ripensare Roosevelt.* Milano: Franco Angeli, 60–95.

Bonazzi T (2004) Europa, Zeus e Minosse, ovvero il labirinto dei rapporti euro-americani. *Ricerche di Storia Politica* vol 7(1): 3–24.

Bonham J (1954) *The Middle Class Vote.* London: Faber & Faber.

Bonn MJ (1932) *The Crisis of Capitalism in America.* New York: John Day Co.

Booth C (1896) *Life and Labour of the People in London.* London: Macmillan.

Borgognone G (2000) *James Burnham: totalitarismo, managerialismo e teoria delle élites.* Aosta: Stylos.

Borgognone G (2015) *Tecnocrati del progresso: il pensiero politico americano del Novecento. Capitalismo, liberalismo e democrazia.* Torino: Utet.

Borkenau F (1932) *Zur Sociologie der Faschismus.* Stuttgart: Archiv fur Soziographischer Versuch auf statistischer Grundlage.

Bourdieu P (2012) Capitale simbolico e classi sociali. *Polis* vol XXVI(3): 401–415.

Bragg R (1996) Big Holes Where the Dignity Used to be. *New York Times,* 5 March, p.1, 16–18.

Brants V (1902) *La petit industrie contemporaine.* Paris: Victor Lecoffre.

Brick H (2006) *Trascending Capitalism. Visions of a New Society in Modern American Thought.* Ithaca: Cornell University Press.

Briggs A (1967) The Language of 'Class' in early Nineteenth-Century England. In: Briggs A and Saville J (eds) *Essays in Labour History.* New York: Macmillan, New York, 43–73.

Briggs A (1959) *The Age of Improvement,* London: Longman, Green & Co., London.

Brinkley A (1996) *The End of Reform. New Deal Liberalism in Recession and War.* New York: Vintage Books.

Brooks J (1966) Mr. White and Mr. Blue: Notes on the New Middle Class. *Harper's Magazine* 1 June: 88–97.

Brophy B et al. (1986) Middle-Class Squeeze. *U.S. News & World Report* 18 August: 36–45.

Broun H (1935) White Collar Into Plume. *The Nation* 10 April: 420.

Browder E (1935a) What is Communism? I. Who Will Lead the Revolution? *New Masses* 21 May: 18–19.

Browder E (1935b) What is Communism? II. Who Will Lead the Revolution? *New Masses* 21 May: 18–19.

Browder E (1935c) What is Communism? III. Who Will Lead the Revolution? *New Masses* 21 May: 9–10.

Browder E (1938) *The People's Front.* New York: International Publishers.

Brown A (1936) *The Fate of the Middle Classes.* London: V. Gollancz ltd.

Bruce-Biggs B (ed.) (1988 [1977]) *The New Class?* New Brunswick: Transaction Books.

Brun C (1929) La grande pitié des classes moyennes. Leur disparition porterait un coup fatal à la vie intellectuel française. *La Réforme sociale:* 417–422.

Brzezinski Z (1970) *Between Two Ages: America's Role in the Technetronic Era.* New York: The Viking Press.

Buchanan J (1936) *White Collars Organize. New Masses* 7 April: 21–22.

Buhle P (1995) *A Dreamer's Paradise Lost: Louis C. Fraina/Lewis Corey (1892–1953) and the Decline of Radicalism in the United States.* Atlantic Highlands: Humanities Press.

Bulmer M (1984) *The Chicago School of Sociology: Institutionalization, Diversity and the Rise of Sociological Research.* Chicago: University of Chicago Press.

Burck G and Parker S (1953) The Changing American Market. *Fortune* August: 99–102.

Burnham J (1941) Is democracy possible? In: DeWitt Talmadge I (ed.) *Whose Revolution? A Study of the Future Course of Liberalism in the United States.* New York: Howell, 188–217.

Burns AE (1936) Work Relief Wage Policies 1930–1936. *Monthly Report of the* FERA June: 22–55.

Burnshaw S (1936) The Passion for Liberty. *New Masses* 7 April: 19–20.

California Study Claim Middle-Class Negroes' Discontent Foments Riots (1967). *Chicago Defender,* 5 August 1967, p. 27.

Cammarano F (2003) Crisi politica e politica della crisi: Italia e Gran Bretagna 1880–1925. In: Pombeni P *Crisi, legittimazione, consenso.* Bologna: il Mulino, 81–132.

Can They Unseat the Sitters? (1937) *Business Week* 27 February: 18.

Cannadine D (1998) *Class in Britain.* New Haven: Yale University Press.

Capital's Sit-Down Strike (1937) *The New Republic* 24 November: 59–60.

Caradog Jones D (1928) The Cost of Living of a Sample of Middle-Class Families. *Journal of the Royal Statistical Society* vol 19(4): 463–518.

Caroppo E (2013) *Per la pace sociale: l'Istituto internazionale per le classi medie nel primo Novecento.* Galatina: Congedo.

Cartosio B (1998) *L'autunno degli Stati Uniti. Neoliberismo e declino sociale da Reagan a Clinton.* Milano: Shake.

Cartosio B (2010) *I lunghi anni Sessanta. Movimenti sociali e cultura politica negli Stati Uniti.* Milano: Feltrinelli.

Cavalli A (1982) Un'ipotesi sull'orgine della sociologia nella Germania guglielmina. In: Bonazzi T (ed.) *Potere e nuova razionalità. Alle origini delle scienze e della società e dello stato in Germania e negli Stati Uniti.* Bologna: Clueb, 59–66.

Centers R (1949) *The Psychology of Social Classes.* Princeton: Princeton University Press.

Cento M (2014) Daniel Bell e lo Stato post-industriale: percorsi di "assemblaggio" dello Stato americano. *Passato e Presente* vol 91(1): 103–126.

Cento M (2015) The Revolution of Rising Entitlements: Daniel Bell and the Logic of Segregation in the Post-Industrial State. In: Buonomo L and Vezzosi E (eds) *Discourses of Emancipation and the Boundaries of Freedom.* Trieste: Edizioni Università di Trieste, 231–242.

Cento M (2019) Il governo delle differenze: Daniel Bell, la Great Society e il "populismo borghese". *Scienza & Politica* vol 31(61): 35–55.

Challenge to the Middle Class (1936) *New Masses* 7 April.

Chamberlain J (1935) Books of the Times. *New York Times*, 11 December.

Chandler AD, Jr (1977) *The Visibile Hand: The Managerial Revolution in American Business.* Cambridge: Belknap Press.

Chase S (1932a) *A New Deal.* New York: Macmillan.

Chase S (1932b) A New Deal for America: The Road to Revolution. *The New Republic* 6 July.

Chase S (1933) *Technocracy. An Interpretation.* New York: John Day Publishing Company.

Chase S (1934) *The Economy of Abundance.* New York: Macmillan.

Chevalier M (1839 [1835]) *Society, Manners and Politics in the United States, Letter XXXI: The Middle Classes.* Boston: Jordan & Company.

Clark JB (1902 [1899]) *The Distribution of Wealth. Theory of Wages, Interest and Profits.* New York: Macmillan.

Clark JB (1903) The Dynamics of the Wages Question. *Publications of the American Economic Association* vol 34(1): 130–142.

Clark JB (1914) *Social Justice without Socialism.* New York: Houghton Mifflin.

Clark JB (1918 [1917]) *Essentials of Economic Theory.* New York: Macmillan.

Clark JB (1896) The Theory of Economic Progress. *Publications of American Economic Association* vol 17(1): 5–22.

Cobban A (1967) The "Middle Class" in France (1815–1848). *French Historical Studies* vol 5: 41–52.

Cohen L (2003) *A Consumers' Republic: The Politics of Mass Consumption in Postwar America.* New York: Vintage.

Cole GDH (1955) The Conception of the Middle Classes. In: Cole GDH *Studies in Class Structure.* London: Routledge and Kegan Paul, 78–100.

Collini S (1979) *Liberalism and Sociology: L.T. Hobhouse and political argument in England (1880–1914).* Cambridge, Cambridge University Press.

Comish NH (1923) *The Standard of Living: Elements of Consumption.* New York: Macmillan.

Commons J (1905) Arbitration, Conciliation, Trade Agreement. In: *Labor, Capital and the Public. A Discussion of the Relations between Employees, Employers, and the Public.* Chicago: Public Policy Publishing, 140–152.

Commons J (1908) Is Class Conflict in America Growing and Is It Inevitable? *American Journal of Sociology* vol 13(6): 756–783.

Commons J (1918) *History of Labor in the United States* vol 1. New York: Macmillan.

Commons J (1926) *History of Labor in the United States* vol 2. New York: Macmillan.

Commons J (1935) Communism and Collective Democracy. *The American Economic Review* vol 25(2): 212–223.

Conk MA (1978) Occupational Classification in the United States Census: 1870–1940. *The Journal of Interdisciplinary History* vol 9(1): 111–130.

Conk MA (1983) Labor Statistics in the American and English Census: Making some Invidious Comparisons. *Journal of Social History* vol 35(4): 83–102.

Conk MA (1988) *The United States Census: A Social History.* New Haven: Yale University Press.

Cooley C (1897) The Process of Social Change. *Political Science Quarterly* vol 12(1): 63–81.

Cooper M (2017) *Family Values Between Neoliberalism and the New Social Conservatism.* Cambridge: The MIT Press.

Corbin J (1922) *The Return of the Middle Class.* New York: Charles Scribner's Sons.

Corey L (1927) How Is Income Distributed? *The New Republic* May: 323.

Corey L (1934) *The Decline of American Capitalism.* New York: Covici-Friede.

Corey L (1935a) The Clash of New and Old Social Systems. *The Annals of the American Academy of Political and Social Science* vol 178(1): 1–8.

Corey L (1935b) The Crisis of the Middle Class. I The Middle Class Under Capitalism. *The Nation* 14 August: 176–178.

Corey L (1935c) The Crisis of the Middle Class. The Middle Class under Fascism. *The Nation* 21 August: 207–210.

Corey L (1935d) The Crisis of the Middle Class. The Middle Class under Socialism. *The Nation* 28 August: 238–241.

Corey L (1935e) Veblen and Marx. *The Nation* vol 139(3625): 745–756.

Corey L (1936) Property and Middle Class. *The Nation* 29 August: 248–249.

Corey L (1937) American Class Relations. *Marxist Quarterly* vol 1(1): 135.

Corey L (1940a) Marxism Reconsidered I. *The Nation* 17 February: 245–249.

Corey L (1940b) Marxism Reconsidered II. *The Nation* 2 March: 272–276.

Corey L (1940c) Marxism Reconsidered III. *The Nation* 16 March: 305–308.

Corey L (1941) The Need Still Is: A New Social Order. In: DeWitt Talmadge I (ed.) *Whose Revolution? A Study of the Future Course of Liberalism in the United States.* New York: Howell, 249–273.

Corey L (1945) Problems of the Peace: The Middle Class. *The Antioch Review* vol 5(1): 68–87.

Corey L (1992 [1935]) *The Crisis of the Middle Class*, New York: Columbia University Press.

Corey Says Middle Class Has Disappeared (1935) *New York Post* 11 November.

Correspondence. Revolt in the Middle West (1935) *The Nation* 5 April: 387.

Cowie J (2016) *The Great Exception. The New Deal and the Limits of American Politics.* Princeton: Princeton University Press.

Coyner SJ (1977) Class Consciousness and Consumption: the New Middle Class during the Weimar Republic. *Journal of Social History* vol 10(3): 310–317.

Croly H (1920) The Eclipse of Progressivism. *The New Republic* 27 October.

Croner F (1937 [1928]) *The White Collar Movement in Germany since the Monetary Stabilization*, xerox, translated by E.E. Warburg and A. Lissance, project supervisor W.R. Dittmar, Ph.D. published by the State Department of Social Welfare and the Department of Social Science, Columbia University, as a report on Project No. 165-97-6999-6027 conducted under the auspices of the Works Progress Administration. Translation held by Columbia University's Butler Library, New York.

Crossick G (1977) The Emergence of the Lower Middle Class in Britain: A Discussion. In: Crossick G *The Lower Middle Class in Britain (1870–1914)*. London: Croom Helm.

Crossick G (1984) Al di là della metafora: studi recenti sui ceti medi inferiori in Europa prima del 1914. *Quaderni storici* vol XIX(56): 573–612.

Crossick G (1996) Formation ou invention des classes moyennes? Une analyse comparée: Belgique-France-Grande Bretagne (1880–1914). *BTNG-RBHC* vol XXVI(3–4): 105–138.

Crouch C (2004) *Post-Democracy*. Cambridge: Polity.

Cuppini N and Ferrari R (2020) Il piano come strategia d'ordine del capitalismo. In: Baritono R and Ricciardi M (eds) *Strategie dell'ordine: categorie, fratture, soggetti*. Quaderno N. 8, Scienza & Politica, 227–260.

Curtis BE (1981) *The Middle-Class Progressivism of William Graham Sumner*. Boston: Twayne.

Davidson C (ed.) (2011) *Revolutionary Youth and the New Working Class: Lost Writings of SDS*. Pittsburgh: Changemaker Publications.

Davis C (2001) The Corporate Reconstruction of Middle-Class Manhood. In: Bledstein JB and Johnston RD (eds) (2001) *The Middling Sorts. Explorations in the History of the American Middle Class*. New York: Routledge, 201–216.

de Chilly L (1924) *La classe moyenne en France après la guerre (1918–1924)*. Bourges: Tardy.

De Feo NM (1992) *Riformismo Razionalizzazione Autonomia operaia. Il Verein für Sozialpolitik (1872–1933)*. Roma-Bari: Lacaita.

De Grazia V (2005) *Irresistible Empire: America's Advance through Twentieth-Century Europe*. Cambridge: Belknap Press of Harvard University Press.

Dennis L (1932) *Is Capitalism Doomed?* New York: Harper & Bros.

Dennis L (1936) *The Coming of American Fascism*. New York: Harper & Bros.

de Tocqueville A (1839) *Democracy in America*. New York: Goerge Adlak.

Debate: "Can Civilization Survive Under Capitalism?", L. Corey vs. H. Agar (1935) 11 April. In: Rare Book and Manuscript Library, Columbia University of New York, Box 10, Corey Paper.

Del Pero M (2014) Gli Stati Uniti, i limiti e i dilemmi della modernizzazione. *Ricerche di Storia Politica* vol 17(2): 187–196.

Deming S (1915) *A Message to the Middle Class*. Boston: Maynard & Company Publishers.

Dempsey JM and Gruver E (2009) "The American System": Herbert Hoover, the Associative State, and Broadcast Commercialism. *Presidential Studies Quarterly* vol 39(2): 226–244.

Desrosières A (1998) *The Politics of Large Numbers. A History of Statistical Reasoning.* Cambridge: Harvard University Press.

Dewey J (1927) *The Public and Its Problems.* New York: H. Holt & Company.

Dewey J (1930) *Individualism Old and New.* New York: Minton Balch.

Dewey J (1931a) The Need for a New Party I: The Present Crisis. *The Nation* 18 March: 115–117.

Dewey J (1931b) The Need for a New Party II: The Breakdown of the Old Order. *The Nation* 25 March: 151–152.

Dewey J (1931c) Who Might Make a New Party? *The Nation* 1 April: 178–179.

Dewey J (1931d) Policies for a New Party. *The Nation* 8 April: 203–205.

Dewey J (1933) The Future of Radical Political Action. *The Nation* 4 January: 8–9.

Dewey J (1935) *Liberalism and Social Action.* New York: Minton Balch.

Didier E (2014) Crises et Rupture: Leçon statistique du moment Roosevelt. *Le Seuil/ Pouvoirs* vol 150(3): 93–102.

Dimitroff G (1935) Working-Class Unity. Bulwark Against Fascism. Report to the Seventh World Congress of the Communist International. *New Masses* 15 October: 8–9, 26–27.

Dobkin Hall P (2010) Rediscovering the Bourgeoisie: Higher Education and Governing-Class Formation in the United States. In: Beckert S and Rosenbaum JB *The American Bourgeoisie: Distinction and Identity in the Nineteenth Century.* New York: Macmillan, 167–192.

Donzelot J (1986) *L'invention du social.* Paris: Fayard.

Dorfman J (1966) *The Economic Mind in American Civilization* vol 2. New York: Augustus M. Kelley.

Draft Resolution of the Eight Convention of the Communist Party of USA (1934) 2–8 April. In: CPUSA Records: Series I, Tamiment Library NYU, BOX 170, Folder 10 and 12.

Draft Resolution on Browder Report (1937) 17–21 June. In: CPUSA Records: Series I, Tamiment Library NYU, BOX 260, Folder 39.

Dreyfuss C (1933) *Beruf und Ideologie der Angestellten.* München-Leipzig: Duncker & Humblot.

Du Bois WEB (1956) How United are Negroes. *National Guardian,* 23 January.

Eakins D (1972) The Origins of Corporate Liberal Policy Research (1916-1922): The Political-Economic Expert and the Decline of Public Debate. In: Israel J (ed.) *Building the Organizational Society: Essays on Associational Activities in Modern America.* New York: Free Press, 163–179.

Earle P (1989) *The Making of the English Middle Class. Business, Society and Family Life in London (1660–1730).* Berkley: University of California Press.

Easton D (1950) Harold Lasswell: Policy Scientist for a Democratic Society. *The Journal of Politics* vol 12(3): 450–477.

Editorial (1935) *New Masses* 17 September: 4.

Editorial Comments. Roosevelt Massage (1936) *New Masses* 14 January: 2–3.

Edwards AM (1911) The Classification of Occupations: The Classification of Occupations, with Special Reference to the United States and the Proposed New Classification for the Thirteenth Census Report on Occupations. *Publications of the American Statistical Association* vol 9(94): 638–645.

Edwards AM (1917) Social Groups of the United States. *Publications of the American Statistical Association* vol 15(118): 643–661.

Edwards AM (1933) A Social-Economic Grouping of the Gainful Workers of the United States. *Journal of the American Statistical Association* vol 28(184): 377–387.

Edwards AM (1934) The "White-Collar Workers". *Monthly Labor Review* vol 38(3): 501–505.

Edwards AM (1936a) Composition of the Nation's Labor Force. *The ANNALS of the American Academy of Political and Social Science* vol 184(1):10–20.

Edwards AM (1936b) The Negro as a Factor in the Nation's Labor Force. *Journal of the American Statistical Association* vol 31(195): 529–540.

Ehrenreich B (1989) *Fear of Falling: The Inner Life of the Middle Class*. New York: Pantheon.

Ehrle LH (1996) The Myth of the Middle Class. *The Humanist* November/December: 17–20.

Eliot TD (ed.) (1931) *American Standards and Planes of Living. Readings in the Social Economics of Consumption*. Boston: Ginn and Company.

Eulau H (1968) The Maddening Methods of Harold Lasswell: Some Philosophical Underpinnings. *The Journal of Politics* vol 30(1): 3–24.

Eulau H (1976) Elite Analysis and Democratics Theory: The Contribution of Harold Lasswell. In: Eulau H and Czudnowski MM *Elite Recruitmen in Democratic Politics*. New York: General Lerning Press, 7–28.

Eulau H and Emor SZ (1999) Harold D. Lasswell's Legacy to Mainstream Political Science: A Neglected Agenda. *Annual Review of Political Science* vol 2: 75–89.

Farr F et al. (2006) The Policy Scientist of Democracy: The Discipline of Harold D. Lasswell. *American Political Science Review* vol 100(4): 579–587.

Fasce F (1980-1981) La "reindustrializzazione dell'America". *Primo Maggio* (14): 31–35.

Fasce F (1983) *Dal Mestiere alla catena. Lavoro e controllo sociale in America (1877–1920)*. Genova: Herodote.

Fasce F (2006) L'impresa irresponsabile. Scandali, potere economico e democrazia in prospettiva storica. *Contemporanea* vol IX(2): 371–379.

Fasce F (2008) Reagan politico. La formazione e le politiche interne. In: Sioli M (ed.) *La parabola di Reagan*. Verona: Ombre Corte, 84–99.

Fasce F (2011) Una Nuova Gilded Age? Grande Impresa e democrazia negli Stati Uniti contemporanei. In: Baritono R and Vezzosi E (eds) *Oltre il secolo americano? Gli Stati Uniti prima e dopo l'11 settembre*. Roma: Carocci, 171–184.

Fasce F (2012) *Le anime del commercio: pubblicità e consumo nel secolo americano*. Roma: Carocci.

Ferrari R (2017) *Beatrice Potter e il capitalismo senza civiltà. Una donna tra scienza, politica e amministrazione*. Roma: Viella.

Feuchtwanger EJ (1985) *Democracy and Empire: Britain 1865–1914*. London: Hodder Education.

Finney RL (1922) *Causes and Cures for the Social Unrest. An Appeal to the Middle Class*. New York: Macmillan.

Fish CR (1927) *The Rise of the Common Man 1830–1850*. New York: Macmillan.

Formisano RP (2015) *Plutocracy in America: How Increasing Inequality Destroys the Middle Class and Exploits the Poor*. Baltimore: John Hopkins University Press.

Foster GG (1850) New York by Gas-Light: With Here and There a Streak of a Sunshine. *New York Tribune* (69).

Fournol E (1933) *Manuel de politique française*. Paris: Éditions des Portiques.

Fox DM (1967) *The Discovery of Abundance. Simon N. Patten and the Transformation of Social Theory*. Ithaca: Cornell University Press.

Fox Piven F and Cloward R (1982) *The New Class War*. New York: Pantheon Books.

Fox Schwartz B (2014) *The Civil Works Administration (1933–1934). The Business of Emergency Employment in the New Deal*. Princeton: Princeton University Press.

Fraina LC (1918) *Revolutionary Socialism. A Study in Socialist Reconstruction*. New York: The Communist Press.

Frazier EF (1962) *Black Bourgeoisie: The Rise of a New Middle Class in the United States*. New York: Collier Books.

Freeden M (1979) *The New Liberalism. An Ideology of Social Reform*. Oxford: Clarendon Press.

Freeman J (1933) The Background of German Fascism. *New Masses* 8 April: 3–7.

Freeman J (1934) The Meaning of Fascism. *New Masses* 2 October: 34–36.

Freeman, J (1936) The Middle Class Today and Tomorrow: The New World of Socialism. *New Masses* 7 April: 35–37.

Freeman J (1936a) The Middle Class and the Election. *New Masses* 1 August: 27–28.

Freeman J (2018) *Behemoth: A History of the Factory and the Making of the Modern World*. New York: Norton.

Frezza D (1986) Democrazia e mass media: il New Deal e l'opinione pubblica. In: Bonazzi T and Vaudagna M (eds) *Ripensare Roosevelt*. Milano: Franco Angeli, 210–239.

Friedman M (1962) *Capitalism and Freedom*. Chicago: University of Chicago Press.

Friedman M (1970) The Social Responsibility of Business is to Increase its Profits. *New York Times Magazine* 13 September: 17–21.

Frustrated Middle Class Will Shake Up Politics (1982). *U.S. News & World Report*, 11 October, p.41–42.

Fukuyama F (1992) *The End of History and the Last Man*. London: Hamish Hamilton.

Galambos L (1970) The Emerging Organizational Synthesis in Modern American History. *Business History Review* vol 44(3): 279–290.

Galbraith JK (1958) *The Affluent Society*. Boston: Houghton Mifflin.

Galbraith JK (1998 [1967]) *The New Industrial State*. Boston: Houghton Mifflin.

Gallup G (1937) Voters Favor Laws Regulating Strikes. *Washington Post*, 4 July.

Gambino F (1975) Composizione di classe e investimenti diretti statunitensi all'estero. In: Ferrari Bravo L (ed.) *Imperialismo e classe operaia multinazionale*. Milano: Feltrinelli, 318–359.

Gambino F (1989) La classe media come categoria della normalità nella sociologia statunitense. In: Pace E *Tensioni e tendenze dell'America di Reagan*. Padova: CEDAM, 63–87.

Gary B (1999) *The Nervous Liberals. Propaganda Anxieties from World War I to the Cold War*. New York: Columbia University Press.

Geary D (2009) *Radical Ambition. C. Wright Mills, the Left, and American Social Thought*. Berkley: University of California Press.

Geiger T (1930) Panik im Mittelstand. *Die Arbeit, Zeitschrift für Gewerkschaftspolitik und Wirtschaftskunde* (10): 637–652.

Gemelli G (1994) Enciclopedie e scienze sociali negli Stati Uniti fra l'età di Hoover e la Guerra fredda. *Passato e Presente* vol XII(32): 33–68.

George H (1879) *Progress and Poverty*. New York: Dodo Press.

Gerstenberger H (1982) Sull'elaborazione della Grande depressione da parte dello Stato e delle scienze dello Stato. In: Bonazzi T (ed.) *Potere e nuova razionalità. Alle origini delle scienze e della società e dello stato in Germania e negli Stati Uniti*. Bologna: Clueb, 13–44.

Gerteis J (1998) Political Alignment and the American Middle Class (1974–1994). *Sociological Forum* vol 13(4): 639–666.

Gerth H and Mills CW (eds) (1946) From Max Weber: Essays in Sociology. Oxford: Oxford University Press.

Giddings F (1901) *Inductive Sociology*. New York: Macmillan.

Giddings F (1922) Resurgent Middle Class. *New York Times*, 31 December, p.39–40.

Giddings F (1926) Is there a Class Psychology? *Journal of Abnormal and Social Psychology* vol XXI: 231–233.

Gillen S (1987) *Politics and Vision: The ADA and American Liberalism 1947–1985*. Oxford, Oxford University Press.

Gioia V (1990) *Gustav Schmoller: la scienza economica e la storia*. Galatina: Congedo.

Goblot E (1925) *La barrière et le niveau: étude sociologique sur la bourgeoisie française moderne*. Paris: Alcan.

Goffman E (1963) *Stigma. Notes on the Management of Spoiled Identity.* Englewood Cliffs: Prentice-Hall.

Goldman L (1986) The Social Science Association (1857–1886): A Context for Mid-Victorian Liberalism. *The English Historical Review* vol 101(95): 95–134.

Goldman L (1987) A Peculiarity of the English? The Social Science Association and the Absence of Sociology in Nineteenth Century Britain. *Past & Present* vol 114(1): 133–171.

Goldman L (1998) Exceptionalism and Internationalism: The Origins of American Social Science Reconsidered. *Journal of Historical Sociology* (1): 1–36.

Goldman L (2004) *Science, Reform and Politics in Victorian Britain. The Social Science Association (1857–1886).* Cambridge: Cambridge University Press.

Goodman D (2011) *Radio's Civic Ambition. American Broadcasting and Democracy in the 1930s.* Oxford: Oxford University Press.

Goodwyn L (1976) *Democratic Promise. The Populist Movement in America.* Oxford: Oxford University Press.

Gordon MM (1958) *Social Class in American Sociology.* Durham: Duke University Press.

Gorman FJ (1936) Artists and Trade Unions. *New Masses* 7 April 1936: 26.

Gouldner A (1970) *The Coming Crisis of Western Sociology.* New York: Basic Books.

Gouldner A (1979) *The Future of Intellectuals and the Rise of the New Class.* New York: Seabury Press.

Gramsci A (2007 [1930–1932]) *Prison Notebooks.* New York: Columbia University Press, Notebook 6, § 49.

Green JR (1998 [1980]) *The World of the Worker.* Chicago: University of Illinois Press.

Gresle F (1993) La notion de classe moyenne indépendante. Un bilan des travaux. *Vingtième Siècle. Revue d'histoire* vol 37(1): 35–44.

Gretton RH (1919) *The English Middle Class.* London: G. Bell and Sons.

Grew R (1980) The Case for Comparing Histories. *American Historical Review* vol 85 (4): 763–768.

Griffith R (1983) The Selling of America: The Advertising Council and American Politics (1942–1960). *Business History Review* vol 57(3): 388–412.

Grimes MD (1991) *Class in Twentieth-Century American Sociology. An Analysis of Theories and Measurement Strategies.* New York: Praeger Publishers.

Groppo B (1989) Socialisme et classes moyennes: quelques remarques d'introduction. *Matériaux pour l'histoire de notre temps* vol 50(17): 1–3.

Guazzaloca G (2004) *Fine secolo. Gli intellettuali italiani e inglesi e la crisi tra Otto e Novecento.* Bologna: il Mulino.

Guizot F (1829–1832) *Histoire de la civilisation en France depuis la chute de l'Empire romain jusqu'en 1789.* Paris: Imprimerie de la Barbier.

Gunn S (1988) The 'Failure' of the Victorian Middle Class: A Critique. In: Seed J and Wolff J (eds) *The Culture of Capital,* Manchester: Manchester University Press, 17–43.

Gunn S (2004) Class, Identity and the Urban: The Middle Class in England (1790–1950). *Urban History* vol 31(1): 29–47.

Gunn S (2012) Between Modernity and Backwardness. The Case of the English Middle Class. In: Lopez AR and Weinstein B (eds) *The Making of the Middle Class. Toward a Transnational History.* Durham: Duke University Press, 58–74.

Gunn S and Bell R (2002) *Middle Classes. Their Rise and Sprawl.* London: Weidenfeld and Nicolson.

Gunnell JG (1993) *The Descent of Political Theory. The Genealogy of an American Vocation.* Chicago: Chicago University Press.

Gunnell JG (1996) The Founding of the American Political Science Association: Discipline, Profession, Political Theory, and Politics. *American Political Science Review* vol 100(4): 479–486.

Habermas J (1991 [1962]) *The Structural Transformation of the Public Sphere. An Inquiry into a Category of Bourgeois Society.* Cambridge: The MIT Press.

Hacker L (1935) Addresses to the Middle Class. *The Nation* November: 625–626.

Haessler C (1936) Program for Professionals. *New Masses* 31 March: 20.

Halbwachs M (1905) Remarques sur la position du problème sociologique des classes. *Revue de métaphysique et de morale* vol XIII: 890–897.

Halbwachs M (1939) *Les Classes moyennes.* Paris: Félix Alcan.

Halbwachs M (1955) *Esquisse d'une psychologie des Classes sociales.* Paris: Marcel Rivière et Cu.

Haldane R (1888) The Liberal Creed. *The Contemporary Review* (54): 465–474.

Haldane R (1905) Notes on Current Events. *Independent Review* (7).

Haney DP (2008) *The Americanization of Social Science. Intellectuals and Public Responsability in the Post War United States.* Philadelphia: Temple University Press.

Hansen AH (1920) Industrial Class Alignments in the United States. *Quarterly Publications of the American Statistical Association* vol 17(132): 417–425.

Harris AL (1939) Pure Capitalism and the Disappearance of the Middle Class. *The Journal of Political Economy* vol 47(3): 328–356.

Hart D (1998) Herbert Hoover's Last Laugh: The Enduring Significance of the "Associative State" in the United States. *Journal of Policy History* vol 9(4): 419–444.

Hartley GC (1951) The Middle Class, Alas! *Harper's Magazine* 1 February: 39–47.

Hartman A (2015) *A War for the Soul of America. A History of the Culture Wars.* Chicago: The University of Chicago Press.

Hartz L (1960 [1955]) *La tradizione liberale in America: interpretazione del pensiero politico americano dopo la rivoluzione.* Milano: Feltrinelli.

Haskell TL (1977) *The Emergence of Professional Social Science: The American Social Science Association and the Nineteenth-Century Crisis of Authority.* Urbana: University of Illinois Press.

Hays S (1972) Introduction: The New Organizational Society. In: Israel J (ed.), *Building the Organizational Society: Essays on Associational Activities in Modern America.* New York: Free Press, 1–17.

Headlines Proclaim the Rise of Fascism and Communism in America. *Life* 1937 (4): 19–26.

Hector L (1927) *Le problème des classes moyennes.* Dison: Winandy.

Heimann E (1938) The "Revolutionary Situation" and the Middle Classes. *Social Research* vol v(2): 227–236.

Henderson AM and Parsons T (eds.) (1947) *Max Weber: The Theory of Social and Economic Organizations.* Oxford: Oxford University Press.

Hilferding R (1910) *Das Finanzkapital: Eine Studie über die jüngste Entiwicklung des Kapitalismus.* Vienna: Verlag der Wiener.

Hill S (1934) Technicians in Revolt. *New Masses* 4 September: 17–18.

Hobsbawm EJ (1964) The Fabians Reconsidered, in Hobsbawm EJ *Labouring Men. Studies in the History of Labour.* London: Weidenfeld & Nicolson, 255–271.

Hobsbawn EJ (1989) La "classe media" inglese (1780-1920). In: Kocka J (ed.) *Borghesie europee dell'Ottocento.* Venezia: Marsilio, 100–106.

Hobson JA (1903) The Dynamics of the Wages Question-Discussion. *Publications of the American Economic Association* vol 4(1): 143–153.

Hodgson G (1976) *America in Our Time.* Garden City: Doubleday.

Hofstadter R (1955) *The Age of Reform: From Bryan to F.D.R.* New York: Vintage Books.

Hofstadter R (1966) *The Paranoid Style in American Politics and Other Essays.* New York: Knopf.

Holcombe AN (1940) *The Middle Classes in American Politics.* Cambridge: Harvard University Press, Cambridge.

Holli MG (2002) *The Wizard of Washington: Emil Hurja, Franklin Roosevelt, and the Birth of Public Opinion Polling.* New York: Palgrave.

Holsendolph E (1969) Middle-Class Blacks are Moving off the Middle. *Fortune* December: 90–99.

Hopkins AG (2002) *Globalization in World History.* New York: Norton.

Hopkins H (1938) *What is the "American Way". An Address delivered at the Chautauqua Institution Chautauqua.* Washington DC: U.S. Government Print.

Horowitz IL (1983) *C.W. Mills: An American Utopian.* New York: Free Press.

Hourwich IA (1911a) The Social Economic Classes of the Population of the United States I. *Journal of Political Economic* vol 19(3): 188–215.

Hourwich IA (1911b) The Social-Economic Classes of the Population of the United States II. *Journal of Political Economy* vol 19(4): 309–337.

Howard DS (1943) *The WPA and Federal Relief Policy.* New York: Russel Sage Foundation.

Hunt W (1897) Workers at Gainful Occupations at the Federal Censuses of 1870, 1880 and 1890. *Bulletin of the Department of Labor* vol II(1): 393–433.

Hunt W (1899) The Scope and Method of the Federal Census. In: *The Federal Census. Critical Essays by Members of the American Economic Association, Collected and Edited by a Special Committee*. New York: Macmillan, 466–494.

Hunt W (1909) The Federal Census of Occupations. *Publications of the American Statistical Association* vol 9(86): 467–485.

Huntington SP et al. (1975) *The Crisis of Democracy: Report on the Governability of Democracies to the Trilateral Commission*. New York: New York University Press.

Hyman L (2011) *Debtor Nation. The History of America in Red Ink*. Princeton: Princeton University Press.

Ihlder J (1925) The Business Man's Responsibility. *Nation's Business* 13 November: 52.

Incorporate Union of Middle Class (1920) *Washington Post*, 8 February.

Inventory. An Appraisal of Results of the Works Progress Administration (1938) Washington DC: U.S. Government Print Washington.

Is the Sit-Down Unfair? (1937) *The New Republic* 17 February: 32–33.

Jacobs M (2002) Inflation: "The Permanent Dilemma" of the American Middle Classes. In: Zunz O et al. (eds) *Social Contracts under Stress: The Middle Classes of America, Europe, and Japan at the Turn of the Century*, New York: Russel Sage Foundation, 131–153.

Jacobs M (2005) *Pocketbook Politics: Economic Citizenship in Twentieth-Century America*. Princeton: Princeton University Press.

Jessup JK (1943) America and the Future. *Life* September: 105–106.

Johnson JF (1919) Business clearly Explained. In: Powell LP (ed.) *The Social Unrest: Capital, Labor, and Public Turmoil* vol 1. New York: The Review of Reviews Company, 97–120.

Johnson L (1982) *Class and Social Development: A New Theory of the Middle Class*. Los Angeles: Sage.

Johnson P (1993) Class Law in Victorian England. *Past & Present* (141): 147–169.

Josephson M (1936) New Proletarians. *The New Republic* 29 January.

Kahn H (1979) *World Economic Development. 1979 and Beyond*. Boulder: Westview Press.

Karim MW (1984) Is Middle Class Really Doomed to Shrivel Away? *U.S. News & World Report*, 20 August, pp.65–67.

Karsh B (1959) White-Collar Labor. *The Nation* 31 January: 93–96.

Katznelson I (2002) Public Policy and the Middle-Class Racial Divide After the Second World War. In: Zunz O et al. (eds) *Social Contracts under Stress: The Middle Classes of America, Europe, and Japan at the Turn of the Century*, New York: Russel Sage Foundation, 157–177.

Katznelson I (2003) *Desolation and Enlightenment. Political Knowledge after Total War, Totalitarianism, and the Holocaust*. New York: Columbia University Press.

Katznelson I (2006) *When Affirmative Action was White: An Untold History of Racial Inequality in Twentieth-Century America*. New York: Norton.

Kaysen C (1957) The Social Significance of the Modern Corporation. *The American Economic Review* vol 47(2): 311–319.

Kazin M (1998) *The Populist Persuasion*. Ithaca: Cornell University Press.

Kelley R (1969) *The Transatlantic Persuasion. The Liberal Democratic Mind in the Age of Gladstone*. New York: Taylor & Francis.

Kellner H and Heuberger FW (1992) *Hidden Technocrats: The New Class and New Capitalism*. New Brunswick: Transaction Books.

Kerby P (1967) Revolt Against the Poor. The Reagan Backlash. *The Nation* 25 September: 262–267.

King LP and Szelény I (2004) *Theories of the New Class: Intellectuals and Power*. Minneapolis: University of Minnesota Press.

Kingsley D and Moore W (1945) Some Principles of Stratification. *American Sociological Review* vol 10(2): 242–249.

Kirchheimer O (1966) Private Man and Society. *Political Science Quarterly* 81(1): 1–24.

Kleher H (1976) Leninism, Lewis Corey, and the Failure of American Socialism. *Labor History* vol 18(2): 249–256.

Klingender FD (1935) *The Condition of Clerical Labour in Britain*. London: Martin Lawrence.

Kloppenberg J (1986) *Uncertain Victory: Social Democracy and Progressivism in European and American Thought (1870–1920)*. Oxford: Oxford University Press.

Kocka J (1973) The First World War and the Mittelstand: German Artisans and White Collar Workers. *Journal of Contemporary History* vol 8(1): 101–123.

Kocka J (1980 [1977]) *White Collar Workers in America 1890–1940. A Social-Political History in International Perspective*. Beverly Hills: SAGE.

Kocka J (1982) Marxist Social Analysis and the Problem of White Collar Employees. *State, Culture and Society* vol 1(2): 137–151.

Kocka J (1995) The Middle Class in Europe. *The Journal of Modern History* vol 67(4): 783–806.

Koepp S et al. (1986) Is the Middle Class Shrinking? Experts Debate the Impact of Job-Market Upheavals on Income Distribution. *Time* March: 54–57.

Kolko G (1963) *The Triumph of Conservatism: A Re-Interpretation of American History (1900–1916)*. Chicago: Quadrangle.

Komroff M (1919) High Cost of Living, In: Powell LP (ed.) *The Social Unrest: Capital, Labor, and Public Turmoil* vol 2. New York: The Review of Reviews Company, 505–508.

Kornhauser AW (1939) Analysis of Class Structure of Contemporary American Society. Psychological Bases of Class Divisions. In: Hartman GW and Newcomb T (eds) *Industrial Conflict: A Psychological Interpretation*. New York: The Cordon Company: 199–264.

Krakauer S (1930) *Die Angestellte*n. Frankfurt: Frankfurter Societäts-Druckerei.

Kramnick I (1990) *Republicanism and Bourgeois Radicalism: Political Ideology in Late Eighteenth-Century England and America.* Ithaca: Cornell University Press.

Kristol I (1970) When Virtue Loses All Her Loveliness-Some Reflections on Capitalism and The Free Society. *The Public Interest* (21): 3–13.

Kristol I (1971) On Capitalism and the Free Society. *The Public Interest* (22): 105.

Kristol I (1972) About Equality. *Commentary.* November: 41–47.

Kristol I (1973) Capitalism, Socialism, and Nihilism. *The Public Interest* (31): 3–13.

Kristol I (1974) Taxes, Poverty, and Equality. *The Public Interest* (37): 6–7, 27–28.

Kristol I (1975a) Corporate Capitalism in America. *The Public Interest* (41): 124–125.

Kristol I (1975b) Business and the "new class". *Wall Street Journal*, 19 May, p.8.

Kristol I (1978) On Conservatism and Capitalism. In: Kristol I *Two Cheers for Capitalism.* New York: Basic Books, 139–140.

Kristol I (1979) The 'New Class' Revisited. *Wall Street Journal*, 31 May, p.24.

Krugman P (2014) The Realities of Class Begin to Sink. *New York Times*, 27 January. Available at: https://krugman.blogs.nytimes.com/2014/01/27/the-realities-of-class-begin-to-sink-in/.

Kuenzli IR et al. (1949) Democracy vs. All-Inclusive Labor. *Labor and Nation* May/June: 20–23, 32–37.

Kutnets (1934) National Income, 1929-1932. New York: NBER. Available at: https://www.nber.org/system/files/chapters/c2258/c2258.pdf.

Labor and NRA. *The New Republic* 25 October 1933: 169.

Labor, Capital and the Public. A Discussion of the Relations between Employees, Employers and the Public. Chicago: Public Policy Publishing, 1905.

Labor. The Longest White-Collar Walkout. *Fortune* March 1952: 49–52.

Labor's Interest in Law and Order. Editorial: Chicago Chronicle. In: *Labor, Capital and the Public. A Discussion of the Relations between Employees, Employers and the Public.* Chicago: Public Policy Publishing, 1905, 174–175.

Lambrechts H (1935) *Contribution à l'histoire de l'Institute international des classes moyennes.* Dison: Winandy.

Landy A (1940) Mr. Corey Reconsidered. The Case of the Spurious Marxist. He Abandons the Socialism he never Possessed. *New Masses* 26 March: 22–26.

Lapin A (1937) Middle Classes. Left or Right? Experiences in the Steel Strike Show Why both Labor and Capital Try to Organize Them as Comrades-in-arms. *New Masses* 10 August: 7.

Lash C (1991) *The True and Only Heaven: Progress and Its Critics.* New York: Norton.

Lasswell HD (1933a) The Psychology of Hitlerism. *Political Quarterly* vol 4(3): 373–384.

Lasswell HD (1933b) The Problem of World-Unity: In Quest of a Myth. *International Journal of Ethics* vol 44(1): 68–93.

Lasswell HD (1935) The Moral Vocation of the Middle-Income Skill Group. *International Journal of Ethics* vol 45 (2): 127–137.

Lasswell HD (1937) The Relation of Skill Politics to Class Politics and National Politics. *Chinese Social and Political Science Review* (21): 298–313.

Lasswell HD (1941a) *Democracy through Public Opinion.* Menasha: George Banta Publishing.

Lasswell HD (1941b) Radio as an Instrument of Reducing Personal Insecurity. *Studies in Philosophy and Social Science* vol 9(1): 49–65.

Lasswell HD (1943), *Public Opinion in War and Peace. How Americans Make Up Their Minds.* Washington. National Council for the Social Studies, National Association of Secondary-School Principals, Departments of the National Education Association.

Lasswell HD (1949) "Inevitable" War: A Problem in the Control of Long-Range Expectations. *World Politics* vol 2(1): 1–3.

Lasswell HD (1950 [1934]) World Politics and Personal Insecurity. In: Lasswell HD et al. *A Study of Power.* Glencoe. The Free Press, 3–327.

Lasswell HD (1977) *On Political Sociology.* Chicago: Chicago University Press.

Lasswell HD and Blumenstock D (2012 [1939]) *World Revolutionary Propaganda. A Chicago Study.* London: Forgotten Books.

Lasswell HD and Kaplan A (1950) *Power and Society; A Framework for Political Inquiry.* New Haven: Yale University Press.

Lasswell HD et al. (1943) *War and The Middle Class: A Radio Discussion* by The University of Chicago Round Table No. 278 (490TH Broadcast in Cooperation with the National Broadcasting Company, July 18, 1943).

Laswell HD (1938) *Continental Security; an American Program of Peaceful Unity, Democracy and Abundance.* Washington DC: William Alanson White Psychiatric Foundation, Material for the Study of Propaganda No. 1 of the *Political Symbol Series.*

Laswell HD (1943) *Public Opinion in War and Peace. How Americans Make Up Their Minds.* Washington DC: National Council for the Social Studies, National Association of Secondary-School Principals, Departments of the National Education Association.

Laswell HD (1947) Toward a Skill commonwealth: A Workable Goal of World Politics. In: Bryson L et al. *Approaches to Group Understanding, Sixth Symposium of the Conference on Science, Philosophy and Religion in Their Relation to the Democratic Way of Life.* New York: Harper & Bros, 290–301.

Lauck WJ (1929) *The New Industrial Revolution and Wages.* New York: Funk & Wagnalls.

Laudani R (ed.) (2012) *Il nemico tedesco: scritti e rapporti riservati sulla Germania nazista (1943–1945).* Bologna: il Mulino.

Laufenburger H (1933) Classes moyennes et national-socialisme en Allemagne. *Revue politique et parlementaire* 10 April: 46–60.

Laurie B (1997) *Artisans into Workers. Labor in Nineteenth-Century America.* New York: Hill & Wang.

Laurie B (2001) "We are not afraid to work": Master Mechanics and the Market Revolution in the Antebellum North. In: Bledstein BJ and Johnston RD (eds)

The Middling Sorts. Explorations in the History of the American Middle Class. New York: Routledge, 50–68.

Le Béguec G (1993) Prélude à un syndicalisme bourgeois. L'association de défense des classes moyennes (1907–1939). *Vingtième Siècle. Revue d'histoire* vol 37: 93–104.

Lears J (2009) *Rebirth of a Nation: The Making of Modern America (1877–1920).* New York: Harper Collins.

Lederer E (1931) *Technischer Fortschritt und Arbeitslosigkeit.* Tübingen: Mohr.

Lederer E (1937 [1912]) *The Problem of the Modern Salaried Employee: Its Theoretical and Statistical Basis,* xerox, translated by E.E. Warburg, project supervisor W.R. Dittmar, Ph.D. published by the State Department of Social Welfare and the Department of Social Science, Columbia University, as a report on Project No. 165-97-6999-6027 conducted under the auspices of the Works Progress Administration. Translation held by Columbia University's Butler Library, New York.

Lederer E and Marschak J (1937 [1926]) *The New Middle Class,* xerox, translated by S. Ellison, project supervisor W.R. Dittmar, Ph.D. published by the State Department of Social Welfare and the Department of Social Science, Columbia University, as a report on Project No. 165-97-6999-6027 conducted under the auspices of the Works Progress Administration. Translation held by Columbia University's Butler Library, New York.

Leighton GR (1932) And If the Revolution comes ...? *Harper's Magazine* March: 466–476.

Leonhard J (2007) Progressive Politics and the Dilemma of Reform: German and American Liberalism in Comparison (1880–1920). In: Vaudagna M (ed.) *The Place of Europe in American History: Twentieth-Century Perspectives.* Torino: Otto, 115–132.

Lerner M (1937) A Third Party for 1940? *The Nation* 4 September: 234–235.

Lerner M (1938) Six Errors of Marxism. *The New Republic* 16 November: 37–38.

Lerner M (1940) The Left: End and Beginning. *The Nation* 10 February: 164–166.

Lerner M (1957) *America as a Civilization: Life and Thought in the United States Today.* New York: Simon & Schuster.

Leuchtenburg WE (1976) *Roosevelt e il New Deal (1932–1940).* Roma-Bari: Laterza.

Lewis HG (1939) The Negro Business, Professional, and White-Collar Worker. *The Journal of Negro Education* vol 75(3): 430–445.

Lewis R and Maude A (1953) *The English Middle Classes.* London: Penguin Books.

Lewis S (1922) *Babbitt.* Harcourt, Brace & Co.

Lichtenstein N (1989) From Corporatism to Collective Bargaining: Organized Labor and the Eclipse of Social Democracy in the Postwar Era. In: Fraser S and Gerstle G *The Rise and Fall of the New Deal Order (1930–1980).* Princeton: Princeton University Press, 122–152.

Lindley EK (1974 [1933]) *The Roosevelt Revolution.* New York: Da Capo Press.

Lippmann W (1922) *Public Opinion.* New York: Macmillan.

Lippmann W (1925) *Phantom Public.* Harcourt, Brace & Company.

Lipset SM (1963) *The First New Nation: the United States in Historical and Comparative Perspective.* New York: Basic Books.

Lipset SM and Bendix R (1951) Social Status and Social Structure: A Re-Examination of Data and Interpretations. *The British Journal of Sociology* vol 11(3): 230–254.

Living on the Ragged Edge, Family Income vs. Family Expenses (1925) *Harper's Magazine* December.

Llyod H (director) (1923) *Safety Last* [Motion picture]. Hal Roach Studios: Culver City.

Lockwood D (1958) *The Blackcoated Worker. A Study in Class Consciousness.* Oxford: Clarendon Press.

Loeb H (1933) *Life in a Technocracy.* New York: Viking.

Lola de San Carlos (1893) Middle-Class Life in France. *The North American Review* vol 156(437): 478–484.

Longworth RC and Neikirk B (1979) The Changing American Worker. A Special Report. *Chicago Tribune*, 16 September, pp.1, 18.

Lopez AR and Weinstein B (2012) Introduction. We Shall be All: Toward a Transnational History of the Middle Class. In: Lopez AR and Weinstein B (eds) *The Making of the Middle Class. Toward a Transnational History.* Durham: Duke University Press, 1–28.

Lorini A (1980) *Ingegneria umana e scienze sociali negli USA (1890–1920).* Messina-Firenze: G. D'Anna.

Lovett RM (1936) Revolt or Revolution? *The New Republic* 3 June: 109.

Lovin HT (1971) The Fall of Farmer-Labor Parties (1936–1938). *The Pacific Northwest Quarterly* vol 62(1): 16–26.

Low AM (1913) What is Socialism? IV Some Reasons for the Present Discontent. *The North American Review* vol 197(689): 556–565.

Lynd R and Lynd H (1929) *Middletown. A Study in Modern America Culture.* New York: Harcourt Brace.

Lynd R and Lynd H (1965 [1937]) *Middletown in Transition. A Study in Cultural Conflict.* New York: Harcourt Brace.

Magil AB (1936) Pipers of Reaction. *New Masses* 7 April: 18.

Magil AB (1938a) Who is the Little Business Man? *New Masses* 5 April: 10.

Magil AB (1938b) The New Deal and Labor. *New Masses* 12 July: 17.

Magil AB (1940) How FDR Killed the New Deal. *New Masses* 5 November: 7.

Maier CS (1988) *In Search of Stability. Exploratios in Historical Political Economy.* Cambridge: Cambridge University Press.

Maier CS (2006) *Among Empires. American Ascendancy and Its Predecessors.* Cambridge: Harvard University Press.

Malatesta M (2011) *Professional Men, Professional Women: the European Professions from the Nineteenth Century until today.* Los Angeles: Sage.

Malthus TR (1826) *An Essay on the Principle of Population.* London: Reeves and Turner.

Mangoni L (1985) *Una crisi di fine secolo. La cultura italiana e la Francia fra Otto e Novecento*. Torino: Einaudi.

Mangoni L (1988) *La terza repubblica e la sociologia di Durkheim*. Bologna: il Mulino.

Mann M (2012) *The Sources of Social Power. Volume II: The Rise of Classes and Nation-States (1760–1914)*. Cambridge: Cambridge University Press.

Mannheim (1929) *Ideology and Utopia: An Introduction to the Sociology of Knowledge*. New York: Mariner Books.

Marshall A (1873) *The Future of the Working Classes*. London: T. Tofts: Available at: https://catalogue.nla.gov.au/Record/6096802.

Marshall TR (1919) The Awakening Middle Class. Reprinted from the New York Times, Sunday October 5, 1919. In: Powell LP (ed.) *The Social Unrest: Capital, Labor, and Public Turmoil* vol 1. New York: The Review of Reviews Company, 325–334.

Marx K (1979 [1852]) The Eighteenth Brumaire of Louius Bonaparte. In: *Karl Marx Frederick Engels Collected Works*, vol. 11. London: International Publishers Co, 99–197.

Marx K (1986 [1871]) The Civil War in France. In: *Karl Marx Frederick Engels Collected Works*, vol. 22. London: International Publishers Co, 435–570.

Mason R and Morgan I (2017) *The Liberal Consensus Reconsidered. American Politics and Society in the Postwar Era*. Gainesville: University of Florida Press.

Masterman CFG (1909) *The Condition of England*. London: Methue & Co.

Masterman CFG (1922) *England After the War*. London: Hodder and Stoughton.

Mattson K (2002) *Intellectuals in Action: The Origins of the New Left and Radical Liberalism (1945–1970)*. Philadelphia: Pennsylvania University Press.

Mayer A (1975) The Lower Middle Class as a Historical Problem. *Journal of Modern History* vol 47(3): 409–411.

Mayo E (1933) *The Human Problems of an Industrial Civilization*. New York: Macmillan.

McAdams J (2015) *The New Class in Post-Industrial Society*. New York: Macmillan.

McComb M (2006) *Great Depression and the Middle Class. Experts, Collegiate Youth and Business Ideology (1929–1941)*. New York: Routledge.

McDougal MS and Reisman WM (1979) Harold Dwight Lasswell 1902–1978. *The American Journal of International Law* vol 88(4): 655–660.

McGee R (1959) White-Collar Explosion. *The Nation* 7 February: 112–115.

McGerr M (2005) *A Fierce Discontent: The Rise and Fall of the Progressive Movement in America*. Oxford: Oxford University Press.

McKibbin R (1998) *Classes and Cultures: England (1918–1951)*. Oxford: Oxford University Press.

McLeod H (1977) White Collar Values and the Role of Religion. In: Crossick G *The Lower Middle Class in Britain (1870–1914)*. London: Croom Helm, 58–62.

Meltzer CH (1919) The Intermediate Millions. *North American Review* (209): 225–233.

Merriam CE (1939) *The New Democracy and the New Despotism*. New York: McGraw-Hill Book Company.

Merrill L (1941) *Defense and Salaried Employee*, reprint of an address by L. Merrill delivered May 18, 1941. New York: UOPWA.

Merrill L (1943) *A Salary Policy to Win the War*. New York: UOPWA.

Merrill L (1944) *The White Collar Worker and the Future of the Nation*. Testimony to the Senate Sub-Committee on Wartime Health and Education, January 1941. New York: UOPWA.

Merrill L (1946) Memo to Professionals. *New Masses* 8 January: 15.

Merton RK (1938) Social Structure and Anomie. *American Sociological Review* vol 3(5): 672–682.

Meusel A (1933) Middle Class. In: Seligman ERA et al. (eds) *Encyclopaedia of the Social Sciences*, vol. 10, Macmillan: New York, 407–415.

Meyer BD and Sullivan JX (2013) Consumption and Income Inequality and the Great Recession. *The American Economic Review* vol 103(3): 178–183.

Michelmore MC (2012) *Tax and Spend. The Welfare State, Tax politics and the Limits of American Liberalism*. Philadelphia: University of Pennsylvania Press.

Michels R (1909) Sulla scadenza della classe media industriale antica e sul sorgere di una classe media industriale moderna nei paesi di economica spiccatamente capitalistica. *Giornale degli economisti* vol XXXVIII (2): 85–103.

Middle Class Strengthens Economic Role. *Chicago Daily Tribune*, 3 January 1956: 2.

Middle-Class Blues. *National Review* 7 November 1994: 14–15.

Mill JS (1859) *On Liberty*. London: John W. Parker and Son.

Mill JS (1978 [1823]) Essay on Government, Jurisprudence, Liberty of the Press, Education, and Prisons and Prison Discipline. In: Lively J and Rees J (eds) *Utilitarian Logic and Politics*. Oxford: Oxford University Press.

Miller L (1936) The Negro Middle Class. The Failure of Emancipation. *New Masses* 7 April: 20–21.

Mills CW (1942) Review of W. Lloyd Warner and Paul S. Lunt, The Social Life of a Modern Community. *American Sociological Review* vol 7(2): 263–271.

Mills CW (1943) The Professional Ideology of Social Pathologists. *American Journal of Sociology* vol 49(2): 165–180.

Mills CW (1949a) Notes on White Collar Unionism. *Labor and Nation* March/April: 17–21.

Mills CW (1949b) White Collar Unions-Labor-Democracy. *Labor and Nation* May/June: 17–20.

Mills CW (2006 [1959]) *The Sociological Imagination*. Oxford: Oxford University Press.

Mills CW (2012 [1951]) *White Collar. The American Middle Classes*. London: Forgotten Books.

Minton B (1935) Work or Starve! *New Masses* 10 September: 16–18.

Mistura S (ed.) (2001) *Figure del feticismo*. Torino: Einaudi.

Mondolfo R (1925) *Il problema delle classi* medie. Milano: La Giustizia.

Montgomery D (1974) The 'New Unionism' and the Transformation of Workers' Consciousness in America (1909–1922). *Journal of Social History* vol 7(4): 509–529.

Montgomery D (1993) *Citizen Worker*. Cambridge: Cambridge University Press.

Moskowitz M (2012) Arent' We All? Aspiration, Acquisition and the American Middle Class. In: Lopez AR and Weinstein B (eds) *The Making of the Middle Class. Toward a Transnational History*. Durham: Duke University Press, 75–86.

Moulin L and Aërt L (1954) Les classes moyennes. Essai de bibliographie critique d'une définition. *Revue d'Histoire économique et social* vol 32(3): 168–181.

Mouriaux R (1989) La CGT et les classes moyennes non-fonctionnaires pendant l'entre-deux-guerres. *Matériaux pour l'histoire de notre temps* (17): 32–35.

National Labor Relation Board Annual Reports (1936–1938) Washington DC: Government Printing Office.

Negro Middle Class. *Chicago Daily Defender* 21 August 1967: 13.

Nelson D (1980) *Frederick W. Taylor and the Rise of Scientific Management*. Madison: University of Wisconsin Press.

Niebuhr R (1932) The German Election. *The New Republic* 16 November: 6.

Niebuhr R (1933) The Opposition in Germany. *The New Republic* 28 June: 169–171.

Ninkovich F (2009) *Global Dawn. The Cultural Foundation of American Internationalism (1865–1890)*. Cambridge: Harvard University Press.

Nixon R (1971) *Address to the Nation on Labor Day* 6 September. Available at: https://www.presidency.ucsb.edu/documents/address-the-nation-labor-day.

Noble DF (1986) *Forces of Production: A Social History of Industrial Automation*. Oxford: Oxford University Press.

Novak M (1978) *The American Vision. An Essay on the Future of Democratic Capitalism*. Washington DC: American Enterprise Institute for Public Policy Research.

Novak M (1992) Middle Class "meltdown"? *Forbes* 20 January: 94–95.

Nygreen GT and Schreiber EM (1970) Subjective Social Class in America (1945–1968). *Social Forces* vol 48(3): 348–356.

O'Noyle L (1966) The Middle Class in Western Europe (1815–1848). *The American Historical Review* vol 71(3): 826–845.

Oakwood J (1922) Will Labor Maintain Its Lead over "White-Collars"? *Forbes* 11 November: 141–142.

Ogburn W (1922) *Social Change with Respect to Culture and Original Nature*. New York: B.W. Huebsch.

Ogburn WF and Peterson D (1916) Political Thought of Social Classes. *Political Science Quarterly* vol 31(2): 300–317.

On the White Collar Front (1934) *New Masses* 19 June: 9.

One Big Family. A Management Chart (1949) *Fortune* February: 65–67.

Ormsbee H (1912) The Man who Failed. *The Atlantic Monthly* (109): 508.

Ortner SB (2002) Subjects and Capital: A Fragment of a Documentary Ethnography. *Ethnos* vol 67(1): 9–32.

Ottanelli FM (1991) *The Communist Party of the United States. From Depression to World War II*. New Brunswick: Rutgers University Press.

Page CH (1964) *Class and American Sociology: From Ward to Ross*. New York: Octagon Books.

Palm FC (1936) *The Middle Classes Then and Now*. New York: Macmillan.

Palmer RR (1959) *The Age of the Democratic Revolution: a Political History of Europe and America (1760–1800)*. Princeton: Princeton University Press.

Parker R (1972) *The Myth of the Middle Class*. New York: Harper Colophon Books.

Parrington VL (1927) *The Colonial Mind 1620–1800*. New York, Harcourt, Brace & Co.

Parsons T (1937) *The Structure of Social Action*. New York: McGraw Hill.

Parsons T (1940) An Analytical Approach to the Theory of Social Stratification. *American Journal of Sociology* vol 45(6): 841–862.

Parsons T (1967) *Structures and Process in Modern Societies*. Glencoe: The Free Press.

Parsons T (1993 [1940]) Memorandum: The Development of Groups and Organizations Amenable to Use against American Institutions and Foreign Policy and Possible Measures of Prevention. In Gerhardt U *Talcott Parsons on National Socialism*. New York: Walter de Gruyter, 101–130.

Passos DJ (1935) *The Role of the Middle Class in Social Development. Fascism, Populism, Communism, Socialism*. In: *Economic Essays in Honor of Wesley Clair Mitchell*. New York: Columbia University Press, 395–423.

Patel KK (2017) *The New Deal. A Global History*. Princeton: Princeton University Press.

Patten SN (1896) *The Theory of Social Forces*. Philadelphia: American Academy of Political and Social Sciences.

Patten SN (1907) *The New Basis of Civilization*. New York: Macmillan.

Peixotto JB (1927) *Getting and Spending at the Professional Standard of Living: a Study of the Costs of Living an Academic Life*. New York: Macmillan.

Pells RH (1973) *Radical Visions and American Dreams. Culture and Social Thought in the Depression Years*. New York: Harper Torchbooks.

Pells RH (1985) *The Liberal Mind in a Conservative Age: American Intellectuals in the 1940s and 1950s*. New York: Harper & Row.

Pendleton Herring E (1940) *The Politics of Democracy. American Parties in Action*. New York: Rinehart & Company.

Perkin H (1969) *The Origins of Modern English Society 1780–1880*. London: Ark Paperbacks.

Perkin H (1989) *The Rise of Professional Society*. London: Routledge.

Perlman S (1928) *A Theory of Labor Movement*. New York: Macmillan.

Pfautz HW (1953) The Current Literature on Social Stratification: Critique and Bibliography. *American Journal of Sociology* vol 58(4): 391–418.

Phillips K (1992) *Boiling Point. Republicans, Democrats, and the Decline of Middle-Class Prosperity*. New York: Random House.

Phillips-Fein K (2009) *Invisible Hands: The Businessmen's Crusade Against the New Deal*. New York: Norton.

Pilbeam PM (1990) *The Making of the Middle Class? The Middle Classes in Europe (1789–1914): France, Germany, Italy and Russia*. Chicago: Lyceum Books.

Pinkey DH (1964) The Myth of the French Revolution of 1830. In: Ropp T *A Festschrift for Frederick B. Artz*. Chapel Hill: University of North Carolina Press, 52–71.

Potter D (1954) *People of Plenty: Economic Abundance and the American Character*. Chicago: Chicago University Press.

Potthof H (1989) Syndicats et classes moyennes à l'époque de Weimar. *Matériaux pour l'histoire de notre temps* (17): 36–41.

Powell LF Jr (1971) *Attack of American Free Enterprise System* 23 August. Available at: https://lawdigitalcommons.bc.edu/cgi/viewcontent.cgi?article=1078&context =darter_materials.

Pratt Fairchild H (ed.) (1944) *Dictionary of Sociology*, Greenwood Press: Westport.

Preston Y (1967) Tragedy of the Black Middle-Class. *Afro-American* 11 November: 17.

Productivity is the Sticking Point. *Business Week* 10 July 1971: 17–19.

Prosperous ... Restless ... Demanding ... New Breed of Workers. *U.S. News & World Report*, 3 September 1979, pp. 35–41.

Purcell EA Jr (1973) *The Crisis of Democratic Theory. Scientific Naturalism and the Problem of Value*. Lexington: University Press of Kentucky.

Ramsey D (1935a) The Dilemma of the Middle Class. *New Masses* 17 December: 40–42.

Ramsey D (1935b) Middle Class Attitude. Review of Insurgent America e An Exclusive Labor Party. *New Masses* 16 July: 7, 39–40.

Recent Social Trends in United States. Report of the President's Research Committee on Social Trends (1933). New York: McGraw-Hill.

Reich R (1991) *The Work of Nations*. New York: Vintage Books Edition.

Report of the Committee of the Senate upon the Relations between Labor and Capital, and Testimony taken by the Committee (1885). Washington DC: Government Printing Office.

Report on Organization (1938), May. In: CPUSA Records: Series I, Tamiment Library NYU, BOX 170, Folder 17.

Report on the Works Program (1936) Division of Research, Statistics, and Records. Washington DC: Government Printing Office.

Research Work on Projects of the Works Administration. Reprinted from the Hearings before the Subcommittee of the Committee on Appropriations, House of Representatives, on the Emergency Relief Appropriation Act of 1938 and Public Works Administration Appropriation Act of 1938. Washington DC: Government Print, 1938.

Resolutions of the Ninth Convention of the Communist Party (1936), 24–28 June. In: CPUSA Records: Series I, Tamiment Library NYU BOX 170, Folder 17.

Resolutions of the Tenth Convention of the Communist Party (1938), 27–31 May. In: CPUSA Records: Series I, Tamiment Library NYU BOX 170, Folder 19.

Ricciardi M (2007) Performance, potere, azione politica. Appunti per una discussion. *Scienza & Politica* vol 19(36): 43–57.

Ricciardi M (2008) L'ordine ritrovato. Le scienze sociali statunitensi e la politica della teoria. In: Mezzadra S (ed.) *Cantieri d'Occidente. Scienze sociali e democrazia tra Europa e Stati Uniti dopo la Seconda guerra mondiale.* Soveria Mannelli: Rubbettino, 65–86.

Ricciardi M (2013a) Ascesa e crisi del costituzionalismo societario. Germania (1840–1900). *Ricerche di storia politica* vol 16(3): 283–300.

Ricciardi M (2013b) Dallo Stato moderno allo Stato globale. Storia e trasformazione di un concetto. *Scienza & Politica* vol 25(48): 75–93.

Rice SA (1934) Statistical Opportunities and Responsibilities. *Journal of the American Statistical Association* vol 29(185): 1–10.

Richman LS (1990) Why the Middle Class is Anxious. *Fortune* May: 106–112.

Richman LS (1990) The New Middle. *Fortune* August: 104–113.

Riesman D (1964) Abundance for What and Other Essays. Garden City: Doubleday.

Rimer S (1996) A Hometown Feels Less Like Home. *New York Times*, 6 March, pp. 1, 16–18.

Rivière L (1910) La notion des classes moyennes, in *Les classes moyennes dans le commerce et l'industrie*, 29° congrès de la Société internationale de l'économie sociale et des Unions de la paix, Société d'économie sociale.

Rizas S (2018) *The End of Middle Class Politics?* Newcastle: Cambridge Scholars Publishing.

Robbins MW (2017) *Middle Class Union. Organizing the Consuming Public in Post-World War I America.* Ann Arbor: University of Michigan Press.

Robinson DL (1999) *The Measures of Democracy: Polling, Market Research, and Public Life (1930–1945).* Torino: University of Toronto Press.

Rochester A (1931) The Middle-Class Budget. In: Eliot TD (ed.) *American Standards and Planes of Living. Readings in the Social Economics of Consumption.* Boston: Ginn and Company, 553–563.

Rodgers DT (1982) In Search of Progressivism. *Review in American History* vol 10(4): 113–132.

Rodgers DT (2000) *Atlantic Crossings. Social Politics in a Progressive Age.* Cambridge: The Belknap Press of Harvard University Press, Cambridge, 2000.

Rodgers DT (2011) *Age of Fracture.* Cambridge: Cambridge University Press.

Roediger D (1991) *Wages of Whiteness. Race and the Making of the American Working Class.* London: Verso.

Roediger D (2020) *The Sinking Middle Class. A Political History.* New York: Or Books.

Rogow AA (ed.) (1969) *Politics, Personality and Social Science in the Twentieth Century. Essays in Honor of Harold D. Lasswell.* Chicago: Chicago University Press.

Romanelli R (1989) Borghesia/Burgentum/Bourgeoisie. Itinerari europei di un concetto. In: Kocka J (ed.) *Borghesie europee dell'Ottocento*. Venezia: Marsilio, 69–94.

Romano P (1994 [1947]) L'operaio americano. In: Montaldi D *Bisogna sognare. Scritti 1952–1975*. Milano: Colibri.

Romero F (2009) *Storia della guerra fredda. L'ultimo conflitto per l'Europa*. Torino: Einaudi.

Roosevelt FD (1932a) *Radio Address from Albany, New York: The Forgotten Man Speech*. 7 April. Available at: https://www.presidency.ucsb.edu/documents/radio-address-from-albany-new-york-the-forgotten-man-speech.

Roosevelt FD (1932b) *Address Accepting the Presidential Nomination at the Democratic National Convention in Chicago*. 2 July. Available at: https://www.presidency.ucsb.edu/documents/address-accepting-the-presidential-nomination-the-democratic-national-convention-chicago-1.

Roosevelt FD (1932c) *Address to the American Legion Convention, Chicago, Illinois*. 31 October. Available at: https://www.presidency.ucsb.edu/documents/address-the-american-legion-convention-chicago-illinois.

Roosevelt FD (1933a) *Campaign Address on a Program for Unemployment and Long-Range Planning at Boston, Massachusetts*. 2 October. Available at: https://www.presidency.ucsb.edu/documents/campaign-address-program-for-unemployment-and-long-range-planning-boston-massachusetts.

Roosevelt FD (1933b) *Statement on N.I.R.A.* 16 June. Available at: http://docs.fdrlibrary.marist.edu/odnira.html.

Roosevelt FD (1934) *Address Delivered at Green Bay, Wisconsin*. 9 August. Available at: https://www.presidency.ucsb.edu/documents/address-delivered-green-bay-wisconsin.

Roosevelt FD (1935a) *Statement Fixing Jurisdictions of P.W.A. and W.P.A.* 3 July. Available at: https://www.presidency.ucsb.edu/documents/statement-fixing-jurisdictions-pwa-and-wpa.

Roosevelt FD (1935b) *Address at Atlanta, Georgia*. 29 November. Available at: https://www.presidency.ucsb.edu/documents/address-atlanta-georgia.

Roosevelt FD (1935c) *Address on Receiving the 1935 Award for Distinguished Service to Agriculture, Chicago, Illinois*. 9 December. Available at: https://www.presidency.ucsb.edu/documents/address-receiving-the-1935-award-for-distinguished-service-agriculture-chicago-illinois.

Roosevelt FD (1936a) *Fireside Chat*. 6 September. Available at: https://millercenter.org/the-presidency/presidential-speeches/september-6-1936-fireside-chat-8-farmers-and-laborers.

Roosevelt FD (1936b) *Acceptance Speech for the Renomination for the Presidency*. 27 June. Available at: https://www.presidency.ucsb.edu/documents/acceptance-speech-for-the-renomination-for-the-presidency-philadelphia-pa.

Roosevelt FD (1938) *Address at Denton, Maryland* 5 September. Available at: https://www.fdrlibrary.org/utterancesfdr.

Roosevelt FD (1940) *Statement on Peace Time Universal Selective Service.* 16 September. Available at: https://www.presidency.ucsb.edu/documents/statement-peace-time -universal-selective-service.

Roosevelt FD (1942) *Message to Congress on Stabilizing the Economy.* 7 September. Available at: https://www.presidency.ucsb.edu/documents/message-congress-stab ilizing-the-economy.

Roosevelt FD (1943a) *Veto of H. R. 2869.* 2 July. Available at: https://www.presidency .ucsb.edu/documents/veto-h-r-2869.

Roosevelt FD (1943b) *Excerpts from the Press.* 15 June. Available at: https://www.preside ncy.ucsb.edu/documents/excerpts-from-the-press-conference-14.

Roosevelt FD (1944) *Remarks at Hartford, Connecticut.* 4 November. Available at: https://www.presidency.ucsb.edu/documents/address-hartford-connecticut.

Roosevelt T (1905) The Remedy of Wrongs. From Various Messages to Congress. In: *Labor, Capital and the Public. A Discussion of the Relations between Employees, Employers and the Public.* Chicago: Public Policy Publishing, 181–189.

Roosevelt T (1906) *Sixth Annual Message to the Senate and House of Representatives.* 3 December. Available at: https://www.presidency.ucsb.edu/documents/sixth-ann ual-message-4.

Rosenberg E (1982) *Spreading the American Dream: American Economic and Cultural Expansion.* New York: Hill & Wang.

Rosenberg E (2012) *Consuming the American Century.* In: Bacevich AJ *The Short American Century.* Cambridge: Harvard University Press, 38–58.

Ross D (1997 [1991]) *The Origins of American Social Sciences.* Cambridge: Cambridge University Press.

Ross E (1934) Research and Statistical Program of the Federal Emergency Relief Administration. *Journal of the American Statistical Association* vol 29(187): 288–294.

Ross EA (1896a) Social Control. *American Journal of Sociology* vol 1(5): 513–535.

Ross EA (1896b) Social Control II. Law and Public Opinion. *American Journal of Sociology* vol 1(6): 753–770.

Ross EA (1900a) Social Control. XV. Custom. *American Journal of Sociology* vol 5(5): 604–616.

Ross EA (1900b) Social Control. XIX. Class Control. *American Journal of Sociology* vol 5(3): 381–395.

Ross EA (1914 [1901]) Social Control. A Survey of the Foundations of Order. New York: Macmillan.

Ross FA (1924) The Passing of the German Middle Class. *American Journal of Sociology* vol 29(5): 529–538.

Rostin B (1967) The Militants and the Middle Class. *New York Amsterdam News*, 14 October, p.15.

Rostow WW (1960) *The Stages of Economic Growth: A Non-Communist Manifesto*. Cambridge: Cambridge University Press.

Roversi A (1984) *Il magistero della scienza. Storia del Verein für Sozialpolitik dal 1872 al 1888*. Milano: Franco Angeli.

Rubenstein E (1991) Middle-Class Malaise. *National Review* 2 December: 16.

Rugg H (1933) *The Great Technology*. New York: John Day Company.

Ruhlmann J (1989) Les classes moyennes, le Parti socialiste de France et le Plan: l'impossible ralliement. *Matériaux pour l'histoire de notre temps* vol XVII(1): 47–52.

Saint-Léon EM (1905) Die Mittelstandsfrage in Frankreich. In: *Internationaler Kongress des städtischen und ländlichen Mittelstandes*, 16–18 August, p.1–2.

Saint-Léon EM (1910) L'organisation corporative des classes moyennes. In: Saint-Léon EM, *Classes moyennes industrielles et commerciales*. Paris: Alcan, 166–175.

Salvati M (2000) *Da Berlino a New York. Crisi della classe media e futuro della democrazia nelle scienze sociali degli anni trenta*. Milano: Mondadori.

Salvatorelli L (1923) *Nazionalfascismo*. Roma: Libero.

Samuel R (1983) The Middle Class Between Wars. *New Socialist* January/February (1).

Sargent DJ (2015) *A Superpower Transformed: The Remaking of American Foreign Relations in the 1970s*. Oxford: Oxford University Press.

Sassen S (2013) The Middle Classes. An Historic Actor in Today's Global World. *Juncture* vol 20(2): 125–128. Available at: http://www.saskiasassen.com/PDFs/publications/the-middle-classes.pdf.

Schanberg SH (1982) Era of the New Sadism. *New York Times*, 30 October.

Schiera P (1987) *Il laboratorio borghese: scienza e politica nella Germania dell'Ottocento*. Bologna: il Mulino.

Schiera P and Tenbruck F (eds) (1989) *Gustav Schmoller e il suo tempo: la nascita delle scienze sociali in Germania e in Italia*. Bologna: il Mulino.

Schlesinger AM (1930) *Political and Social History of the United States*. New York: Macmillan.

Schlesinger AM, Jr. (1949) *The Vital Center*. Boston: Houghton Mifflin.

Schor JB (1992) *The Overworked American: The Unexpected Decline of Leisure*. New York: Basic Books.

Schor P (2017) *Counting Americans: How the US Census Classified the Nation*. Oxford: Oxford University Press.

Schulter DB (1979) Economics and the Sociology of Consumption: Simon Patten and early Academic Sociology in America. *Journal of the History of Sociology* (1): 132–162.

Seaver E (1934) White Collar Workers and Students Swing Into Action. *New Masses* 5 June: 16–17.

Seed J (1992) From 'Middling Sort' to Middle Class in Late Eighteenth and Early Nineteenth-Century England. In: Bush ML *Social Orders and Social Classes in Europe since 1500*. Manchester: Manchester University Press: 114–135.

Seidelman R. (1985) *Disenchanted Realists. Political Science and the American Crisis*. New York: SUNY Press.

Seligman ERA (1903) Economics and Social Progress. *Publications of American Economic Association* vol 4(1): 52–70.

Settis B (2016) *Fordismi. Storia politica della produzione di massa*. Bologna: il Mulino.

Shachtman M (1940a) The Marxists Reply to Corey I. *The Nation* February 17.

Shachtman M (1940b) The Marxists Reply to Corey II. *The Nation* February 24.

Shachtman M (1940c) The Marxists Reply to Corey III. *The Nation* March 9.

Shaw GB (1993 [1894]) *Socialism and Superior Brains*. London: Routledge.

Shlakman V (1951/1952) Status and Ideology of Office Workers. *Science & Society* vol 16(1): 1–26.

Sick KP (1993) Le concept de classes moyennes. Notion sociologique ou slogan politique? *Vingtième Siècle. Revue d'histoire* (37): 14–16.

Siegfried A (1930) *Tableau des partis en France*. Paris: Grasset.

Simmel G (1896) Superiority and Subordination as Subject-Matter of Sociology II. *American Journal of Sociology* vol 2(3): 392–415.

Simmel G (1904) The Sociology of Conflict. *American Journal of Sociology* vol 9(4): 490–525.

Simon WE (1978) *A Time for Truth*. New York: McGraw-Hill Book Company.

Sklar MJ (1988) *The Corporate Reconstruction of American Capitalism*. Cambridge: Cambridge University Press.

Skowroneck S (1982) *Building a New American State. The Expansion of National Administrative Capacities (1877–1920)*. Cambridge: Cambridge University Press.

Sloan DE (1967) Our Middle Class Forgets Too Soon. *Afro-American* 25 November: 5.

Small A (1904) The Subject Matter of Sociology. *American Journal of Sociology* vol 9(3): 285–298.

Small A (1905) *General Sociology. An Exposition of the Main Development in Sociological Theory from Spencer to Ratzenhofer*. Chicago: Chicago University Press.

Small A (1906) The Relation Between Sociology and Other Sciences. *American Journal of Sociology* vol 12(1): 11–31.

Small A (1907) Points of Agreement Among Sociologists. *American Journal of Sociology* vol 13(5): 633–655.

Small A (1912) Socialism in the Light of Social Science. *American Journal of Sociology* vol 17(6): 811–815.

Small A (1915) The Bonds of Nationality. *American Journal of Sociology* vol 20(5): 629–683.

Smith MC (1994) *Social Science in the Crucible. The American Debate Over Objectivity and Purpose (1918–1941)*. Durham: Duke University Press.

Sogge TM (1933) Industrial Classes in the United States in 1930. *Journal of the American Statistical Association* vol 28(182): 199–203.

Soule GH (1934a) *The Coming American Revolution*. London: Routledge.

Soule GH (1934b) Why Capitalism is Declining. *The New Republic* 19 September: 164.

Speier H (1934) The Salaried Employee in Modern Society. *Social Research* (1): 111–129.

Sprague LW (1919) The Public. In: Powell (ed.) LP *The Social Unrest: Capital, Labor, and Public Turmoil* vol 1. New York: The Review of Reviews Company, 121–128.

Sproule JM (1997) *Propaganda and Democracy. The American Experience of Media and Mass Persuasion*. Cambridge: Cambridge University Press.

Stagner R (1935) Fascist Attitudes: An Exploratory Study. *The Journal of Social Psychology* vol 7(3): 309–319.

Stannard Baker R (1903) Capital and Labor Hunt Together. Chicago the Victim of the New Industrial Conspiracy. *McClure's* vol 21(5): 451.

Starch in the White Collar (1943) *New Masses* 14 December: 20–21.

Stearns PN (1979) The Middle Class: Toward a Precise Definition. *Comparative Studies in Society and History* vol 21(3): 377–396.

Stedman Jones G (1982) The Language of Chartism. In: Epstein J and Thompson D (eds), *The Chartist Experience: Studies in Working-Class Radicalism and Culture (1830–1860)*. New York: 3–58.

Stedman Jones G (1983) *Languages of Class. Studies in English Working-Class History (1832–1982)*. Cambridge: Cambridge University Press.

Steinfels P (1980) *The Neoconservatives: The Men Who are changing America's Politics*. New York: Simon and Schuster.

Stessin L (1946a) Crack-Up in White Collar Moral! *Forbes* 1 July: 16–18.

Stessin L. (1946b) White Collar Unions? *Forbes* 15 December: 19.

Stevenson THC (1910) Suggested Lines of Advanced in English Vital Statistics. *Journal of the Royal Statistical Society* vol 73(6/7): 685–713.

Stevenson THC (1928) The Vital Statistics of Wealth and Poverty. *Journal of the Royal Statistical Society* vol 91(2): 207–230.

Stolber B and Winton WJ (1935) *The Economic Consequences of the New Deal*. New York: Brace.

Sugrue TJ (2005) *The Origins of the Urban Crisis: Race and Inequality in Postwar Detroit*. Princeton: Princeton University Press.

Sumner WG (1883) *What Social Classes Owe to Each Other*. New York: Harper & Bros.

Sumner WG (1914) *The Challenge of Facts and other Essays*. New Haven: Yale University Press.

Sumner WG (1918 [1885]) The Science of Sociology. In: Sumner WG (ed.) *The Forgotten Man and other Essays*. New Haven: Yale University Press, 401–408.

Sylvers M (1989) *Politica e ideologia nel comunismo statunitense*. Roma: Jouvence.

Szelény I (1988) The Three Waves of New Class Theories. *Theory and Society* vol 1(17): 645–667.

Szreter SRS (1984) The Genesis of the Registrar-General's Social Classification of Occupations. *The British Journal of Sociology* vol 35(4): 522–546.

Szreter SRS (1993) The Official Representation of Social Classes in Britain, the United States, and France: The Professional Model and "Les Cadres". *Comparative Studies in Society and History* vol 35(2): 285–317.

Tait S (1973) Alle origini del movimento comunista negli Stati Uniti: Louis Fraina teorico della azione di massa. *Primo Maggio* (1): 17–41.

Testi A (1980) *Il socialism americano nell'età progressista: il Socialist-democratic Party del Wisconsin (1900–1920)*. Padova: Marsilio.

Testi A (2000) *Trionfo e declino dei partiti politici negli Stati Uniti*. Torino: Otto.

The American Round Table. Discussions on People's Capitalism (1956) Digest Report by D.M. Potter, sponsored by Yale University and The Advertising Council. New Haven: Yale University Press.

The Black Middle Class. *Ebony*, Special Issue, August 1973.

The Communists and People of Washington. Report to District Conference (1939), 28–29 January. In: CPUSA Records: Series I, Tamiment Library NYU, BOX 258, Folder 18.

The Crisis of the Middle Class (1935) *New Masses* 2 July: 6–7.

The Disenchantment of the Middle Class. Special Report. *Business Week* 25 April 1983: 82–83.

The Downsizing of America. *New York Times*, 3-9 March 1996. Available at: https://arch ive.nytimes.com/www.nytimes.com/specials/downsize/indext.html.

The End of the Trail: Why does a Woman leave Home and Faithful mate after Twenty Years? (1923) *Sunset* (50): 30–33.

The Fate of the Salaried Man (1903). *Independent*, 20 August, p.12.

The Federal Census. Critical Essays by Members of the American Economic Association, Collected and Edited by a Special Committee (1899). New York: Macmillan.

The Great Middle Class Is Beginning to Turn (1920) *New York Tribune*, 11 January.

The Middle Class Must Choose (1934) *New Masses* December: 9–13.

The Myth of the Vanishing Middle Class (1984) *Business Week* 9 July: 85–86.

The New Industrial Relations. Special Report (1981) *Business Week* 11 May: 85–98.

The New Middle. (2016) National Public Radio. Available at http://www.npr.org/series/485129365/the-new-middle.

The Plight of the White-Collar Army (1930) *The Literary Digest* 7 June 1930: 69–70.

The Rich Middle-Income Class (1954) *Fortune* May: 95–98.

The Short Way Home (1920) *New York Times*, 23 May.

The Sit-Down. *The New Republic* 20 January 1937: 343.

The Squeeze on the Middle Class. Inflation and Recession Have Shrunk its Spending Power. *Business Week* 10 March 1975: 52–60.

The Transformation of American Capitalism. *Fortune* February 1951: 79–83, 154–158.

Therborn G (2012) Class in the 21st Century. *New Left Review* (78): 5–29. Available at: https://newleftreview.org/issues/ii78/articles/goran-therborn-class-in-the-21st -century.

Thesis and Resolutions for the Seventh National Convention of the Communist Party of USA, by Central Committee Plenum (1930) 31 March–4 April. In: CPUSA Records: Series I, Tamiment Library NYU, BOX 170, Folder 10.

Thierry A (1827) *Lettres sur l'histoire de France, pour servir d'introduction à l'étude de cette histoire.* Paris: Sautelet.

Thomas N (1934) *The Choice before Us Mankind at the Crossroads.* New York: Macmillan.

Thomson D (1952) *Democracy in France: The Third and Fourth Republics.* Oxford: Oxford University Press.

Tobin W (1995) Studying Society: The Making of Recent Social Trends in the United States (1920–1933). *Theory and Society: Renewal and Critique in Social Theory* vol 24(4): 537–565.

Trevelyan GM (1926) *History of England.* London: Longmans, Green and Co.

Tucker CW (1968) A Comparative Analysis of Subjective Social Class (1945–1963). *Social Forces* vol 46(4): 508–514.

Tugwell RG (1933) The Ideas Behind the New Deal. *New York Times*, 16 July.

U.S. Bureau of Census (1872), *Ninth Census of the United States 1870*, vol. I: *The Statistics of the Population of the United States.* Washington DC: Government Printing Office.

U.S. Department of Commerce, Bureau of the Census (1930) *A Social-Economic Grouping of the Gainful Workers of the United States.* Washington DC: Government Printing Office.

U.S.A.: The Permanent Revolution, by the editors of Fortune in collaboration with R.W. Davenport. New York: Prentice-Hall, 1951.

Uchitelle L and Kleinfield NR (1996) On the Battlefields of Business, Millions of Casualties. *New York Times*, 3 March.

Unionization in White Collar (1934) *New Masses* 25 September: 3–8.

Unions Add White-Collar Members (1937) *Business Week* 22 May: 39–40.

Unions Back Store Strike in Milwaukee. Truck Drivers, Building Service Workers out with Retail Clerks. *Daily Workers* 12 May 1934.

Unions for Technicians. *The New Republic* 24 January 1934: 295–296.

Unions Push White-Collar Drive. *Business Week* 19 June 1937: 43–44.

United Office and Professional Workers of America Records. Tamiment Library NYU, WAG.190, Box 66, Folder 5 and Box 123, Folder 2.

United Office and Professional Workers of America Records. Tamiment Library NYU, Printed Ephemera Collection on Trade Unions: PE.001 Box 42.

Vaudagna M (1986) Successo e declino del patto sociale. In: Bonazzi T and Vaudagna M (eds) *Ripensare Roosevelt.* Milano: Franco Angeli, 112–121.

Vaudagna M (2014) "Is the New Deal Socialism?" Roosevelt and Democratic Socialism in the 1930s. In: Vaudagna M *The New Deal and the American Welfare State. Essays from a Transatlantic Perspective (1933–1945)*. Torino: Otto, 261–292.

Vermeil E (1935) Essai sur les origines sociales de la révolution hitlérienne. *Année politique française et étrangère* (16) : 41–78.

Vezzosi E (2002) *Madri e Stato. Politiche sociali negli Stati Uniti del Novecento*. Roma: Carocci.

Vidich AJ (ed.) (1995) *The New Middle Classes. Life-Styles, Status Claims and Political Orientations*. New York: Macmillan.

Vidor K (director) (1928) *The Crowd* [Motion picture]. Metro-Goldwyn-Mayer: Beverly Hills.

Vinovskis MA (1991) Stalking the Elusive Middle Class in Nineteenth Century America. A Review Article. *Comparative Studies in Society and History* vol 33 (3): 582–587.

Vogel D (1979) Clear As Kristol, Business's "New Class" Struggle. *The Nation* 15 December: 625–628.

Wacquant LJ (1991) Making Class: The Middle Class(es) in Social Theory and Social Structures. In: McNall SG et al. (eds) *Bringing Class Back In: Contemporary and Historical Perspective*. Boulder: Westview Press, 39–64.

Wade J (1842) *History of the Middle and Working Classes*. Edinburgh: Chambers.

Wage Demands Look Explosive (1974) *Business Week* 6 April: 18–19.

Wahrman D (1995) *Inventing the Middle Class. The Political Representation of Class in Britain (1780–1840)*. Cambridge: Cambridge University Press.

Walker FA (1876) *The Wages Question. A Treatise on Wages and Wages Classes*. New York: Holt.

Walker FA (1888) The Eleventh Census of the United States. *The Quarterly Journal of Economics* vol 2(2): 135–161.

Walker FA (1890) Statistics of the Colored Race in the United States. *Publications of the American Statistical Association* vol 2(11/12): 91–106.

Walker FA (1899) *Discussions in Economics and Statistics*, vol. II: *Statistics, National Growth, Social Economics*. New York: Holt.

Walker P (ed.) (1979) *Between Labor and Capital. The Professional-Managerial Class*. Boston: South End Press.

Walkowitz DJ (1999) *Working with Class. Social Workers and the Politics of Middle-Class Identity*. Chapel Hill: The University of North Carolina Press.

Wallas G (1908) *Human Nature in Politics*. London: A. Constable and Co.

Wallech S (1986) Class Versus Rank: The Transformation of English Social Terms and Theories of Production. *Journal of the History of Ideas* vol 47(3): 409–431.

Wallerstein I (2011) *The Modern World-System IV. Centrist Liberalism Triumphant (1789–1914)*. Berkeley: University of California Press.

War H (1936) Forget the Rich. *New Masses* February 1936: 5–6.

Ward LF (1883) *Dynamic Sociology, or Applied Social Science as Based upon Statical Sociology and the Less Complex Sciences*, vol. I. New York: Appleton.

Ward LF (1889) Some Social and Economical Paradoxes. *American Anthropologist* vol 2(3): 119–132.

Ward LF (1900) *Applied Sociology. A Treatise on the Conscious Improvement of Society by Society*. New York: Ginn & Company.

Ward LF (1903) *Pure Sociology. A Treatise on the Origin and Spontaneous Development of Society*. New York: Macmillan.

Ward LF (1908) The Sociology of Political Parties. *American Journal of Sociology* vol 13(4): 439–454.

Warner WL (1936) American Caste and Class. *American Journal of Sociology* vol 42(2): 234–237.

Warner WL (1937) The Society, the Individual and his Mental Disorders. *American Journal of Psychiatry* vol 92(2): 278–279.

Warner WL (1949) *Democracy in Jonesville*. New York: Harper & Row.

Warner WL (1953) *American Life: Dream and Reality*. Chicago: Chicago University Press.

Warren DI (1976) *The Radical Center. Middle Americans and the Politics of Alienation*. Indiana: University of Notre Dame Press.

Warren FA (1966) Alfred Bingham and the Paradox of Liberalism. *The Historian* (2): 252–267.

Waterhouse BC (2014) *Lobbying America: The Politics of Business from Nixon to NAFTA*. Princeton: Princeton University Press.

Webb S (1917) *The Works Manager To-day*. New York: Longmans, Green and co.

Webb S (1920) Can the Middle Class be Organized? *The New Commonwealth* 9 January: 13–14.

Webster N (ed.) (1828) *An American Dictionary of the English Language*, vol. II. S. Converse: New York.

Weems RE and Randolph LA (2001) The National Response to Richard M. Nixon's Black Capitalism Initiative: The Success of Domestic Détente. *Journal of Black Studies* vol 32(1): 66–83.

Weinstein J (1968) *The Corporate Ideal in the Liberal State (1910–1918)*. Boston: Beacon Press.

Wells HG (1906) Socialism and the Middle Classes. *Fortnightly Review* November: 785–795.

Wheatley R (1885) The New York Stock Exchange. *Harper's Magazine* (71): 829–853.

Wheatley R (1886) The New York Produce Exchange. *Harper's Magazine* (73): 189–218.

Wheatley R (1888) The New York Real Estate Exchange. *Harper's Magazine* (77): 928–944.

Wheatley R (1890a) The New York Bank. *Harper's Magazine* (80): 475–473.

Wheatley R (1890b) The New York Maritime Exchange. *Harper's Magazine* (80): 756–766.

Wheatley R (1891) The New York Chamber of Commerce. *Harper's Magazine* (83): 502–517.

White Collar Unions on their Way (1939) *Business Week* 9 August: 30–31.

White Collar Woe. New Organizing drive by CIO (1946) *Business Week* 28 September: 100–104.

White H (1973) *Metahistory: The Historical Imagination in Nineteenth-Century Europe.* Baltimore: Johns Hopkins University Press.

White WA (1937) A Yip from the Doghouse. *The New Republic* 15 December: 160–162.

White-Collar Dilemma. The Middle Classes More and More Cast off Their Upper-Class Illusions (1941) *New Masses* 18 February: 40.

White-Collar Drive (1944) *Business Week* 9 September: 104–105.

White-Collar Man (1946) *Fortune* June: 124, 206.

White Collar Problem? Lyle Dowling and Lewis Merrill argue some questions arising out of Mr. Merrill's recent New Masses article (1944) *New Masses* 4 January: 21.

White-Collar Union Drive (1939) *Business Week* 21 January: 21.

Whitman W (1932 [1858]) *I Sit and Look Out: Editorials from the Brooklyn Daily Times.* New York: Schwarz.

Whitney WD and Smith BE (eds) (1901) *The Century Dictionary and Cyclopedia with a New Atlas of the World*, vol v. New York: The Century Co.

Wiebe R (1967) *The Search for Order (1877–1920).* New York: Macmillan.

Wiebe R (1995) *Self-Rule. A Cultural History of American Democracy.* Chicago: Chicago University Press.

Wilson CP (1992) *White Collar Fictions: Class and Social Representation in American Literature (1885–1925).* Athens: University of Georgia Press.

Wilson W (1919) Unrest as a World Problem. Address before the State Legislature at St. Paul, Minnesota, September 9, 1919. In: Powell LP (ed.) *The Social Unrest: Capital, Labor, and Public Turmoil* vol 1. New York: The Review of Reviews Company, 385–391.

Winkler A (2018) *We the Corporations. How American Businesses Won Their Civil Rights.* New York: Norton.

Winkler HA (1989) Social-démocratie et classes moyennes sous la République de Weimar. *Matériaux pour l'histoire de notre temps* (17): 13–22.

Withheld H (1995) White-Collar Blues. *Harper's Magazine* 1 January: 2–4.

Wolfe A (1993) Clash of the Middle Classes. *Harper's Magazine* October: 5–7.

Wolfson T (1948) White Collar are Yellow. *Labor and Nation* March/April: 23–24.

Wolfson T (1949) White Collar are Yellow. *Labor and Nation* July/August: 23–25.

Wolin SS (1960) *Politics and Vision: Continuity and Innovation in Western Political Thought.* Boston: Little, Brown.

Wolin SS (2017 [2008]) *Democracy Incorporated: Managed Democracy and the Specter of Inverted Totalitarianism.* Princeton: Princeton University Press.

Work Rules: The Main Barrier to Productivity (1971) *Business Week* 28 August: 54–55.

Woytinsky WS (1938) *Labor in the United States, Basic Statistics for Social Security. A Report prepared for the Committee on Social Security.* Washington DC: Committee on Social Security-Social Science Research Council.

Wright EO (1985) *Classes.* London: Verso.

Zadrozny JT (ed.) (1959) *Dictionary of Social Science.* Public Affairs Press: Washington DC.

Zibordi G (1922) *Critica socialista del fascismo.* Bologna-Trieste: Licinio Cappelli Libraio Editore.

Zunz O (1990) *Making America Corporate (1870–1920).* Chicago: University of Chicago Press.

Zunz O (1998) *Why the American Century?* Chicago: Chicago University Press.

Index